NEUROFEEDBACK: EXPLAINED

Neurofeedback: Explained

How Brain Training Works, What the Evidence Says, and How to Choose the Right Approach

by Andrew Hill, PhD & Madeleine McCann

Peak Brain Press LLC
Los Angeles, California

2026

Published by Peak Brain Press, LLC
www.peakbrainpress.com

ISBN: 978-1-971402-08-6
eISBN: 978-1-971402-09-3

First edition, 2026

Dedication

For my late brother, James. Your life continues to inspire my commitment to helping others better understand their brains and to bringing greater compassion, curiosity, and hope to the field of mental health.

And for everyone who has ever felt misunderstood, discouraged, or alone in their mental health journey. May this book ignite a seed of hope that encourages you to keep going.

Madeleine McCann

Acknowledgements

From Madeleine McCann:

I am deeply grateful to Dr. Andrew Hill for his mentorship, generosity, and unwavering commitment to advancing the field of neurofeedback. Thank you for believing in me and encouraging my curiosity and, above all, leading by example. It has been an incredible privilege to learn from you and to collaborate with you on this book. Your work has transformed my life, as well as the lives of countless individuals and families.

To my parents, thank you for giving me the space to explore, to learn, and to become the person I am today. Your unwavering love and support have shaped every step of this journey and ultimately allowed me to help others do the same.

Above all, I thank God for calling me to this work and for continually reminding me that understanding brings hope, and hope makes healing possible.

From Andrew Hill:

My gratitude goes first to the teachers who shaped how I understand the brain. Dr. Eran Zaidel taught me how the brain is organized, and how much there still is to learn about it. Dr. Lawrence Hirshberg taught me neurofeedback, and showed me by example that rigor and kindness belong in the same room. From both of them I learned that you can hold a demanding scientific standard and a deep respect for the person in the chair at the same time.

And to everyone I have worked with across twenty-five years of this work: thank you. Every brain I have had the privilege to map, train, and learn from has taught me something no textbook could. This book exists because of what you were willing to show me.

Contents

How to Use This Book

This book is organized in four sections. You don't have to read it in order, but here's what each section gives you:

Section I: Your Brain Has a Signature (Chapters 1-2). What a brain map is, how to read one, and the sixty-year history of neurofeedback. Start here if you want the foundation.

Section II: How Neurofeedback Actually Works (Chapters 3-6). The mechanism, what sessions look like, what the evidence says, and safety. Start here if you want to cut straight to "does this work and is it safe?"

Section III: Neurofeedback in the Real World (Chapters 7-15). Nine chapters covering specific conditions and goals. Each follows the same structure: what it feels like, what the brain pattern looks like, what training targets, and your next step. Skip to your chapter if you already know what you're looking for.

Section IV: The Bigger Picture (Chapters 16-19). Beyond brainwaves, when training stalls, how to choose a provider, and the full optimization stack. Read this before you spend money.

The Quick Reference Insert that follows gives you the essentials in two minutes. Useful if you want to act before you've finished reading.

How This Book Fits in the Series

Peak Brain Press titles fall into two tiers.

The clinical and trade books go deep for practitioners, researchers, and readers who want technical depth:

- ***QEEG Field Guide*** (with Jonathon Lomeli) documents all thirty-one individual phenotypes and ten composite signatures, with detection rules, normative database comparisons, artifact taxonomy, and report-writing methodology. The clinical reference for practitioners adding QEEG to practice.
- ***Your Brain on Drugs*** is a practitioner's framework for medication-aware QEEG interpretation: how psychotropics, substances, and

medical conditions alter the brain map, and how to account for them in interpretation.

- ***Your Brain on Trauma*** examines recurring, nonspecific EEG observations reported among some trauma-referred clients, with intervention sequencing and clinical decision-making for trauma-informed neurofeedback practice.

The consumer and recovery books meet readers where they are, in plain language:

- ***Gifted and Tortured*** (published) introduces twelve character archetypes, including the Stabilizer, the Supervisor, the Fog, the CEO, the Lifeguard, and others, each mapped to a recognizable brain-behavior pattern. The emotional entry point to the series.
- ***Half a Second More*** covers mindfulness, breath-based training, HRV biofeedback, and the voluntary-skill side of self-regulation, the complement to this book's involuntary, operant training.
- ***Borrowed Peace*** addresses the neuroscience of addiction and recovery: moderation versus abstinence, reward circuitry, and the phenotype-substance map.

This book, *Neurofeedback: Explained,* is the bridge between those two tiers, consumer-readable but technically honest, translating what clinicians see in brain maps into decisions that consumers can act on.

Reading order depends on your entry point:

- Consumer or patient starting from scratch: this book first, then *Half a Second More* for the voluntary-skill dimension.
- Already read *Gifted and Tortured*: this book picks up where the archetypes leave off and grounds them in mechanism.
- Clinician: the *QEEG Field Guide* first for clinical depth, then this book for the consumer-readable translations you can share with clients.

For clinicians: Appendix B has tools specifically for you: referral frameworks, collaboration scripts, and client preparation guides.

For parents: Chapter 14 (The Developing Brain) and Chapter 11 (The Autistic Brain) are written for you. But read Chapter 13 (Sleep) first. It may change everything.

For everyone about to spend money: Appendix I (Consumer Quick Lookup) consolidates provider scripts, red flags, costs and insurance, a "is it working?" self-check rubric, the parent path, and a recording-day prep checklist into one quick-reference section.

Before You Go Any Further

If you're going to Google neurofeedback clinics before finishing this book, read this page first.

Neurofeedback in 90 Seconds

Neurofeedback is operant conditioning of your brain's electrical activity. Sensors on your scalp record real-time brainwaves. A computer provides feedback: a movie plays smoothly when your brain hits the target pattern, dims when it drifts. Over sessions, your brain learns to produce healthier patterns. It's personal training for your brain, not a pill.

Three Red Flags You Can Spot in 30 Seconds

1. **They guarantee results.** No legitimate brain intervention guarantees outcomes. If they promise to cure your ADHD / anxiety / insomnia, walk away.

2. **They don't assess before training.** If there's no brain map, no thorough intake, no measurement before they start, there is no way to know what to train or whether training is working. Your brain deserves a baseline.

3. **They sell a fixed package with no checkpoints.** "40 sessions, $8,000, pay now" with no reassessment built in? That's a business model, not clinical care.

The Evidence Lens (One Sentence Per Question)

Apply these five questions to any neurofeedback claim:

1. **Mechanism:** Is there a brain-based explanation that makes biological sense?

2. **Maps:** Does brain data support what they're targeting in YOUR brain?
3. **Outcomes:** Are they measuring change with real data, not just "how do you feel?"
4. **Trials:** What does the controlled research actually show for this condition?
5. **Replication:** Has anyone besides this clinic reproduced the results?

Where to Start: A Decision Tree

"I'm new to this. I've never had a brain map." Start with Chapter 1 (what a brain signature is), then Chapter 3 (how the training works), then Chapter 5 (the evidence). When you're ready to act, Chapter 17 tells you how to find a good provider.

"I've already had a brain map. I want to understand my results." Chapter 1 covers what the bands and patterns mean. Appendix G is a consumer-readable atlas of twenty QEEG phenotypes. Appendix H is a symptom observation worksheet that helps you organize what you are experiencing before your appointment. Bring these to your next appointment.

"I'm doing neurofeedback and it's not working." Chapter 18. Directly. It covers why training stalls, the diagnostic sequence for figuring out what's wrong, and a concrete decision tree for what to do next.

"I'm a parent considering neurofeedback for my child." Chapter 14 (The Developing Brain) first. Then Chapter 13 (Sleep), because sleep problems drive a surprising amount of what looks like ADHD and behavioral dysregulation in children. Then Chapter 17 to evaluate providers. Chapter 6 covers safety.

"I'm already doing HRV biofeedback or meditation and want to know how neurofeedback fits." Chapter 16 covers HRV biofeedback alongside neurofeedback. Chapter 19 covers how neurofeedback and meditation work together. Chapter 3 explains the voluntary-involuntary distinction that separates these modalities.

"I'm a clinician considering adding neurofeedback to my practice." Chapter 5 (evidence), Chapter 17 (provider evaluation, but read it as self-assessment), Appendix B (clinician-specific tools). For clinical depth on QEEG, see the *QEEG Field Guide*.

Want the Full Guide?

- **Provider evaluation:** Chapter 17
- **The evidence by condition:** Chapter 5
- **Safety and side effects:** Chapter 6
- **When training stalls:** Chapter 18
- **The full phenotype atlas:** Appendix G
- **Symptom observation and referral worksheet:** Appendix H

A Note on This Book and Medical Advice

This book is for educational and informational purposes only. It is not a substitute for professional medical advice, diagnosis, or treatment.

Nothing in this book should be interpreted as medical advice. The information presented here reflects the clinical observations of the authors, published research findings, and general educational content about neurofeedback and related fields. It is not intended to diagnose, treat, cure, or prevent any medical condition.

Talk to your provider before making any decisions about starting, modifying, or stopping any treatment, therapy, or intervention (including neurofeedback), especially if you are managing a diagnosed medical or psychiatric condition, are pregnant or nursing, or are currently taking prescription medication.

The authors and publisher are not responsible for any adverse effects or consequences resulting from the use or application of the information in this book.

Individual results from neurofeedback vary. The accounts and outcomes described in this book represent clinical observations and are not guarantees of similar outcomes for any particular person.

What We Have a Stake In

You should know this before you read our recommendations rather than after. Andrew founded Peak Brain Institute, which provides the assessment and training this book describes. We have a commercial interest in that practice, in the directory and equipment named in these pages, and in the companion resources the book points you toward. Peak Brain appears in the provider directories we recommend, on the same terms as any other qualified practice.

We think that interest is a reason to be more careful, not less. It is why the evidence chapters report the trials that found nothing alongside the ones that found something, why the book tells you a brain map cannot diagnose you, and why it says plainly when the research does not support a claim. Hold us to that. If a recommendation in here only makes sense if you buy something, treat it with suspicion.

A Note on the People in This Book

Every person described in these pages is a composite. Each represents several real people of that type, drawn from twenty-five years of clinical practice. Details have been changed to protect privacy, but the brain patterns, the clinical arcs, and the outcomes are real. No case was invented.

For the Provider Guide, consumer device comparisons, and protocol guidance in this book: all information is educational only. Consult a licensed, qualified neurofeedback clinician before pursuing assessment or training. Selecting and overseeing a neurofeedback program requires professional clinical judgment that no book can replace.

Where This Book Sits in the Peak Brain Press Portfolio

Neurofeedback: Explained is the consumer literacy bridge between two groups of books: those that explain the clinical measurement science, and those that address the human experience of living in a specific kind of brain.

The measurement science side:

- *QEEG Field Guide* (Andrew Hill & Jonathon Lomeli): the clinical reference for practitioners. Everything this book treats at consumer depth, the Field Guide covers at clinical depth: phenotype detection, normative database selection, protocol logic, re-mapping methodology, artifact interpretation, and advanced training approaches.
- *Neurofeedback: Explained* (this book): the consumer translation. What a brain map means, how training works, what the evidence says, and how to make an informed decision.

The human-experience side:

- *Gifted and Tortured* (Andrew Hill): the platform book. Twelve character archetypes organized around peak brain patterns: The Supervisor, The Fog, The Lifeguard, The Stabilizer, and others. Emotional and narrative rather than clinical; the entry point for readers who want to understand their brain through lived character rather than technical pattern.
- *Your Brain on Trauma*: trauma's regulatory architecture, the composite client model, and the clinical arc from dysregulation toward regulatory capacity. If Chapter 10 of this book resonates, *Your Brain on Trauma* goes further.
- *Borrowed Peace*: regulatory dysregulation and self-medication, why the brain reaches for substances and external regulation when internal regulation fails, and what the path toward genuine stability looks like. If Chapter 12 of this book resonates, *Borrowed Peace* goes further.
- *Half a Second More* (Andrew Hill): practical self-regulation for overactive minds, breathwork, HRV, mindfulness, and the day-to-day

practice of calming a nervous system that won't cooperate. The accessible front door. If Chapter 19's discussion of the optimization stack resonates, *Half a Second More* is the practical companion.

The relationship between these books:

No book in this portfolio competes with another. Each addresses a different reader at a different moment: *Gifted and Tortured* for the reader who recognizes themselves in a character. *Your Brain on Trauma* for the reader who needs to understand their clinical path. *Borrowed Peace* for the reader working through self-medication and recovery. *Half a Second More* for the reader who needs practical tools today. *Neurofeedback: Explained* for the reader who needs to understand the measurement technology and make an informed decision about training. *QEEG Field Guide* for the clinician who needs the full technical picture.

You do not need to read any of these books to benefit from this one. But if any chapter in this book points somewhere you want to go further, one of the others is likely where the further goes.

All books listed above are published by Peak Brain Press. Current publication status and ordering information at peakbrainpress.com.

Introduction: Why This Book Exists

The woman sitting across from me is a partner at a law firm. She bills four hundred dollars an hour. She manages teams of twenty. She hasn't slept through the night in three years.

She's tried SSRIs. She's tried therapy, two therapists, actually. She's tried the meditation apps, the weighted blankets, the magnesium supplements her functional medicine doctor recommended. Nothing has stuck. She's here because a friend told her about brain mapping, and she's skeptical but desperate enough to try one more thing.

I put the cap on her head, nineteen electrodes, a little conductive gel, nothing invasive, and we record ten minutes of her brain's electrical activity with her eyes open and ten minutes with them closed. Then I process the data against a normative database and show her something she's never seen before: a quantitative picture of how her brain actually works.

I show her the map. In our clinical framework, her left sensorimotor strip, the region running across the top of the head where the brain's stabilizing rhythms arise, is significantly underengaged. The sensorimotor rhythm (SMR) generated by this strip reflects the brain's capacity to settle the body and sustain calm, focused attention. In our experience, when the left side runs low, the pattern more often tracks with inattentiveness; when the right side is the problem, it more often tracks with impulsivity and disinhibition. This is a tendency we see across clients, not a fixed rule, and individual variation matters. Her pattern suggests the stabilizing circuit isn't holding things steady during the day and isn't downshifting well at night.

We run a continuous performance test (CPT) alongside the map, a twenty-minute behavioral measure of sustained attention and impulse control. It shows the same picture from a different angle: her attention drifts in exactly the pattern the map's underengaged left sensorimotor region would predict. When the physiology and the behavioral performance outline the same phenomenon, the reading becomes more than a guess. It is a convergence of two independent measures pointing at the same regulatory pattern.

"So this is why I can't sleep," she says. Not a question.

"This is one piece of the picture," we tell her. "The map shows a pattern that differs from what we'd expect for your age. It doesn't hand us a diagnosis, but it gives us a hypothesis and a training target. And now that we can see it, we can train it."

That moment lands differently for almost every person who experiences it. Not relief exactly, not yet. But the frame shifts. She's frustrated, yes, three years of bad sleep and nothing working will do that. But she's no longer confused. She's no longer wondering if she's broken or weak or doing something wrong. The data shows a measurable difference in a specific region, one that informs where training can focus. That reframe, from "what is wrong with me" to "here is what my brain is doing and here is what we can train," is why we wrote this book.

The Gap This Book Fills

Neurofeedback has been around for over sixty years. It has thousands of published studies. It's used in clinics on every continent. And yet, if you try to learn about it as a consumer, you'll find:

- **Textbooks** written for clinicians that assume you already know what a Z-score is
- **Pamphlets** from clinics that promise everything and explain nothing
- **Blog posts** that either hype neurofeedback as a cure-all or dismiss it as pseudoscience
- **One really good book:** Jim Robbins' *A Symphony in the Brain*, published in 2000, that's now a quarter-century out of date

What you won't find is a current, honest, evidence-based book that tells you what neurofeedback actually does to your brain, what the research actually shows, and how to make a smart decision about whether it belongs in your life.

We wrote it.

What This Book Does Differently

What we promise:

We'll give you a new frame for understanding yourself: not as a collection of symptoms and diagnoses, but as a brain with measurable regulatory patterns and specific, trainable goals. Most people walk into a neurofeedback clinic thinking about what's wrong with them. We'll help you start thinking about how your brain works, what it's doing, and what you can actually change. Moving from passive sufferer to informed agent is the foundation on which everything else in this book builds, and it makes every brain-based tool you use work better, not just neurofeedback.

We'll show you how to evaluate claims: clinics, devices, protocols, marketing. Neurofeedback is a real science operating in a largely unregulated marketplace. That combination creates opportunity for both excellent care and predatory practice. You'll learn to tell the difference.

We'll be honest about the evidence: including where it's weaker than you might expect. The best sham-controlled studies show that standardized neurofeedback protocols don't always outperform active controls at the group level. We'll explain why that's true, what it means, and why the clinical results we see with individualized, QEEG-guided training look different from the group averages. This book won't sell you certainty. It will give you clarity.

We'll integrate neurofeedback into the bigger picture: sleep, therapy, exercise, meditation, medication. Neurofeedback isn't the only lever. It's one powerful tool in a toolkit. The biohacker who treats it as a standalone fix and the clinician who ignores everything else are both making the same mistake.

We'll give you a decision framework: so you can figure out if neurofeedback is right for you, what to expect if you try it, how to find a good provider, and when to stop if it's not working. Not everyone responds. Good practice means knowing when to adjust and when to walk away.

What Neurofeedback Actually Is (The 90-Second Version)

Your brain produces electrical activity, measurable patterns of oscillation that change depending on what you're doing, thinking, and feeling. These patterns can be recorded with electrodes on your scalp (EEG) and compared against normative databases to create a quantitative map of how your brain operates.

Neurofeedback is operant conditioning of that electrical activity. You sit in front of a screen. Your brain's real-time electrical patterns drive what happens on that screen, a movie plays, a game responds, a tone sounds. When your brain moves toward a target pattern, you get a reward signal. When it moves away, the reward stops.

Your brain doesn't need you to "try." It learns the way any system learns: through repetition and reinforcement. Over sessions, the trained patterns strengthen. Over weeks, those changes consolidate. The result, when it works, is a measurable shift in your brain's regulatory capacity: better sleep, sharper attention, calmer emotional responses, more cognitive flexibility.

This is personal training for your brain, closer to physical therapy than pharmacology, not a pill or a passive treatment that happens to you. Your engagement matters. Your clinician's skill matters. The match between the protocol and your specific brain pattern matters. Get all three right and the results can be remarkable. Get any one wrong and you'll join the statistics of people who tried neurofeedback and "it didn't work."

This book teaches you how to get it right.

How to Read This Book

The book is organized in four sections:

Section I: Your Brain Has a Signature: What a brain map is, how to read one, and the sixty-year history of how we got here. Start here if you want the foundation.

Section II: How Neurofeedback Actually Works: The mechanism, what sessions look like, what the evidence says, and what to watch for. Start here if you want to cut straight to "does this work and is it safe?"

Section III: Neurofeedback in the Real World: Nine chapters covering specific conditions and goals: regulation, anxiety, ADHD, trauma, autism, addiction, sleep, kids, and performance. Each follows the same structure: what it feels like, what the brain pattern looks like, what training targets, and what your next step could be. Skip to your chapter if you already know what you're looking for.

Section IV: The Bigger Picture: How to choose a provider, how neurofeedback fits into the broader optimization stack, and your concrete next steps. Read this before you spend money.

You don't have to read this book in order. But if you read Section IV without reading Section II, you'll be making decisions without understanding the evidence. We'd rather you were informed.

A Note on Who We Are (and Then We'll Move On)

Andrew Hill is a cognitive neuroscientist with a PhD from UCLA. He started reading brain maps in 2000, first in clinical settings before graduate school, then running research subjects through EEG protocols at UCLA, then building his own practices. For fourteen years, he's sat with clients weekly at Peak Brain Institute (www.PeakBrainInstitute.com), walking each person through their QEEG data in real time and watching brain patterns change across months and years of training. Across twenty-five years of this work: more than 25,000 brain maps and 10,000 clients. Andrew also developed a double-blind sham neurofeedback protocol for his doctoral research, showing that real neurofeedback produces measurable brain responses that sham controls do not. What he has come to care most about isn't using a brain map as a diagnostic label. It's teaching people to read their own patterns, connect them to their experience, and understand what's actually trainable and why.

Madeleine McCann is a Senior Neurofeedback Coach and Southeast Program Manager at Peak Brain Institute. She specializes in QEEG-guided neurofeedback, brain mapping, and client education, helping individuals better understand and improve their brain function. Working closely with clients throughout the neurofeedback process, she combines clinical experience with a passion for making neuroscience and brain-based care accessible. Madeleine holds a B.S. in Neuroscience from Boston College and is currently pursuing a Master of Education in Mental Health Counseling at the University of Miami, where she hopes to further integrate neurofeedback with evidence-informed mental health care.

This book lives in the gap between published research and clinical experience, and its purpose is to help you work through that gap, not around it. We've written the book we wish someone had handed us before the first brain map we ever saw.

Let's look at your brain.

For clinicians: If you're a therapist, psychologist, or coach reading this: welcome. This book is written for your clients, but the best thing you can do with it is read it yourself first. We believe clinicians should understand their own brain before they refer clients for brain training. If you want to see your own brain data, Peak Brain Institute offers brain maps to clinicians. The resources you need to refer clients intelligently are in the chapters ahead.

Your Move:

1. **Reflect:** What brought you to this book? Write down your top three brain complaints, the things you'd most want to change about how your mind works.

2. **Act:** Track your sleep quality for the next week. Simple scale: 1 (terrible) to 10 (great), every morning. You'll need this data later.

3. **Share:** If someone in your life is curious about neurofeedback, the Quick Reference at the back of the book gives them the essentials in two minutes.

Ch 1: Your Brain Has a Signature (Here's How to See It)

1.1 A Different Frame

Imagine walking into a cardiologist's office and saying, "I get chest pains when I exercise." And the cardiologist says, "Interesting. Let's skip the EKG and the stress test. Here's a prescription." You'd want someone to actually *look* at your heart before deciding what to do about it.

In mental health, clinical assessment, history-taking, and symptom evaluation are the foundation, and they work. But they rarely include direct measurement of the organ. You describe your symptoms. Someone matches those symptoms to a diagnostic label. The label guides the treatment. A brain map adds another layer of information to that process, an additive measurement that can make the clinical picture more specific.

But the brain is an organ. And we have the technology to measure it. So why don't we use it?

This book is about what happens when you do look. When you measure your brain's electrical activity, compare it to what's expected for your age, and see, for the first time, the actual pattern that's been running your experience.

Your brain produces a measurable electrical signature. That signature shapes how you think, feel, sleep, focus, react, and recover. It's a map, a starting point for understanding what's actually going on in the organ that runs your life.

When you have that map, something shifts: you stop thinking about your struggles as character flaws and start thinking about them as resource problems.

Your brain is an organ that needs resources to run well. Think about a simpler system: if you have low sodium in your bloodstream, your heart rate goes up. You don't label that a "rapid heartbeat disorder" and treat the heart directly. You add electrolytes. The resource imbalance clears and the symptom resolves. It's procedural.

The brain, while more complicated, operates by the same logic. If you're not getting restorative sleep, your brain will try to recover that sleep debt during waking hours, showing up as slow waves on a QEEG when you should be sharp. And that delta intrusion doesn't just make you tired. It chips away at your confidence in a meeting, amplifies anxiety in conversations, and shortens your fuse with your kids. Neurofeedback addresses the resource imbalance at the source, so the downstream symptoms change without you having to fight them one by one.

You are not the problem. You are not broken. Your brain just needs a better pit crew.

1.2 What a Brain Map Actually Is

Let's demystify this.

A quantitative EEG brain map, QEEG for short, is a recording and statistical analysis of your brain's electrical activity. Here's how it works:

You sit in a chair. A technician places a cap on your head, a fabric cap with nineteen small electrodes embedded in it, arranged in a standardized pattern called the 10-20 system. A small amount of conductive gel goes under each electrode to ensure a clean signal. Nothing is injected. Nothing hurts. The cap looks a bit like a swim cap with wires coming out of it.

Then you sit still for about ten minutes with your eyes open, looking at a fixed point on the wall. Then another ten minutes with your eyes closed. That's it. The recording takes less than an hour, and most of that is setup time. Some cases call for longer recordings: traumatic brain injury, seizure history, or presentations where the clinician needs to see how the brain responds to specific cognitive tasks. But for a standard intake map, ten minutes per condition is the clinical norm.

What the electrodes pick up is the summed electrical activity of millions of neurons generating postsynaptic potentials in coordinated rhythms beneath each sensor. (Scalp EEG mostly reflects these synaptic currents, not individual neurons "firing" action potentials; the distinction matters because the signal you see on a brain map is a population-level average of dendritic input, not a count of neurons switching on and off.) This is EEG, electroencephalography. It's the same technology that Hans Berger first demonstrated in 1929, refined over nearly a century into something precise enough to be clinically useful.

The "quantitative" part is what turns it from a simple EEG trace into a brain map. After the recording, software measures your brain's electrical patterns: the power at different frequencies, the connectivity between regions, the symmetry between hemispheres. It compares all of it against a normative database, a statistical model of what's expected for someone your age, built from thousands of typical brains.

The result is a set of topographic maps showing where your brain deviates from the norm and by how much. On screen, these maps use color coding: warm tones (reds, oranges) for areas producing more activity than expected, cool tones (blues) for areas producing less. Green sits at the center of the scale, close to the statistical norm. The further you are from green in either direction, the more your brain deviates from what's typical for your age. When you see your own map in a clinician's office, the pattern is immediately visible. (To see full-color examples of the brain maps discussed in this book, visit neurofeedbackexplained.com/plates. For comprehensive clinical interpretation, see the companion volume *QEEG Field Guide*.)

That's your signature, a quantitative picture of how your brain's electrical patterns compare to what's expected, and a starting point for understanding what those patterns might mean for your experience.

What it feels like to see it for the first time. The room is quiet. The clinician turns the monitor toward you. There's your brain, rendered as a grid of circles, each one showing a topographic view of your head from above. The patterns are immediately visible even before anyone explains them. You see the areas where your brain deviates, and something happens that most people don't expect: recognition. Not "that's interesting." Something closer to "that's *me*." The anxiety you've carried for years, the focus you've never been able to sustain, the sleep that won't come, suddenly has a shape. It's a pattern on a screen, measurable and specific, grounded in physiology. Most people sit with that for a moment before asking the next question. Some get quiet. Some laugh. Some tear up, from the relief of finally seeing what they've only been able to feel.

1.3 Why This Matters

Most mental health and performance interventions start without measuring the organ they're treating.

If you go to a psychiatrist for anxiety, you'll likely get an SSRI or a benzodiazepine, chosen because "anxiety" as a diagnostic category responds to those drugs in many people. If you go for ADHD, you'll likely get a stimulant. For depression, an antidepressant. Standard clinical assessment, history, interview, validated symptom scales, is real and useful. What it typically lacks is direct measurement of what the brain is doing. A brain map adds that measurement.

Across 25,000 brain maps, we see the same thing: the same diagnosis can come from completely different brain patterns. We've mapped people with ADHD whose brains show excess slow-wave activity frontally, the classic "underaroused" pattern. We've mapped other ADHD patients whose brains show the opposite: overactivation, high beta, a brain that's running too fast and can't prioritize. Same diagnosis. Different brains. Different training needs.

The same thing happens with anxiety. Some anxious brains show frontal high beta, a threat-detection system stuck on high alert. Others show alpha suppression, no idle, no neutral gear, no ability to downshift. Others show right-hemisphere overactivation, a vigilance pattern. If you treat all of these the same way, some people will improve and others won't. The ones who don't improve aren't "treatment-resistant." They got the wrong treatment for their brain.

When you know the unique signature of your brain, you can prioritize treatment targets properly. The anxious brain that is suppressing alpha might not be getting deep enough sleep at night; poor sleep drives the next day's anxiety, which suppresses alpha further, which wrecks the next night. The unfocused brain with excess beta might actually be anxious at the root of it, not ADHD at all. By targeting deep sleep in the first case, or anxiety in the second, the root problem gets addressed and the brain can begin to change in a way that feels like a "finally" instead of another medication adjustment.

This shifts how we think about mental health altogether. The traditional model hands you a diagnosis and tells you to learn to live with it. The brain-map model hands you a pattern and tells you what to do about it. Unwanted feelings, difficult behaviors, and stubborn symptoms stop being character flaws or life sentences. They become signals from a nervous system running a specific, identifiable configuration that can be addressed with specific, measurable tools. The diagnosis does not define you. The pattern does not own you. It is a starting point, not a verdict.

A brain map doesn't tell you what's wrong with you. It tells you what pattern your brain is running, adding information to the clinical picture and offering a more specific starting point for choosing an intervention that matches your neurology, not just your label.

1.4 The Difference Between a Picture and a Movie

People sometimes confuse brain maps with brain scans. They're not the same thing.

Structural imaging (MRI, CT) shows you what your brain *looks* like. The physical structure. Tumors, lesions, developmental anomalies. Structural imaging catches a great deal, though it has its own sensitivity and resolution limits and may miss subtle pathology. Most people struggling with anxiety, ADHD, depression, insomnia, or performance issues have structurally normal brains. The MRI comes back clean. "Good news, nothing wrong!" Except you still can't sleep, still can't focus, still feel like you're running on fumes.

Functional imaging (fMRI, PET, SPECT) shows you what your brain *does*. Blood flow, metabolic activity, which regions light up during tasks. PET and SPECT have established clinical roles in specific contexts, including epilepsy localization, dementia evaluation, and oncology, and fMRI is used clinically in presurgical mapping. But for the everyday concerns this book addresses, these tools remain largely research instruments: expensive, slow, and not widely available for routine clinical use outside of specialized centers. Different tests answer different questions.

EEG and QEEG show you what your brain *produces*: its real-time electrical activity. A continuous recording of the oscillations your neurons generate moment to moment. EEG has millisecond precision, it captures how fast your brain responds, how it shifts between states, how different regions coordinate. And QEEG adds the statistical comparison to normative databases, turning that recording into a map you can read.

Think of it this way: an MRI is a photograph of the engine. An fMRI is a thermal image showing which parts are warm. An EEG is the dashboard, RPMs, oil pressure, temperature, fuel mix, all in real time. The QEEG compares your dashboard readings to what's normal for your make and model.

Most of the time, what you need is the dashboard. The engine looks fine. The problem is how it's running.

What a brain map is not. The cardiologist analogy is useful for what it illustrates: that measuring the organ before treating it is more informative than guessing. But the analogy has limits worth naming. A 12-lead EKG has established sensitivity and specificity for specific cardiac diagnoses, validated against decades of outcome trials. A QEEG does not. No guideline body recommends QEEG as a standalone diagnostic for any psychiatric condition. What QEEG offers is different and more modest: a quantitative measurement of your brain's electrical patterns at a moment in time, compared against a normative database. That measurement is affected by your sleep the night before, your caffeine intake, your alertness during the recording, and which normative database the clinician uses. The phenotypes we describe in this book are pattern-recognition heuristics based on clinical observation across thousands of maps. They are reliable enough to guide clinical decision-making. They are not validated biomarkers in the pharmaceutical trial sense, and a clinician who tells you otherwise is overstating the evidence. Imperfect measurement beats no measurement. The map turns on the lights. It does not guarantee what you find there is the final word.

1.5 Reading Your Brain Map: The Five Frequency Bands

Your brain produces electrical activity at different speeds, measured in cycles per second, Hertz (Hz). These speeds cluster into bands, and each band has characteristic associations. A caveat before we start: the band-function pairings below are shorthand, not fixed wiring diagrams. Alpha is not always "idle," theta is not always "release," and the same band can serve different roles in different brain regions and different tasks. Context shapes what a given frequency means. The descriptions that follow are the most common clinical associations, not one-to-one rules. What follows is your decoder.

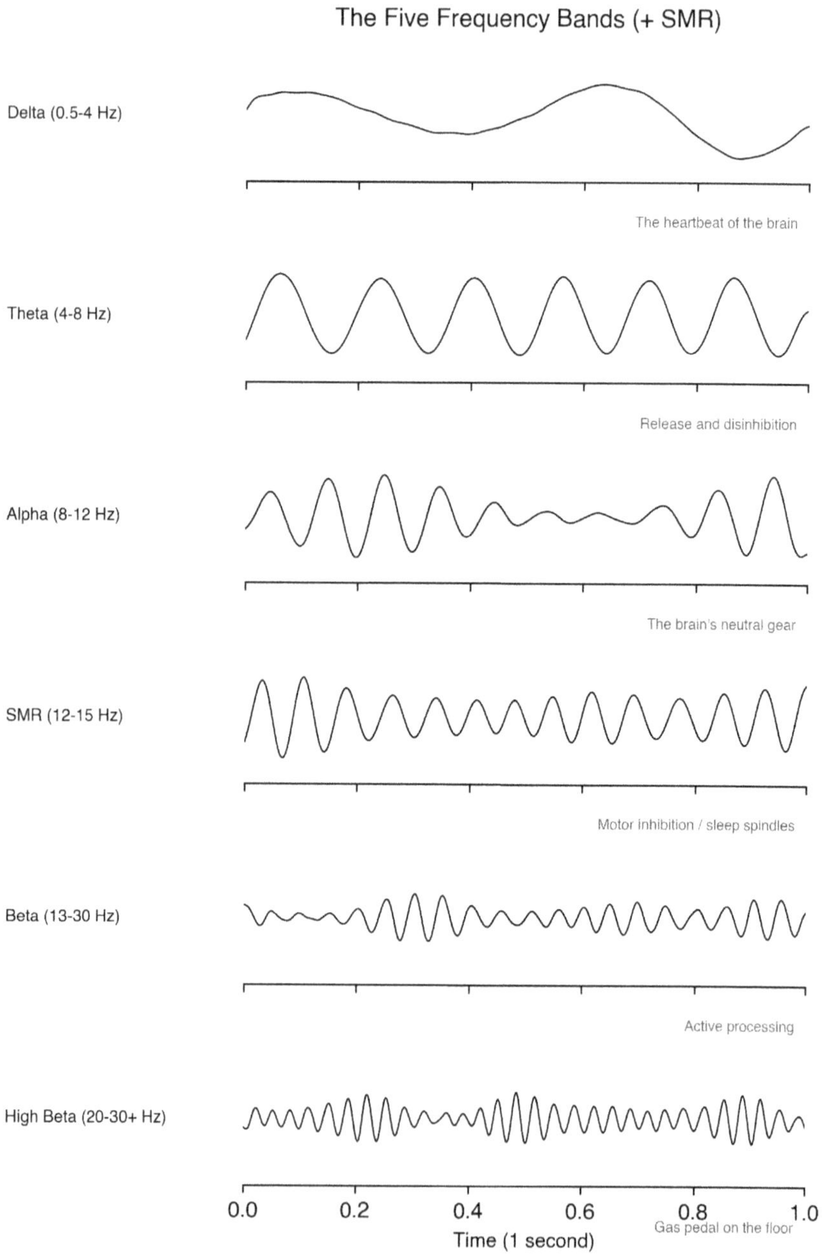

Figure 1.1: The EEG Frequency Bands and SMR

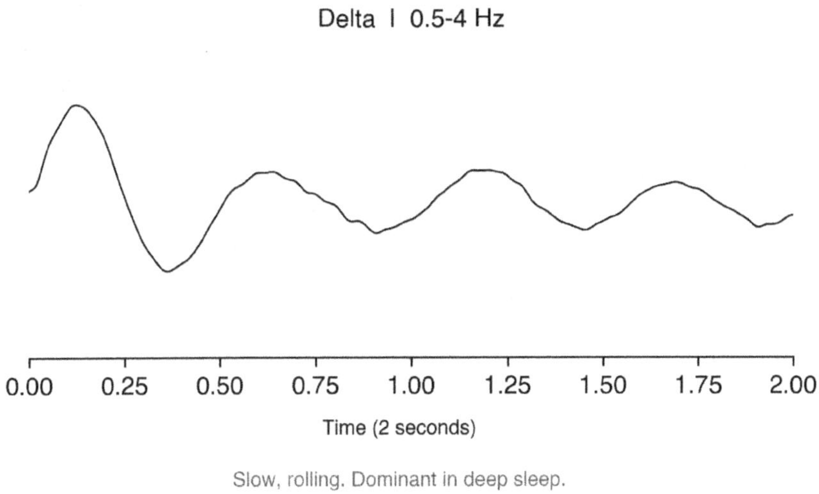

Figure 1.2: Delta waveform

1.5.1 Delta (0.5–4 Hz): The Heartbeat of the Brain

What it is: The slowest brain waves, the brain's deepest, most fundamental rhythm. Think of delta as the heartbeat of the brain: a background pulse of maintenance and infrastructure that runs continuously, beneath your awareness. Delta dominates during deep, dreamless sleep, the deepest stage of non-REM sleep (N3), but it's also present at low levels whenever the brain is doing its deepest repair work: flushing metabolic waste, consolidating learning, rebuilding cellular machinery. It's the rhythm of the brain keeping itself alive and intact.

What it feels like: You don't feel delta, you're unconscious when it's doing its proper job. But when delta shows up prominently in your *waking* EEG, that's a signal. Excess waking delta means something is interfering with cortical function: head injury, medication effects, extreme fatigue, or in some cases, early neurodegeneration. The brain is trying to do deep maintenance work during hours it should be alert.

What it might NOT mean: A bit of frontal delta during a recording can just mean the person was drowsy. Sleep-deprived clients often show delta intrusions in their waking maps, the brain is trying to recover sleep debt during the day because it didn't get the recovery it needed at night. Before interpreting excess delta as pathological, a good clinician checks: did you sleep last night? Are you on sedating medication? Did we record this at 3pm after lunch?

What to do with it: If your map shows significant waking delta, especially in specific regions, it's worth investigating. But delta on its own doesn't tell you *why*, it tells you that cortical function in that area is compromised, and the next step is figuring out the cause.

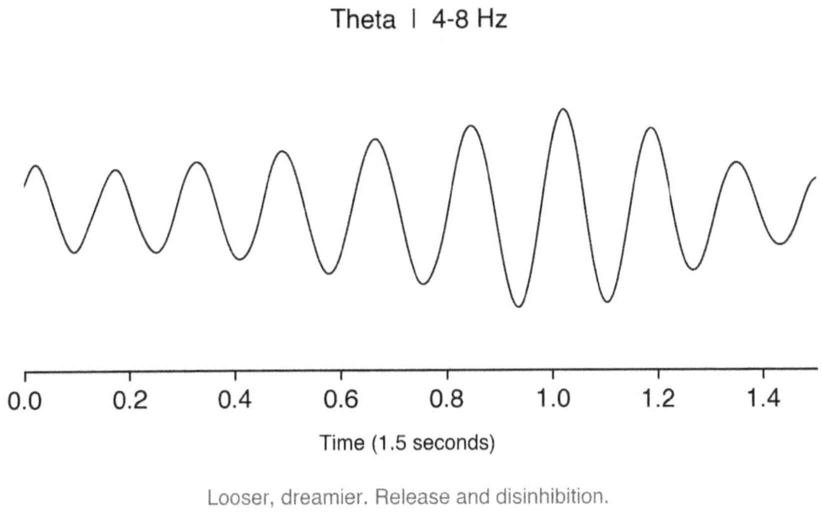

Figure 1.3: Theta waveform

1.5.2 Theta (4–8 Hz): The Release

What it is: Theta is the rhythm of release, of the brain loosening its executive grip and letting go. It dominates when the frontal cortex stands down: during light drowsiness, the hypnagogic threshold before sleep, unfocused inward drifting, deep meditation, and those creative states where the best ideas seem to arrive unbidden. Theta isn't the brain idling (that's alpha's job). It's the brain *disinhibiting*, releasing top-down control so that looser, more associative processing can surface.

What it feels like: You know that feeling when you've been reading the same paragraph three times and none of it is landing? Your eyes are open, but the frontal override is off. That's theta. It's also the highway drive where you "zone out" and find yourself ten miles past your exit, the executive hand on the wheel released, the brain drifting internally. Still active, just unconstrained. During deep meditation or right before sleep, this feels like floating, thoughts arise and dissolve without your usual management of them.

What it might NOT mean: Elevated theta doesn't automatically mean ADHD. It can mean sleep deprivation, and this matters enormously. The theta-beta ratio was once considered the hallmark ADHD biomarker, until researchers realized that elevated TBR often reflects drowsiness and slow alpha peak frequency rather than ADHD-specific pathology (Arns, Conners & Kraemer, 2013; Lansbergen et al., 2011; Gloss et al., 2016). A child who's sleeping six hours a night can look identical on theta metrics to a child with genuine attentional difficulties. The mechanism is the same: in both cases, the frontal cortex isn't holding the controls firmly. Whether the cause is trait-level underactivation or state-level exhaustion requires a clinician who asks the right questions.

What to do with it: If your map shows excess frontal theta, the first question is: are you sleeping enough? If yes, theta excess often points to chronic underactivation, the frontal cortex releasing control when it should be holding it. This is trainable, and it's one of the most common targets in neurofeedback.

What chronic underactivation looks like from the outside is often mistaken for laziness or defiance. It is the sharp twelve-year-old zoning out in a class that bores her, not because she cannot do the work but because her frontal cortex will not hold the controls for material that does not grab her. It is the creative adult stuck in a job with no outlet, fogging over by two in the afternoon because nothing in the environment demands the engagement her brain needs to stay online. In every case the frontal cortex can activate; it just will not do so without a strong enough signal. Neurofeedback trains that threshold down so the brain holds the controls at lower levels of stimulation.

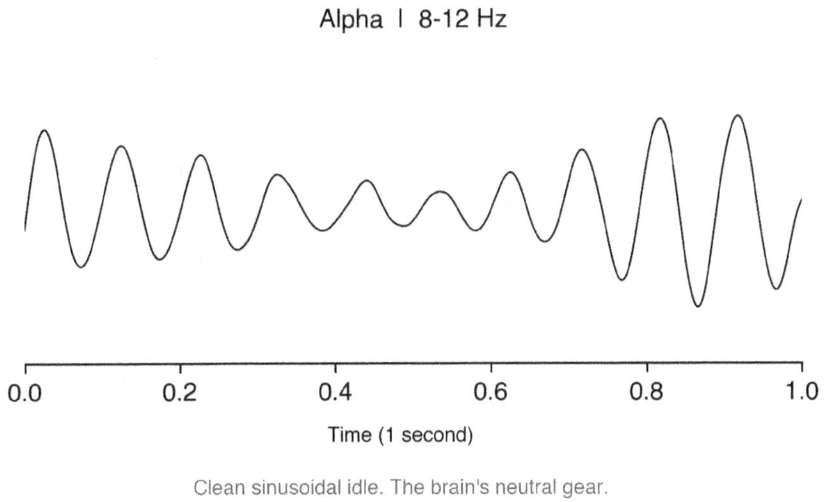

Figure 1.4: Alpha waveform

1.5.3 Alpha (8–12 Hz): The Idle

What it is: Alpha is the brain's idle, the neutral gear between engaged processing and sleep. When a cortical region is awake but not currently working, it produces alpha. Close your eyes right now: within a few seconds, your visual cortex will start humming at 8–12 Hz. Open them, and alpha drops as the region comes back online. Alpha is the resting hum of a brain that's on but not in gear.

Beyond just idling, alpha does something active: it *suppresses* regions that aren't needed. When you're focused on a conversation in a noisy room, alpha increases over the brain areas you're deliberately not using, the visual cortex when you're listening, the auditory cortex when you're looking. This is the brain's noise-cancellation mechanism, and it only works when alpha production is robust. A healthy alpha rhythm means you can be quiet without being asleep, present but not straining.

What it feels like: When alpha is healthy, you can rest. Sit in a chair without something to do and not feel itchy or anxious about it. Fall asleep at night because your brain knows how to downshift from "on" into neutral before sliding into sleep. When alpha is suppressed, when you can't produce enough of it, you have no neutral gear at all. Clients describe it as: "I can never just *be*. My brain is always running." They're not wrong, without alpha, the brain has no way to idle.

What it might NOT mean: Alpha varies by age, state, and activity. Low alpha during eyes-open recording in a bright room is normal, the brain is supposed to be engaged. Low alpha during eyes-closed rest when you're supposed to be relaxing? Worth investigating. High alpha everywhere, even during demanding tasks? That can mean disengagement, the brain is idling when it should be working. Context is everything.

What to do with it: Alpha is one of the most trainable rhythms. Suppressed alpha with anxiety, insomnia, or an inability to disengage is a clear training target. Excessive alpha during tasks points toward a different approach, getting the idle to disengage when engagement is called for.

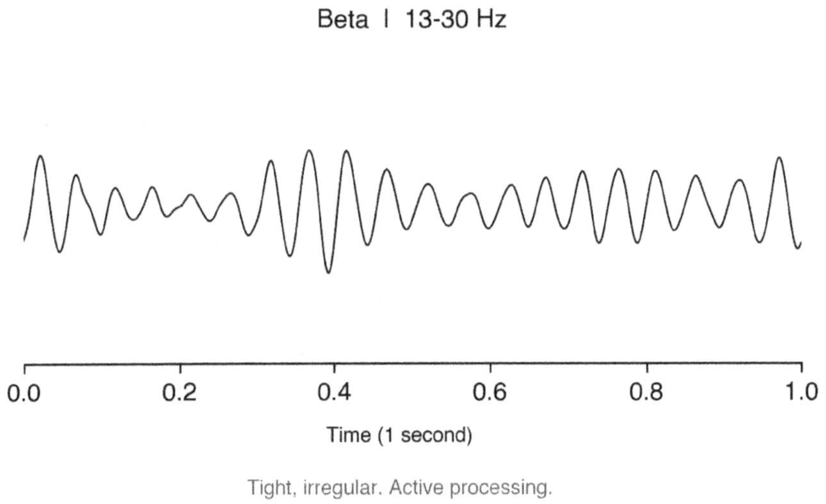

Figure 1.5: Beta waveform

1.5.4 Beta (13–30 Hz): The Processing Brain

What it is: Beta is the processing rhythm, the electrical signature of a brain doing cognitive work. It shows up in two flavors. *Focal beta* is localized: a specific region lighting up because it's the one doing the task right now, your motor cortex firing as you type, your language regions activating as you formulate a sentence. *Distributed beta* is network-level: larger coordinated assemblies processing complex information across multiple regions simultaneously, the kind of integration that underlies reasoning, decision-making, and executive function. Both are beta. What differs is the scale of the tissue involved and the breadth of the network engaged.

What it feels like: Healthy beta feels like being in it, focused, decisive, productive. Information is moving, choices feel clear. Low beta, insufficient activation in the regions that should be working, feels like trying to start a car with a weak battery. The fog, the stall, the "I know what I need to do and I can't make myself start." That's a processing deficit, not a character flaw.

What it might NOT mean: Elevated beta isn't always a problem. Fast processors, complex thinkers, and high performers often show robust beta across broad networks, their brains are running large, co-ordinated operations. The question isn't the level; it's the context and the voluntariness. Can it turn off when you need to rest? If elevated beta correlates with anxiety, poor sleep, and an inability to downshift, the beta isn't the problem, the inability to modulate it is.

What to do with it: Low frontal beta is a common training target, building the capacity for sustained engagement. High beta, particularly if it's chronic and disrupting sleep or emotional regulation, is addressed through protocols aimed at restoring the brain's ability to downshift.

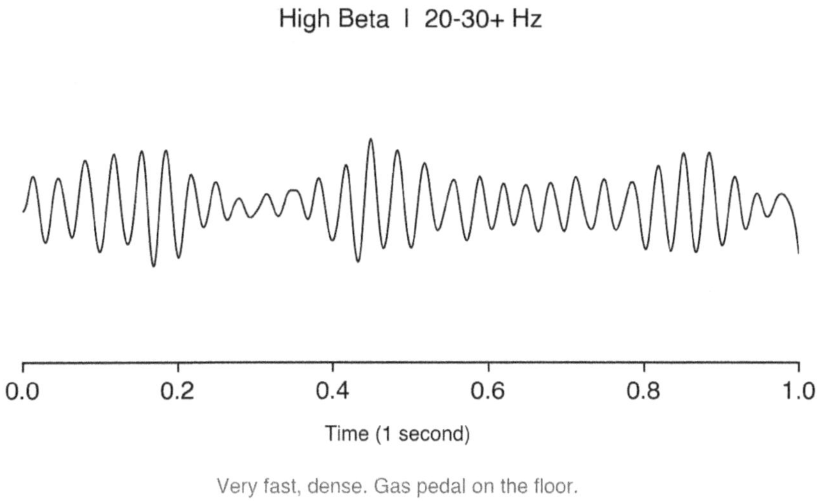

Figure 1.6: High-beta waveform

1.5.5 High Beta (20–30 Hz): The Gas Pedal

What it is: High beta is the gas pedal, the brain running in high gear. It is the upper, faster portion of the beta range, singled out because chronically elevated fast activity carries distinct clinical meaning. At the fast end of the beta range (roughly 20-30 Hz), elevated high beta can represent cortical tissue under heavy activation demand, but it has an important mimic: scalp muscle artifact (EMG). Frontalis, temporalis, and masseter muscles produce electrical activity that peaks in the same 20-30 Hz range, and on a recording it can look identical to cortical high beta. Before interpreting any fast-frequency elevation as a cortical finding, a competent reader inspects the raw EEG waveform and checks for muscle contamination. When the elevation is genuinely cortical, high beta is appropriate and even desirable in the right context: an athlete in the final seconds of a competition, a surgeon making a precise decision under pressure, an executive in a crisis. The brain needs high gear sometimes. The problem is when the pedal is stuck, when high beta persists at rest, during low-demand tasks, or at 2am when nothing is actually happening.

What it feels like: Acutely, high gear feels like being fully alive, sharpened, fast, present to every detail. That's high beta doing its job. Chronically, it feels like the engine running hot all the time: racing thoughts, physical tension (jaw clenching, tight shoulders) that may not respond to stretching. Some of this tension is cortically driven; some of it also feeds back into the EEG as muscle artifact that inflates the high-beta reading itself (see the EMG caveat above). Separating cortical fast activity from muscular fast activity requires raw-waveform review, not just the color map. Alongside the tension: an inability to stop the mental activity even when you want to. The 2am mind that's reviewing everything and solving nothing. The body that can't soften even in a warm bath. The brain generating urgency in the complete absence of urgency.

What it might NOT mean: First, not all elevated 20-30 Hz activity on a brain map is cortical. EMG from scalp and facial muscles (frontalis, temporalis, masseters) produces fast-frequency energy in exactly this range and is one of the most common EEG artifacts. If your map shows "high beta" at frontal or temporal sites and the raw EEG was not reviewed for muscle contamination, the finding may be partly or entirely artifact rather than a cortical pattern. Ask your clinician whether the raw waveform was inspected and whether artifact channels were checked. This distinction matters for every condition chapter that follows: whenever this book discusses elevated high beta, the EMG differential applies. Second, high beta during a demanding task isn't a problem, it's the point. An athlete mid-competition, a musician mid-performance, a developer deep in a hard problem: these brains should show elevated fast activity. The clinical question is always: *when* and *where*? Frontal high beta at rest, in someone who's lying down trying to sleep, is a very different finding from central high beta during a complex motor task.

What to do with it: When high beta is chronically elevated at rest, particularly frontal, and correlates with anxiety, rumination, or insomnia, it's one of the clearest and most responsive targets in neurofeedback. Training the brain to release unnecessary high-gear production during rest is among the most reliable changes we see.

1.6 Beyond Power: How Your Brain Talks to Itself

Frequency bands tell you what's happening at each electrode site. But your brain isn't nineteen independent generators, it's a network. The relationships *between* sites matter as much as what each site is doing on its own.

Coherence measures the statistical coupling between two brain regions at a given frequency: how correlated their oscillations are over a window of time. High coherence means the two signals are tightly coupled; low coherence means they are relatively independent.

A caveat before we go further: coherence is a statistical measure, not a direct readout of neural communication. It depends on the recording reference, is inflated by volume conduction (electrical spread through tissue and skull) and by common noise sources, and varies with alertness, task, and preprocessing choices. Two regions can show high coherence because they are genuinely coordinating, because a shared electrical source is bleeding into both electrodes, or because the reference montage creates an artificial correlation. A skilled reader accounts for all of these before interpreting coherence as a meaningful connectivity finding.

With that caveat in place: both extremes of coherence can be clinically relevant. If two regions that should be coordinating show low coherence, their functional coupling may be weak. If two regions show excessive coherence, locked together too tightly, the system may lose flexibility. It's the difference between a jazz ensemble (flexible coordination) and a marching band (rigid synchronization). Your brain needs both modes, and the ability to shift between them.

Phase measures the timing relationship between regions, not just whether they're oscillating at the same frequency, but whether they're doing it in sync. Are they peaking at the same moment, or offset? Phase relationships are how your brain coordinates processing across distant regions, the frontal cortex talking to the temporal cortex, the left hemisphere coordinating with the right.

You don't need to understand the math. What you need to know is this: your brain map doesn't just show whether each region is producing the right frequencies. It shows the statistical coupling between regions, which clinicians use as one window into how those regions may be coordinating. Some of the most important clinical findings are in the connectivity metrics, the coupling between areas, not just the activity within them. (Remember the coherence caveat above: these metrics are informative but not a direct photograph of neural communication.)

1.7 What Maps Can Show, And What They Can't Prove

Here's what a brain map is and isn't.

A brain map IS:

- A quantitative measurement of your brain's electrical patterns at a moment in time
- A comparison of those patterns against age-matched norms
- A tool for generating hypotheses about what's contributing to your symptoms
- A guide for selecting neurofeedback protocols and tracking progress
- Reproducible, a well-done map taken today should look similar to one taken next month (assuming nothing major has changed)

A brain map is NOT:

- A diagnosis. "Your brain map shows ADHD" is a misuse of the technology. Your brain map shows a *pattern* that is often *associated* with ADHD. Those are different statements.
- A guarantee. A brain map can suggest a protocol direction. It can't promise that protocol will work for you.
- A sales tool. If a clinic uses your brain map primarily to sell you a training package, that's a red flag. A map should inform your options, not close a sale.

- The whole picture. Your brain map is one source of information. Your history, symptoms, goals, medications, sleep, and life circumstances are the others. A good clinician integrates all of them.

The most visible misuse of brain mapping is in marketing. We've seen clinics show prospective clients a brain map full of red and yellow, "Look how abnormal your brain is!", as a conversion tool. Clinics often skip this: *everyone's* brain map has some deviations from the norm. A deviation isn't necessarily a problem. A two-standard-deviation reading in a region that corresponds to your specific complaint? That's clinically meaningful. A scattering of yellow across a map in someone who's functioning well? That's normal variation. If a clinic can't explain the difference, find a different clinic.

1.8 Norms, Confounds, and Why Context Is Everything

A brain map compares your data to a normative database, a statistical model of what's expected for your age. This is powerful, but it has limitations you should understand.

Age matters. A healthy 8-year-old's brain looks very different from a healthy 40-year-old's. The database adjusts for this, but the quality of the database matters. Some databases have thin coverage at certain ages. A good clinician knows which database they're using and what its limitations are.

State matters. Your brain map is a recording of your brain on one particular day, at one particular time, in one particular state. If you were sleep-deprived, over-caffeinated, anxious about the recording, or on certain medications, your map will reflect that. These are *state* influences, not stable traits. A responsible clinician asks about all of them before interpreting your data.

Medications matter. Many common medications alter EEG patterns. Stimulants change theta-beta ratios. Benzodiazepines boost fast activity. SSRIs can affect alpha. If you're on medication during your recording, the map shows your brain *on that medication*, not your brain at baseline. Some clinicians prefer to map off medication when possible. Others map on medication and interpret accordingly. Either approach is valid if the clinician accounts for it.

Sleep matters enormously. We've said it before and we'll say it throughout this book: sleep deprivation distorts everything. A chronically sleep-deprived brain can look like an ADHD brain, a depressed brain, or a cognitively declining brain on a map, because sleep debt impairs the same circuits. Before concluding that your brain map shows a trait pattern, rule out the state of exhaustion (see Chapter 13 for the full story on sleep and EEG).

Statistical deviation isn't automatically clinical. A Z-score of 2.0 means your reading is two standard deviations from the norm. In a population, about 4.6% of healthy people will naturally fall at or beyond that level in either direction for any given measure. And a standard brain map examines dozens of measures across multiple sites and frequency bands, so many nominal outliers are expected by chance alone. If your map shows one or two readings at 2.0 and you're otherwise functioning well, that's probably normal variation, not pathology. If multiple readings cluster at 2.0 or beyond in regions that correspond to your reported difficulties? That's a pattern worth investigating.

The skill of brain map interpretation is in the integration, reading the colors and connecting them to the person sitting in front of you.

1.8.1 How We Know What We Know

Throughout this book, we'll make observations based on our experience with over 25,000 quantitative EEG brain maps. What that number actually means, and what it doesn't:

Those 25,000 maps come from Peak Brain Institute, the neurofeedback practice Andrew founded. The people who come to us are not a random sample of the population. They're a *referral population,* people who sought out brain mapping because something wasn't working. The most common presentations are ADHD, anxiety, sleep issues, trauma, and cognitive performance concerns. We see fewer people with, say, stable depression who are well-managed on medication and not looking for alternatives.

This means the patterns we describe are patterns we see *in the people who come through our doors.* We're confident in them because they repeat across thousands of cases. But we're also honest about the fact that our sample is biased toward certain presentations, and that patterns we see frequently may not generalize to populations we see less often.

Every map in our dataset meets specific quality standards. We use rigorous artifact rejection, removing segments contaminated by eye blinks, muscle tension, movement, or electrical noise before the statistical comparison is run. We compare against established normative databases and cross-reference findings with clinical history. We track outcomes over time.

When we say "this is what we often see," we mean it literally: this pattern appears repeatedly, across many cases, in the context of specific complaints. When we're extrapolating beyond our data, we'll tell you. When we're sharing clinical observation rather than citing published research, we'll tell you that too.

Transparency about method is what separates authority from assertion. You deserve to know how the sausage gets made.

1.9 What "Clinical-Grade" Means (And Why It Matters)

You'll hear the term "clinical-grade" throughout this book, so let's define it once.

There is no regulatory body that certifies equipment as "clinical-grade," so the term is informal. When we use it in this book, we mean a system that meets all of the following measurable specifications together; no single feature (including channel count) is sufficient on its own:

- **Medical-grade EEG hardware:** a full 19-channel (or more) recording system with proper electrode impedance, amplification, and artifact handling. Not a consumer headband with 2-4 sensors. Channel count is necessary for adequate spatial coverage, but a 19-channel system with poor impedance, inadequate amplifier resolution, or no artifact management does not become clinical-grade by channel count alone.
- **Standardized recording conditions:** eyes open and eyes closed, in a controlled environment, with specific instructions to minimize artifact.
- **Normative database comparison:** your data compared statistically against a validated, age-matched reference population.
- **Qualified interpretation:** someone who understands neurophysiology, artifact, confounds, and clinical context reading your map. Not an algorithm alone.
- **Integration with clinical history:** the map interpreted alongside your symptoms, goals, medications, sleep habits, and life circumstances.

Consumer EEG devices, Muse, FocusCalm, and similar headbands, can pick up some brain signals. They're not useless. But they're recording from a handful of sites with lower-quality sensors in uncontrolled conditions. They can give you a rough sense of whether your brain is calm or active. They can support meditation practice. What they can't do is generate the kind of detailed, multi-site, normatively compared data that guides clinical decision-making.

The distinction matters because the quality of the data determines the quality of the decisions you make with it. Chapter 17 goes deeper into how to evaluate providers and devices. For now: if someone is making clinical claims based on consumer-grade hardware, ask questions.

1.10 Your Brain Is One of a Few Dozen Recurring Patterns

Across the population, brains don't produce an infinite variety of electrical signatures. This surprises most people the first time they hear it. They produce a finite set of recurring patterns.

We've looked at more than 25,000 brain maps. The same patterns appear again and again. Elevated frontal theta with low beta: the underaroused brain. Globally elevated high beta with suppressed posterior alpha: the hyperaroused brain. Low-voltage fast activity everywhere: the brain running on fumes. Slowed individual alpha frequency with poor frontal activation: the processing-speed deficit. Each pattern has a recognizable shape, a set of conditions it tends to show up in, and a set of protocols that target it.

The technical term for these recurring patterns is **phenotype**: a stable, observable configuration of brain electrical activity that recurs across individuals. The concept is borrowed from genetics, where a phenotype is any observable trait produced by the interaction of genes and environment. In the EEG context, a phenotype is a recognizable combination of power, frequency, and connectivity features that shows up reliably in enough brains to be documented.

There are roughly thirty to thirty-five of these that a skilled clinician can identify (the exact count depends on how finely you split related patterns; the *QEEG Field Guide* documents thirty-one individual phenotypes at full clinical depth). Some are common (frontal theta excess appears in a substantial minority of all clients). Others are rare (temporal dysrhythmias with paroxysmal features). Twenty of the most consumer-relevant appear in Appendix G of this book: what each is, what it feels like, what conditions it shows up in, what protocols target it, and whether it's the kind of pattern that changes with training or the kind that's wired in for life.

This is the concept that ties the rest of this book together. When you read the condition chapters in Section III, each one describes a set of brain patterns associated with that condition. ADHD isn't one pattern; it's at least four. Anxiety isn't one pattern; it's at least three. Trauma reshapes patterns in specific, recognizable ways. The diagnosis is the surface label. The phenotype is the brain underneath it. And the phenotype is what determines which protocol will help.

The *QEEG Field Guide,* which launches alongside this book, documents the full set at clinical depth. *Gifted and Tortured* introduces twelve character archetypes (the Stabilizer, the Supervisor, the Fog, the Lifeguard, and others) that map onto these same patterns in a different register. This book gives you the consumer-readable version: enough to understand your own brain, ask good questions, and evaluate whether the protocol your provider chose actually targets the pattern your map revealed.

1.11 Your Brain Is Probably Two or Three of These at Once

One more thing the pattern concept requires you to know: most real brains don't present with a single clean phenotype. They present with two or three stacked.

The client whose map shows underaroused frontal theta often also shows a frontal alpha asymmetry suggesting withdrawal-motivation bias. The client with globally elevated high beta often also shows suppressed posterior alpha, because the hyperarousal and the inability to idle are two faces of the same regulatory failure. The client with a slowed alpha peak frequency often also has elevated frontal theta, because both reflect a brain whose timing circuits are running slow.

This matters because it explains why "one protocol for everyone" fails so often. If your brain has both excess theta and excess high beta, and your provider targets only the theta, the high beta continues driving anxiety and sleep disruption. Half the problem gets addressed; half remains. A competent provider looks at the full pattern, identifies the primary driver, targets it first, and adjusts as the brain shifts.

Composite signatures are the norm. The human brain is a complex system, and complex systems rarely fail in exactly one dimension. The condition chapters in Section III describe the most common combinations for each diagnosis. Chapter 18 explains what to do when training stalls because the protocol is hitting one pattern and missing the others.

1.12 DSM Categories Cluster Around Brain Systems

Diagnostic labels (ADHD, anxiety, PTSD, depression) are built from symptom clusters, not from brain mechanisms. Two people with the same diagnosis can have completely different brain patterns; two people with different diagnoses can share the same pattern. The brain doesn't organize itself by DSM category. It organizes itself by functional systems: arousal regulation, threat detection, cognitive control, sleep-wake cycling. Different combinations of functional-system dysregulation produce different symptom profiles, and the same combination earns different diagnostic labels depending on which clinician is doing the labeling. The phenotype model moves from "what are your symptoms called?" to "which brain systems are involved?" That shift is what makes the rest of this book legible.

This raises a question worth answering directly: if a brain map is not a diagnosis, is it something less?

No. It is something different. The DSM began as a counting instrument. Its direct ancestor, a statistical manual first published in 1917 to tally patients in psychiatric institutions, grew out of nineteenth-century census tallies of "idiocy" and "insanity." DSM-I, published in 1952, described itself as a continuation of that manual.

The 1980 revision brought real gains. Robert Spitzer's task force replaced loose clinical impressions with explicit symptom checklists, and diagnostic reliability improved. But the revision was deliberately atheoretical about causes. It described what clinicians observe, not what the brain is doing, and that agnosticism has persisted through every edition since. In 2013, Thomas Insel, then director of the National Institute of Mental Health, put it directly: the DSM's diagnoses "are based on a consensus about clusters of clinical symptoms, not any objective laboratory measure" (Insel, 2013).

The DSM organizes clinical communication, treatment guidelines, and insurance coverage, and it does that work. But it was never designed to map brain mechanism. Using it as a description of what your brain is doing is asking it for something it does not offer.

A QEEG phenotype is a measured, reproducible feature of your brain. It compares your electrical patterns against thousands of people your age and identifies what is stably, individually yours. Map the same person months later, nothing major changed, and the same patterns appear. That stability is not a limitation. It is the point. Your phenotypes are not symptoms you reported on a questionnaire. They are features your brain produced while you sat in a chair, and they will produce them again.

The value is not in replacing a diagnosis. It is in understanding how your resources actually work. A diagnosis tells you which club you have been sorted into. A phenotype tells you which circuits are running loud, which are running quiet, and where the regulatory bottlenecks sit. In the specific sense of being individual, physiological, and stable across time, that is the more valid measurement. For choosing what to train, what to address first, and what to expect, it is often the more useful one.

None of this means the phenotype taxonomy is a finished science. This book says so plainly, earlier in this chapter: the patterns are clinical heuristics, reliable across thousands of maps but not validated biomarkers in the pharmaceutical trial sense. Large-scale EEG reviews do document reproducible subtypes within single diagnoses (Clarke et al., 2001; Slater et al., 2022), and imaging work converges on the same principle (Pan et al., 2026). The evidence is real. The taxonomy built on it is still maturing. Hold both.

1.13 How the Bands Talk to Each Other

Those functional systems don't run on single frequencies. The five bands described earlier in this chapter were presented separately for clarity, but they don't operate in isolation. A major discovery in modern neuroscience is that brain rhythms nest: slow rhythms organize when fast rhythms fire, and the quality of that nesting determines how well your brain integrates information.

Theta-gamma coupling is the best-studied example. Theta (4 to 8 Hz) provides a slow scaffold. Gamma bursts (30 to 100 Hz or higher) ride on specific phases of the theta wave, like notes placed at precise moments within a musical measure. This is how the hippocampus encodes and retrieves memories: the theta rhythm provides the timing structure, and gamma carries the content. When the coupling is strong, learning and memory consolidation work well. When it's weak, information gets lost or stored unreliably.

Alpha gating is the second mechanism worth knowing. Alpha doesn't just idle. It actively suppresses cortical regions that aren't needed for the current task. When you focus on a voice in a crowded room, alpha increases over visual cortex (you're not using it), freeing resources for auditory processing. This is sensory gating: alpha decides what gets through and what gets filtered out. Clients with poor alpha production often report feeling overwhelmed by sensory input, because the gate that would normally filter it is broken.

The reason this matters for neurofeedback: when you train a single band, you're not just changing that band in isolation. You're tuning a relationship. Training SMR (12 to 15 Hz) at the sensorimotor cortex strengthens sleep spindle production (which is cross-frequency coupled to delta during sleep) and improves the theta-to-SMR transition that marks a brain settling from drift into alert stability. Training alpha strengthens the gating mechanism that allows focused processing. The bands are a system, not separate dials.

Chapter 13 develops the sleep-QEEG connection at greater length.

1.14 Your Brain, Your Data

Stated plainly:

Your brain is an organ. Like any organ, it produces measurable outputs. Like any measurement, those outputs can be compared against norms, tracked over time, and used to guide intervention. You don't need to understand every frequency band or every connectivity metric. You need to understand that your brain's patterns are *visible, measurable,* and *changeable,* and that having this information adds specificity that standard clinical assessment alone does not provide.

A doctor who never ordered a blood panel has less to go on when evaluating your cardiovascular risk. A clinician who has never measured your brain has less to go on when evaluating what's driving your symptoms.

A brain map doesn't answer every question. But it turns on the lights. And once the lights are on, everything that follows, the training, the lifestyle changes, the clinical decisions, can be informed by data instead of driven by assumption.

That's what this book is about: literacy. The ability to see your own brain clearly and make smart decisions about it.

Decision Point: If you're intrigued by the idea that your brain has a readable pattern, one that might explain why you struggle with the things you struggle with, Chapter 3 explains exactly how neurofeedback works to change those patterns. If you want the sixty-year backstory of how we got here first, that's Chapter 2.

1.14.1 Going Deeper

- For the full clinical picture of what a brain map reveals, see *QEEG Field Guide* Chapter 1.
- For the twelve character archetypes that map to the phenotypes introduced here, see *Gifted and Tortured*.
- For the consumer phenotype atlas covering twenty common patterns, see Appendix G in this book.

Your Move:

1. **Reflect:** Think about the last time you tried to change something about how your mind works, sleep, focus, anxiety, energy. Did anyone measure anything before recommending an intervention? If not, how did they decide what to try?

2. **Act:** If you've ever had a brain map, pull it out and look at it with fresh eyes. If you haven't, consider whether the patterns described in this chapter match anything in your experience.

3. **Start a conversation:** Ask your therapist, doctor, or coach: "Have you ever recommended a brain map for someone like me? Why or why not?" Their answer will tell you a lot about how they think about brain-based assessment.

Ch 2: A Short, Weird History of Neurofeedback

Neurofeedback has one of the strangest origin stories in modern medicine. It starts with cats, rocket fuel, and a lab at UCLA. It winds through Vietnam-era VA hospitals, counterculture meditation experiments, and decades of turf wars between competing schools of practice. It was championed by clinicians, ignored by mainstream psychiatry, and funded by nobody with deep pockets. And it's only now, sixty years in, finally getting the rigorous scrutiny it deserved all along.

This history won't teach you how neurofeedback works, that's Chapter 3. But it will explain something you'll encounter as soon as you start researching: why the field looks fragmented, why the evidence base is messier than it should be, and why the strongest critics and the strongest advocates are often both partially right.

2.1 Sterman's Cats (1960s–1970s)

The story begins in the mid-1960s at UCLA, where a neuroscientist named Barry Sterman was studying sleep and wakefulness in cats. He had electrodes implanted over their sensorimotor cortex, the strip of brain that controls movement, and he noticed something interesting. When the cats sat motionless but alert, a specific rhythm appeared in their EEG: a 12–15 Hz oscillation he called the sensorimotor rhythm, or SMR.

Sterman wanted to know if the cats could learn to produce more of this rhythm. So he set up a simple conditioning experiment: whenever a cat's brain produced SMR for about half a second, a food dispenser clicked and delivered a small reward. Over sessions, the cats' brains produced more SMR. The rhythm strengthened.

This is important to get right, because the popular version of this story often implies the cats *chose* to produce SMR, as if they sat there thinking, "I'll make my brain do that 12 Hz thing now." They didn't. This was operant conditioning, the same process by which a rat learns to press a lever or a child learns that saying "please" gets results. The brain's electrical patterns were shaped by reinforcement, not by conscious effort. The cats didn't decide to change their brainwaves any more than you decide to salivate when you smell dinner. Their nervous systems learned because the environment rewarded a specific pattern.

Neurofeedback isn't mind-over-matter. It's conditioning. That distinction matters for everything that follows.

Then came the rocket fuel.

Around the same time, NASA asked Sterman to study monomethylhydrazine, a rocket propellant known to cause seizures, to estimate safe exposure levels for astronauts. Sterman exposed cats to hydrazine, expecting seizures at predictable doses. Most seized on schedule. But a few resisted seizures far longer than expected.

When Sterman checked his records, he realized these seizure-resistant cats were the same ones he'd previously trained on SMR. In the initial study, just three trained cats and three untrained controls received the same dose. The controls seized at about fifty-five minutes; the trained cats averaged nearly three times that, and none of the early toxic symptoms were delayed, only the seizure itself (Sterman, LoPresti & Fairchild, 1969).

A controlled replication followed: thirty cats in three groups of ten, unoperated, operated with electrodes but no conditioning, and operated with three months of SMR training. The surgery alone increased seizure susceptibility, shortening latencies significantly. SMR conditioning countered that effect: trained cats showed seizure latencies comparable to or exceeding the unoperated animals, with marked individual variability in how much protection the conditioning conferred (Sterman, 1976). The operant conditioning of a brain rhythm had made those brains harder to push into pathological firing.

That accidental discovery, space-program toxicology meets conditioned cat brainwaves, is the origin of neurofeedback. Sterman pub-

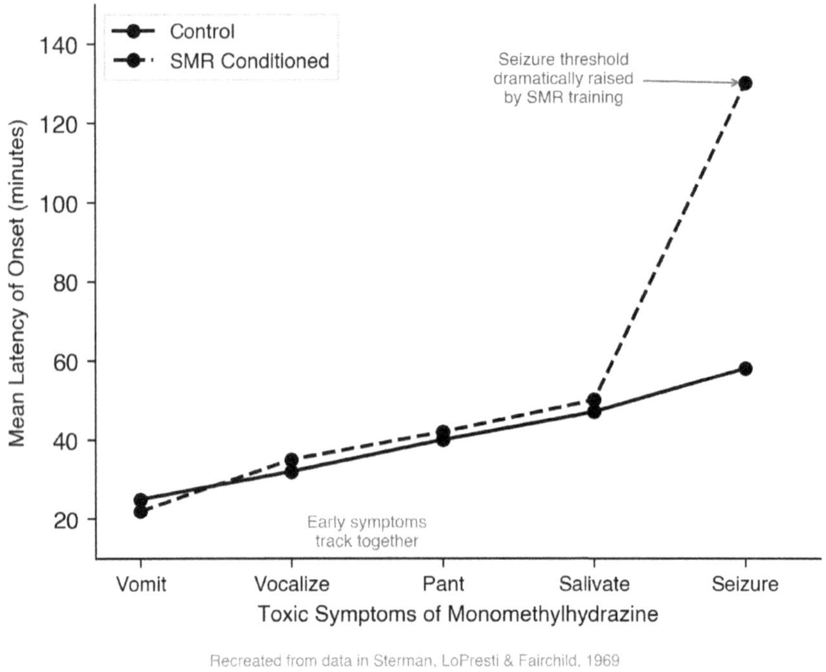

Figure 2.1: Sterman's SMR-conditioned cats showed dramatically delayed seizure onset after monomethylhydrazine exposure, while early toxic symptoms tracked together in both groups. Recreated from data in Sterman, LoPresti & Fairchild, 1969.

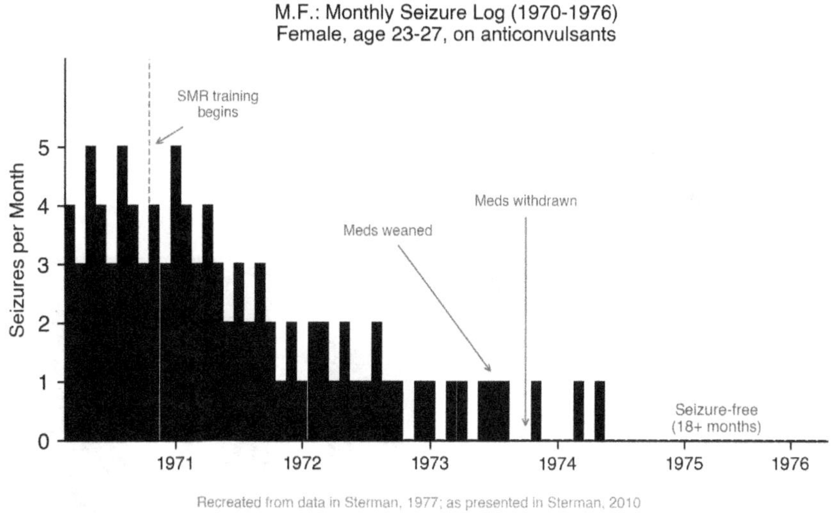

Figure 2.2: M.F.'s monthly seizure log shows the gradual decline after SMR training began, continuing through medication withdrawal, to sustained seizure freedom. Recreated from data in Sterman, 1977; as presented in Sterman, 2010.

lished the foundational cat work with Wanda Wyrwicka, first identifying the rhythm and then showing it could be operantly conditioned in the waking cat (Wyrwicka & Sterman, 1968; Sterman, Wyrwicka & Howe, 1969). He showed that SMR conditioning facilitated spindle-burst sleep in *Science* in 1970, and translated the approach to humans with intractable epilepsy in the early 1970s. His first patient was a twenty-three-year-old VA laboratory technician who had suffered grand mal seizures since age eight, uncontrolled on anticonvulsants. After several months of SMR training her seizures declined steadily. Her medications were eventually weaned and withdrawn entirely, and she remained seizure-free long enough to obtain a driver's license for the first time in her life (Sterman & Friar, 1972).

A later review tabulated every published clinical series from 1972 to 1996: of 174 patients, 142 (about 82 percent) showed a significant reduction in seizure frequency, which that review defined as greater than 30 percent, with the average reduction exceeding 50 percent (Ster-

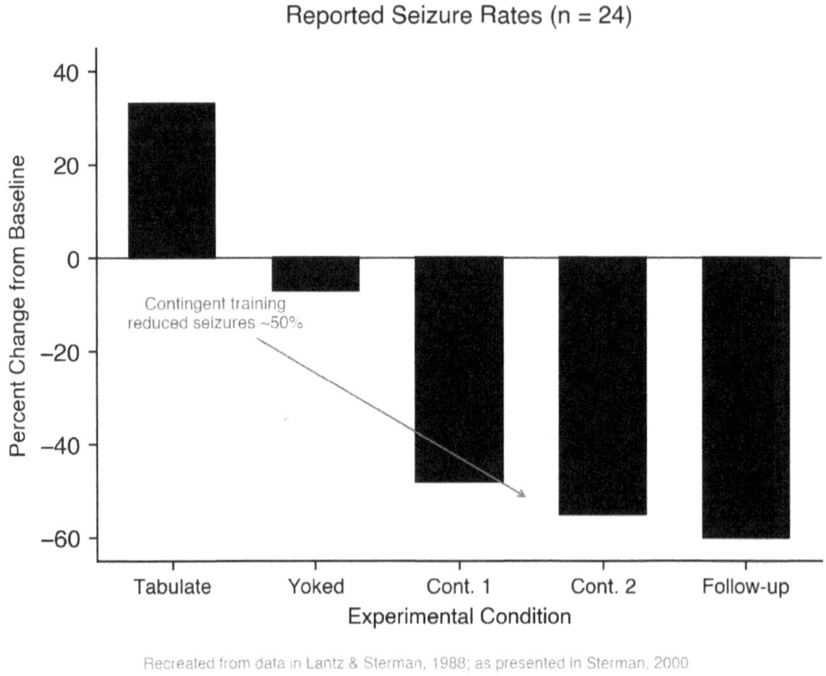

Figure 2.3: Sterman's controlled human epilepsy data: seizure rates increased during baseline tabulation, showed minimal change with yoked (non-contingent) feedback, dropped sharply during contingent SMR training phases, and persisted at follow-up. Recreated from data in Sterman, 2000.

man, 2000). Roughly 5 percent became seizure-free for the periods tabulated. The controlled data told the same story: in a reversal design with twenty-four epilepsy patients, seizures actually increased during a baseline tracking period, barely changed with non-contingent (yoked) feedback, dropped roughly 50 percent during contingent SMR training, and the reduction persisted at follow-up (Sterman, 2000).

Those are drug-refractory patients who had already failed medication, which is what makes the numbers remarkable, and they come from small, mostly uncontrolled series, which is what keeps them from being proof. Later histories would call him the father of neurofeedback.

2.2 Kamiya and the Alpha Seekers (1968)

While Sterman was conditioning cats at UCLA, a researcher named Joe Kamiya at UCSF was running a different kind of experiment. He filtered EEG for alpha waves, the 8–12 Hz rhythm that appears when the brain is awake but not actively processing, and trained human subjects to recognize when they were in a high-alpha state.

The protocol was simple. Subjects sat with eyes closed. Every few seconds, a tone sounded, and they had to guess whether their brain was producing alpha or not. Kamiya gave them immediate feedback on whether they were right.

Within about seven one-hour sessions, nine of twelve subjects could discriminate their own alpha states above chance and intentionally shift into high-alpha on cue. The subjective reports were strikingly consistent: when in high-alpha, people described "not thinking," "letting go," and "feeling tranquil, calm, and alert."

Kamiya published this in *Psychology Today* in 1968 (Kamiya, 1968), a popular magazine rather than a scientific journal. He explicitly linked alpha waves to meditation-like serenity and noted that Zen meditators in his sample excelled at producing alpha. Some subjects reportedly begged to "go back into that state."

That article hit the counterculture like a match hitting gasoline. Alpha waves became a doorway to altered consciousness. Suddenly, neurofeedback wasn't just about seizures and cats, it was about expanding the mind. The 1970s saw a wave of alpha-training enthusiasm that was part legitimate science, part spiritual seeking, and part carnival.

This was both the best and worst thing that could have happened to the field. The enthusiasm brought funding and public interest. The association with consciousness expansion and meditation gave neurofeedback a countercultural stain that would cost it decades of scientific credibility. The field wandered into a no-man's land between science and religion, and mainstream academia wanted nothing to do with it.

2.3 Lubar and the ADHD Connection (1970s–1990s)

While Sterman worked on seizures and Kamiya's alpha work rippled through the culture, a researcher named Joel Lubar was pursuing a different question: could neurofeedback help children with attention problems?

He started where Sterman had. His 1976 report followed a single hyperkinetic boy through months of SMR training over sensorimotor cortex, rewarding 12–14 Hz and inhibiting 4–7 Hz, with independent observers counting behavior in the classroom rather than parents filling out forms (Lubar & Shouse, 1976). The hyperactivity fell when the training ran and returned when the contingency was reversed, which is the part that mattered: the behavior tracked the reinforcement. It was one child, and the drug-withdrawal phase had not yet reported.

From there Lubar moved toward the pattern the field would live on for thirty years. Larger QEEG studies through the late 1980s and 1990s characterized excess slow theta and reduced fast beta as a group-level ADHD signature, and the protocol became: train theta down, train beta up, over frontal and central sites.

By the early 1990s, Lubar and colleagues had formalized this as the theta-beta protocol and published QEEG data showing elevated theta-beta ratios as a consistent ADHD marker. This became the canonical neurofeedback protocol for ADHD, the one that would be studied, debated, and eventually challenged more than any other.

The Lubar lineage shaped the field for decades: identify the theta-beta abnormality, train theta down and beta up, measure the change. It was clean, logical, and seemed to work. It also tied neurofeedback's credibility to a single metric, the theta-beta ratio, that would later prove more fragile than anyone expected.

2.4 Peniston and the VA (1980s)

In the 1980s, at a VA hospital, a clinician named Eugene Peniston developed something completely different: an alpha-theta neurofeedback protocol for Vietnam veterans with alcoholism.

The Peniston protocol used eyes-closed training, usually at O1, a site over the left occipital cortex. Participants were rewarded for producing theta and alpha simultaneously, combined with guided imagery about recovery and sobriety. The sessions had a hypnotic quality, deep relaxation, altered states, sometimes vivid imagery or emotional release.

In a small VA trial, Peniston reported dramatically lower relapse rates in the alpha-theta group compared with treatment-as-usual over thirteen-month follow-up (Peniston & Kulkosky, 1989). A subsequent study extended the approach to Vietnam veterans with PTSD, reporting reductions in depression and PTSD symptoms over approximately thirty-month follow-up (Peniston & Kulkosky, 1991).

These studies became legendary in neurofeedback circles, highly cited, methodologically fragile, and emotionally powerful. They seeded the idea that alpha-theta training could reach deep trauma and addiction circuitry, an idea that Bessel van der Kolk would later popularize in *The Body Keeps the Score*.

2.5 The School Wars

By the 1990s, neurofeedback had splintered into competing camps, each with its own philosophy, its own protocols, and its own personalities. Understanding these camps helps explain why the field looks chaotic from the outside.

The Sterman lineage emphasized SMR conditioning as a physiology-first approach, rooted in animal models and epilepsy research. Conservative, lab-driven, skeptical of overclaiming.

The Lubar lineage focused on theta-beta ratios and ADHD, tied to QEEG-guided subtyping and behavioral outcomes. Data-driven, education-focused, oriented toward research credibility.

The Othmer lineage came from a different place than the others. Sue and Siegfried Othmer entered the field after using neurofeedback with their son Brian, who had severe epilepsy and behavioral challenges that conventional treatment had not resolved. That personal origin shaped everything that followed. Starting in the late 1980s, they pushed symptom-based, multi-site training, arguing that rigid protocols and fixed QEEG markers were too simplistic. Over the following decades, their approach evolved toward increasingly slow frequencies, culminating in infra-low frequency (ILF) training below 0.1 Hz by the mid-2000s. Adjust based on what the client reports in real time, not just what the map says.

These schools disagreed about what to train, how much to trust QEEG, and how strictly to follow published protocols. The disagreements were sometimes scientific and sometimes personal, and they contributed to neurofeedback's reputation as a fragmented, quasi-tribal field. Different approaches work for different presentations. But the infighting cost the field credibility and research dollars at a time when it could afford neither.

2.6 The Decade the Brain Forgot Neurofeedback (1990s)

The 1990s were branded the "Decade of the Brain," and most of that decade's attention went elsewhere. fMRI was transforming neuroscience. Prozac was transforming psychiatry. Neurofeedback had no large blinded trials, no pharmaceutical sponsors, and a lingering association with 1970s alpha-wave experimentation. It was an intervention that was inexpensive, technician-deliverable, and would reduce long-term medication use, which made it commercially uninteresting to the institutions that fund medical research. So it stayed on the fringe: scientifically intriguing, clinically promising in skilled hands, and largely invisible to mainstream medicine.

2.7 The Pharma Shadow

CHADD, the largest ADHD advocacy organization in the United States, received approximately $1 million from pharmaceutical companies between 1991 and 1994 alone. By 2009, money from pharmaceutical companies, counting both direct grants and advertising, represented over a third of CHADD's total revenue. The DEA took notice.

Its 1995 background paper on methylphenidate quoted a Ciba-Geigy spokesman describing CHADD as "essentially a conduit" for reaching patients, and the agency's own conclusion was blunter: the relationship "raises serious concerns about CHADD's motive in proselytizing the use of Ritalin." A 2002 Congressional hearing directly confronted CHADD's leadership.

Stimulant medications do work, for many people. But when the organizations that shape public understanding of ADHD are funded by companies that sell ADHD medication, non-pharmacological alternatives face structural headwinds that have nothing to do with their scientific merit. Neurofeedback has no pharmaceutical sponsor, no patent, and no sales force. It was always going to struggle for institutional attention in that environment. The evidence base looks the way it does not because the science is weak, but because the money and infrastructure that produce large-scale trials never flowed its way.

2.8 The QEEG Revolution

One development changed everything: normative databases.

Starting in the 1980s, Robert Thatcher and other researchers began assembling large, age-stratified EEG databases. For the first time, a clinician could compare an individual's brain activity against a statistical model of what's expected for their age and derive Z-score maps showing specific deviations.

This gave birth to QEEG-guided neurofeedback, training based on what your brain actually shows, not just what your symptoms suggest. Instead of giving everyone with ADHD the same theta-beta protocol, clinicians could look at the individual's map and target the specific patterns that deviated. Different brains got different protocols.

It also gave birth to Z-score training, neurofeedback that rewards movement toward normative values rather than raw changes in power or frequency. This was a philosophical shift: from "change this one thing" to "normalize the system."

The database approach wasn't perfect, databases have their own limitations, and the quality varies, but it represented the field's most important methodological advance since Sterman's cats. It turned neurofeedback from guesswork into measurement.

2.9 The Books That Changed the Conversation

Two books shaped public awareness of neurofeedback more than any clinical trial.

Jim Robbins' *A Symphony in the Brain* (2000) turned the origin stories into pop-science narrative: cats in rocket-fuel chambers, Sterman's epilepsy patients, Lubar's ADHD kids, Peniston's VA addicts. It framed neurofeedback as a rebel technology, overlooked by mainstream medicine, full of oddball characters, running on a mix of lab science and California experimentation. For many early adopters, this was the first time they heard that you could train your own brainwaves.

Bessel van der Kolk's *The Body Keeps the Score* (2014) devoted a chapter to trauma, EEG, and neurofeedback. It described traumatized brains stuck in survival rhythms and highlighted neurofeedback as a way to re-regulate. The book became a global bestseller and put neurofeedback on the radar of trauma therapists, EMDR practitioners, and desperate patients worldwide, massively increasing demand without a parallel increase in rigorous trials.

Together, these books did for neurofeedback what Michael Pollan later did for psychedelics: they created a public narrative that outran the evidence and forced the field to catch up.

2.10 Where We Are Now (2021–2026)

In the last five years, three shifts have reshaped the field.

The sham-controlled reckoning. The double-blind trials that critics demanded finally arrived, and their results were sobering. The 2021 Arnold trial in children with ADHD found no superiority of neurofeedback over sham at post-treatment or thirteen-month follow-up. A 2025 JAMA Psychiatry meta-analysis reached the same conclusion at the group level. For sleep, a rigorous 2017 sham trial (Schabus et al., 2017) found no specific benefit, and a 2024 meta-analysis went further: pooled across randomized trials, the control conditions beat neurofeedback on sleep quality (Recio-Rodriguez et al., 2024). Read that twice. Not a null. The comparison groups, mostly active ones like cognitive behavioral therapy for insomnia, did better than the training.

This doesn't mean neurofeedback does nothing, both groups in these studies improved. It means that standardized protocols applied to mixed populations don't consistently beat well-designed placebo conditions on group-level symptom measures. The field has had to reckon with the difference between "neurofeedback helps people" and "neurofeedback's specific mechanism is what helps people." Chapter 5 goes deep on this.

The pivot to personalization. Simultaneously, tools emerged that could predict who benefits. The Brainmarker-I work (Voetterl et al., 2023) retrospectively stratified ADHD patients by individual alpha peak frequency and found 29–36 percent higher remission rates when treatment happened to match the biomarker, validating it as a predictor of treatment response, though the study did not prospectively test QEEG-guided treatment selection. Machine-learning models began identifying responders from baseline QEEG features. One-size-fits-all is giving way to individualized, QEEG-guided treatment selection.

The technology democratization. Consumer EEG headbands, cloud-based remote training platforms, and VR-enhanced neurofeedback moved training out of clinics and into homes. Whether that's a good thing depends entirely on how it's done, Chapter 17 helps you evaluate those options.

The quiet accumulation of clinical wisdom. There is a fourth shift that does not make headlines. Decades of clinical practice have produced a body of individualization knowledge that often outpaces the publication record. Experienced clinicians who have mapped and trained thousands of brains know things that formal RCTs have not yet tested: which phenotype combinations respond to which sequencing, when to change a protocol at session twelve versus session twenty, how medication interactions alter the training curve. That knowledge is a genuine strength of the field. It is also a vulnerability. Claims built on clinical experience without published data invite skepticism, and some of that skepticism is earned. The best practitioners hold both truths at once: clinical pattern recognition is real, and it is not a substitute for evidence.

2.11 What This History Tells You

You're entering a field that is simultaneously sixty years old and still growing up. The science is real, operant conditioning of brain electrical activity is well-established, and the clinical observations across thousands of practitioners are consistent. The evidence base is improving but uneven. The marketplace is largely unregulated. And the institutions that could have built the evidence faster, universities, NIH, pharmaceutical companies, had incentives that pointed them elsewhere.

As a consumer, this means you need to be literate, someone who can read the evidence and the marketplace with clear eyes. The rest of this book gives you the tools.

Your Move:

1. **Reflect:** Did anything in this history surprise you? If you came in skeptical of neurofeedback, did the structural reasons for the evidence gap change your thinking? If you came in enthusiastic, did the sham-controlled results give you pause?

2. **Act:** Look up one of the key papers or books mentioned in this chapter, Wyrwicka & Sterman's 1968 paper on conditioning sensorimotor spindles in the waking cat, Robbins' *A Symphony in the Brain*, or van der Kolk's neurofeedback chapter in *The Body Keeps the Score*. Read it with fresh eyes.

3. **Start a conversation:** The next time someone tells you neurofeedback "doesn't work" or "isn't proven," you now know enough to ask: "Proven how? By whom? With what protocols, on what populations, for how many sessions?" Those questions change the conversation.

Ch 3: Operant Conditioning for Your Brainwaves

3.1 The Category That Matters

Neurofeedback is personal training for your brain. Like physical therapy for a torn ligament, like vocal coaching for a singer: you show up, a skilled practitioner reads the data, sets targets, and adjusts the program as you progress. The changes happen because your nervous system is adapting, building capacity, strengthening regulatory circuits. Unlike physical therapy or vocal coaching, however, most neurofeedback protocols require no voluntary effort from you during the session. The brain learns through operant conditioning without conscious participation. (The exception is SCP training and certain other protocols that ask you to shift your brain's readiness state on cue; these require active engagement. And younger or disengaged clients sometimes need enough buy-in to sit still and attend to the screen. But for the majority of protocols, the conditioning runs below conscious effort.)

You're not ingesting a substance. What you've built is capacity, not a chemical effect that disappears when you stop taking it. How long that capacity lasts depends on the condition and the protocol. For some presentations, follow-up data show gains persisting months after training ends. For others, the durability picture is less clear, and whether periodic maintenance sessions are needed is an open question the field has not settled. The follow-up evidence is discussed condition by condition in Section III. Your clinician's skill matters. The match between the protocol and your specific brain pattern matters. If someone promises you results without ever seeing your brain data or adjusting as you go, that's a vending machine, not neurofeedback done well.

3.2 How Your Brain Learns Without You Trying

The core mechanism, stripped to its essentials:

Your brain produces electrical activity in real time, the rhythms we covered in Chapter 1. In a neurofeedback session, sensors on your scalp pick up that activity and feed it to a computer that processes the signal instantly. The computer compares what your brain is doing right now against a set of targets, frequencies to increase, frequencies to decrease, thresholds to meet.

When your brain's activity moves toward the target, something happens: a movie plays more smoothly, a game character advances, a tone sounds, a puzzle piece appears. When your brain moves away from the target, the reward stops. The movie dims. The game stalls. The tone goes silent.

That's it. That's the loop. Your brain produces a pattern, the computer evaluates it, and the environment responds with a reward or its absence. Over hundreds of these micro-events per session, across dozens of sessions, your brain's electrical patterns shift.

Most people are surprised to discover: **you don't have to try.** The first few minutes of a session, most people are trying anyway: tensing slightly, concentrating, willing the screen to respond. Then something shifts. The shoulders drop half an inch. The breathing slows. The hands, which were gripping the armrest, open. The movie brightens and stays bright, and the person realizes they weren't doing anything when it happened. That moment, when effort gives way and the brain takes over, is when the real training begins.

You don't have to concentrate on producing the right brainwave. You don't have to visualize anything or think specific thoughts. In fact, trying usually gets in the way. Your brain learns the way Sterman's cats learned, through operant conditioning. The reward signal shapes the pattern. The conscious mind is mostly a spectator.

This is counterintuitive. We're used to learning being effortful, studying, practicing, repeating. But operant conditioning works below the level of conscious effort. Your brain detects the contingency between its own state and the environmental reward, and it adjusts

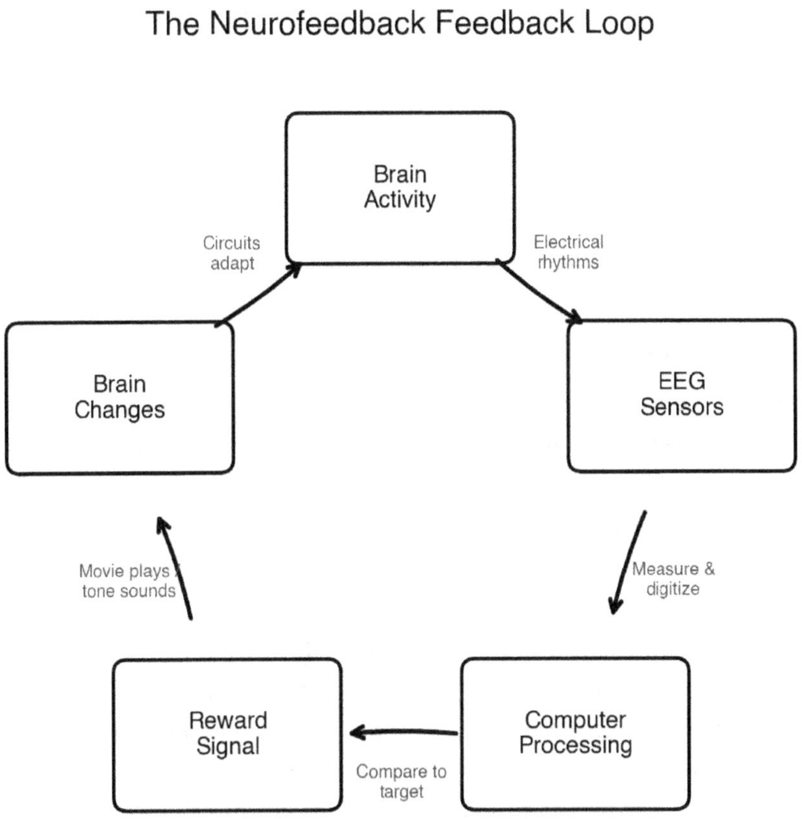

Figure 3.1: The Neurofeedback Feedback Loop

without conscious instruction. That's what brains do when reinforcement is present.

Andrew's doctoral research demonstrated this directly. When participants were given real neurofeedback, where the reward signal was contingent on their actual brain activity, their brains produced measurable electrical events (event-related spectral perturbations) at the trained frequency, at the trained site. When participants were given sham feedback, identical-looking sessions where the reward signal was driven by someone else's pre-recorded brain data, those specific events vanished. The brain knew the difference, even though the participant couldn't tell which condition they were in.

The learning is real. It's specific to the frequency being trained and the brain site being targeted. And it happens whether or not you're aware it's happening.

What's actually happening at the circuit level? When your brain produces a pattern that earns a reward, several things occur in parallel. The neurons firing at the trained frequency strengthen their connections to each other, a process called Hebbian plasticity: neurons that fire together wire together. The reward signal, even when it's just a movie playing smoothly, engages the brain's reinforcement circuitry. Dopamine and related neuromodulators tag the preceding neural activity as "worth repeating." Over hundreds of repetitions, the circuits that produce the target pattern become easier to access, more likely to fire spontaneously, and more resistant to being overridden by competing patterns. You're not memorizing a fact. You're training your brain to spend more time in healthier, more efficient patterns of activity. The brain that used to default to high beta at rest starts defaulting to alpha more often. The brain that couldn't sustain SMR learns to hold that rhythm for longer. It's the same process that lets a pianist's fingers find the right keys without thinking, except the "keys" are frequency bands and the "practice" is the feedback loop.

Why it feels invisible. Most learning we're familiar with is explicit: you study for a test, you practice a chord progression, you notice yourself getting better, and you can describe what you learned. Neurofeedback is implicit learning. The skill builds below the level of verbal awareness, closer to learning how to balance on a bicycle than to memorizing a fact. The reinforcement happens too fast for conscious processing, hundreds of micro-events per minute. You can't introspect your way into producing more alpha or less theta. The brain changes the habit before you can describe what changed. Clients often say they have no idea what they're "doing" during sessions. That's the point. The brain is doing it. Your job is to show up and let the loop run.

The immediacy that makes it work. What makes operant conditioning so effective here is the timing. The reward arrives within milliseconds of the brain producing the target pattern. In animal learning, delay of reinforcement by even a few seconds dramatically weakens learning. Neurofeedback delivers the signal in real time. The brain doesn't have to remember what it did five minutes ago. The association is instant: this pattern, right now, produced that outcome. That immediacy is why thirty minutes of training can contain thousands of learning trials, each one reinforcing the circuits you want to strengthen. It's also why the feedback has to be genuinely contingent on your brain. Sham feedback, where the reward is driven by someone else's brain or a random algorithm, produces no learning. The brain is exquisitely sensitive to whether the reward actually follows from its own activity. When it does, the circuits change. When it doesn't, they don't.

3.3 The Regulation Problem: Thermostat vs. Jazz

What are we actually training when we do neurofeedback? Not a single brainwave. We're training *regulation,* the brain's ability to control its own states.

Think of it as two different kinds of control.

Thermostat regulation is stability. Your brain needs to maintain certain baselines, a level of arousal that matches what you're doing, a sleep architecture that cycles properly through the night, an emotional reactivity that responds appropriately without overreacting. When these baselines drift, you get symptoms: chronic anxiety (arousal too high), ADHD-like fog (arousal too low), insomnia (sleep architecture disrupted), emotional volatility (reactivity uncalibrated).

Jazz improvisation is flexibility. Your brain also needs to shift states fluidly, from focused to creative, from alert to relaxed, from engaged to recovering. A brain that's stuck in one gear, even a productive gear, eventually crashes. Rigidity is its own form of dysregulation.

Good neurofeedback trains both: the stability to hold useful states and the flexibility to shift between them. The specific protocol determines which aspect you're working on. SMR training tends to build stability. Alpha-theta training tends to build flexibility. Most people need both, and a good protocol plan sequences them based on what your brain map shows.

3.4 Biofeedback You Feel; Neurofeedback You Don't

This distinction runs through the rest of the book.

HRV biofeedback is voluntary. A device measures your heart rate variability. You learn a skill: paced breathing at your resonance frequency, conscious recruitment of the vagal brake. You feel the shift happening. You know when you're doing it well. The gains depend on whether the skill transfers into daily life. Do you use the breath when you need it? In traffic, before a presentation, during an argument? If HRV biofeedback "doesn't work," the question is usually about skill acquisition and practice. Did you learn the technique? Do you recruit it under stress? Chapter 16 develops this in depth. *Half a Second More* goes deeper still.

Neurofeedback is involuntary. The brain learns from contingent reinforcement of its own electrical activity without you consciously trying to do anything. Sterman's cats didn't decide to produce more SMR. Their thalamocortical circuits learned because the contingency was set up correctly. Your cortex does the same thing. You sit in the chair, the sensors read your EEG, the software rewards specific patterns, and the brain adjusts. You don't feel the learning as you feel your breathing slow during HRV training. The operant conditioning occurs below conscious effort.

The consequence of this distinction runs through two later chapters and you should have it in mind from here forward. When HRV biofeedback "doesn't work," the question is usually: did the skill transfer? When neurofeedback "doesn't work," the question is usually: did we pick the right target? The wrong exercise does not produce the right change. For neurofeedback, because the learning is involuntary, target selection and protocol quality matter far more than effort, attitude, or compliance. Chapter 16 covers the voluntary-skill case in depth. Chapter 18 covers the wrong-target case in depth.

3.5 What's Trainable, What's Wired In

Not every brain pattern responds equally to training. Some shift within fifteen to thirty sessions. Others are wired in for life and respond slowly or not at all. Understanding where your patterns fall on this spectrum is the best expectation calibration you can do before starting neurofeedback.

The spectrum runs from **regulatory** patterns (state-dependent, responsive to training, meaningfully plastic) to **constitutional** patterns (trait-like, highly heritable, stable across decades). Most patterns fall somewhere between, but the extremes illustrate the range.

Highly constitutional patterns. Your individual alpha peak frequency (IAF), the speed at which your alpha rhythm cycles, is among the most heritable EEG traits: twin studies estimate heritability around 0.81 (Smit et al., 2006). Three timescales help make sense of what "stable" means here. (a) *Short-term test-retest:* in healthy adults measured weeks apart under consistent conditions, IAF is highly stable, which is what makes it useful as a stratification metric. (b) *Developmental and aging change:* IAF rises through childhood and adolescence, peaks in early adulthood, and declines gradually in later adulthood. These shifts are real but slow, playing out over decades. (c) *Experimental trainability:* some studies report small shifts in IAF with neurofeedback, but reported changes are modest and the durability of those shifts is debated. Your overall spectral shape, the relative distribution of power across frequency bands, is roughly 70 percent heritable. These are the brain's version of bone structure: trainable at the margins, but the architecture is substantially set. If your IAF is 8.5 Hz, training is not going to make it 11 Hz. What training can do is improve how well the brain uses the rhythm it has and how efficiently it deploys alpha in context.

Highly regulatory patterns. Frontal theta excess shows moderate heritability, often estimated in the ballpark of 30 to 50 percent (van Beijsterveldt & van Baal, 2002; Smit et al., 2005), with the rest driven by sleep quality, arousal state, and cortical activation habits. It responds well to training in many clients. High beta at rest is substantially state-driven: chronic stress, poor sleep, and threat-scanning can generate it, and removing those drivers (plus targeted training) often brings it down substantially. SMR at the sensorimotor strip is one of the most responsive training targets in the field.

What this means for you. Ask your provider which of your patterns are likely regulatory (and therefore responsive to training within a typical course) and which are likely constitutional (and therefore require managing expectations about how far training can move them). A provider who promises to "normalize everything" without distinguishing between these categories is either poorly informed or overselling. When you get to Chapter 17's provider scorecard, this is one of the questions worth asking: does this provider set different expectations for regulatory patterns versus constitutional ones?

The *QEEG Field Guide* Chapter 7 covers the constitutional-regulatory spectrum at clinical depth, with heritability estimates for each major phenotype. If you want the full picture, that's the reference.

3.6 What Actually Changes When You Learn

The popular image of neurofeedback learning is straightforward: the brain produces more of the target frequency, the "wave gets bigger," and you improve. The reality is more interesting and more useful.

Alpha neurofeedback, the most-studied of the protocol families, doesn't work by making alpha waves taller. Research on alpha-band learning (Ossadtchi et al., 2017, among others) shows that training produces lasting increases in alpha power, but the mechanism is subtler than "wave gets bigger." Clinical observation and microstructure analysis suggest the brain often learns to trigger alpha bursts more frequently rather than inflating individual burst amplitude. How often the thalamocortical system initiates a synchronized burst may change before average amplitude does.

This is one reason the same "alpha-up" instruction at the screen produces different results across people. Some brains have strong burst-initiation capacity and learn quickly. Others lack the thalamocortical flexibility to trigger bursts reliably, and progress is slower. The substrate for learning varies, and that variance is part of what Chapter 18 addresses when training stalls.

For clinicians and informed consumers tracking session data, the practical takeaway: watch incidence-rate and threshold-crossing statistics in the first five to ten sessions, not just average amplitude. If burst frequency is increasing, the brain is learning, even if amplitude looks flat. If burst frequency hasn't changed by session ten, the protocol may need adjustment.

3.7 The Protocol Families: Tools in a Toolbox

What confuses most people about neurofeedback is the number of different approaches. Walk into five different clinics and you might encounter five different methods, each claiming to be the right one. Multiple approaches are valid, and the question isn't which method is "best" in the abstract. It's which method is best matched to your brain pattern and your goals.

Think of these as tools in a toolbox, not competing religions.

3.7.1 Amplitude Training (and Why SMR Is the Foundation)

The most traditional form. One or two electrode sites. Train specific frequencies up or down, increase SMR, decrease theta, reduce high beta. This is what Sterman used, what Lubar developed for ADHD, and what most research studies have tested. Straightforward, well-studied, and effective when the target is well-chosen.

SMR deserves special mention because it's arguably the most foundational protocol in all of neurofeedback. SMR (12-15 Hz over sensorimotor cortex) trains the brain's thalamocortical inhibitory circuits, the same circuits that produce sleep spindles at night, suppress seizures, calm motor restlessness, and stabilize arousal. It's one protocol, but it sits at the hub where sleep, movement, arousal, and plasticity intersect. That's why SMR training shows up in treatment plans for ADHD, anxiety, insomnia, epilepsy, and performance, not because it's a generic cure-all, but because inhibitory regulation is foundational to all of them. Chapter 13 (The Brain Asleep) explains the SMR-spindle connection in detail.

In practical terms, stronger inhibitory regulation means your brain gets better at saying "no" to itself. Your attention wants to chase the next shiny distraction, and now the frontal cortex can override that pull and keep you on task. A child's nervous system wants to escalate into a meltdown when a toy is taken away, and instead, the arousal doesn't spike as hard, the reaction is smaller, the recovery is faster. These aren't abstract neurological changes. They're the moments in daily life where regulation shows up.

3.7.2 Z-Score Training

Instead of training raw power up or down, Z-score protocols train your brain toward normative values, what's statistically expected for your age across multiple sites and frequencies simultaneously. The targets come directly from your QEEG comparison to the normative database. This is a more comprehensive approach that can address multiple deviations at once, but it requires good QEEG data and a clinician who understands what normalization means (and when deviation from the norm is actually fine). Z-score training is particularly useful for complex presentations like traumatic brain injury, where multiple metrics are disrupted simultaneously and you need to move the whole system toward typical function rather than targeting one frequency at a time.

3.7.3 Coherence and Connectivity Training

Targets the *relationships* between brain regions rather than the activity at any single site. If two areas that should be coordinating show low coherence, or two areas that should be independent are locked together, connectivity training addresses that. This is particularly relevant for conditions involving network-level dysfunction, trauma, TBI, and some complex ADHD presentations.

3.7.4 Slow Cortical Potential (SCP) Training

Trains the brain's ability to shift between activation and deactivation states, the slow electrical shifts that underlie cortical readiness. Well-studied for ADHD and epilepsy, particularly in European research. Requires sustained attention from the trainee, because the training asks you to intentionally shift your brain's readiness state on cue, which demands active engagement that passive movie-watching protocols don't. This makes SCP training harder for young children but potentially powerful for adults and older kids who can participate actively.

3.7.5 LORETA/sLORETA Neurofeedback

Uses mathematical modeling to estimate where in the brain the surface-level electrical patterns may originate, then targets those estimated source locations. The honest limits are worth stating plainly: source localization solves an inverse problem that is mathematically ill-posed, meaning multiple different source configurations can produce the same pattern at the scalp. The spatial resolution of any solution is limited, and a 19-channel recording provides far fewer data points than the number of possible source locations. The result is a statistical estimate, not a direct measurement of deep-brain activity. Naming a specific deep structure (the anterior cingulate, the insula) from a 19-channel surface recording should be understood as a model estimate with wide uncertainty, not as an observed anatomical fact.

With those limits in mind: LORETA and sLORETA add a dimension that pure surface-level training does not. The electrodes still sit on the surface of your scalp; nothing is going deep into your brain. The "depth" is mathematical, not physical. The software uses the pattern across all nineteen surface sensors to estimate which source regions are plausible generators, then designs training protocols aimed at influencing those estimated sources through the surface recordings. More technically demanding, requires specialized software, and the precision of the estimates depends heavily on the number and quality of recording channels.

3.7.6 Infra-Low Frequency (ILF) / Othmer Method

Trains at very slow frequencies, below 0.1 Hz, based on the idea that the brain's slowest oscillations regulate overall stability. The Othmer approach adjusts frequencies and training sites based on the client's real-time symptom response rather than fixed QEEG targets. More phenomenological than data-driven: rather than locking in fixed frequency targets from a QEEG, the clinician adjusts in real time based on what the client reports feeling. Some researchers find this imprecise; many experienced clinicians find it powerful, particularly for complex presentations where a rigid protocol framework misses the person.

3.7.7 LENS and Direct Neurofeedback

These are passive approaches, the client doesn't have to engage with feedback. Instead, a very weak electromagnetic signal is delivered to the scalp, offset from the brain's own dominant frequency by a small amount. The theory is that this micro-stimulation nudges stuck patterns without requiring the operant learning loop. LENS is faster per session (sometimes just a few minutes) and is sometimes used as a precursor to more traditional training.

3.7.8 Beyond Brainwaves: HEG, HRV, and Other Modalities

Not all neurofeedback trains electrical patterns. HEG (hemoencephalography) trains **prefrontal metabolic activity** through optical or thermal proxy signals that reflect local blood oxygenation and heat output (with extracranial confounds; see Chapter 16 for the measurement details). HRV biofeedback trains **autonomic regulation:** the body's balance between activation and recovery. These modalities complement EEG neurofeedback rather than competing with it.

Chapter 16 covers these tools in detail, including why blood flow training may work by training the brain's vascular oscillations (vasomotion), and how HRV biofeedback pairs with EEG neurofeedback for a top-down plus bottom-up approach to regulation.

3.8 Why We Prefer QEEG-Guided Over Symptom-Only

Protocol choice has direct practical consequences.

If a clinician picks your protocol based solely on your symptoms, "you have ADHD, so we'll do theta-beta training", they're making the same mistake as the psychiatrist who prescribes based on a diagnosis without measuring anything. Your symptoms might come from high theta, or from low alpha, or from connectivity issues, or from sleep deprivation mimicking the whole picture. Same label, different brain, different optimal target.

QEEG-guided neurofeedback means the protocol is chosen based on what your brain *actually shows*, the specific deviations, the specific regions, the specific relationships between sites. It means two people with the same diagnosis might get different protocols. And it means the protocol can change as your brain changes, because you're tracking objective data, not just subjective reports. In practice, this is not "the map dictates everything." It is a dynamic conversation between the objective QEEG data, the client's subjective reports session to session, and the individual goals that brought them through the door. The map starts the conversation. The client's experience steers it.

This is the fundamental argument of this book: **individualize the intervention to the brain, not the diagnosis.** It's why the clinical results we see with QEEG-guided protocols don't match the group averages in studies that give everyone the same protocol. The studies are testing a standardized approach on a heterogeneous population.

The clinic is matching the approach to the individual. Those are different things, and they produce different outcomes. We should be clear: this is our clinical position, not a proven advantage. No randomized head-to-head trial comparing QEEG-guided protocol selection against symptom-based selection has been published, and Chapter 5 addresses what the controlled evidence can and cannot tell us about individualization.

3.9 The "Different" vs. "Better" Trap

A word of caution about protocol shopping.

Some clinics market their specific method as the one true approach, the only valid neurofeedback. This is a red flag. The research supports multiple approaches for multiple conditions. The question isn't "which method is best?" but "which method is best for *this brain*, with *these goals*, at *this point* in training?"

A good clinician has multiple tools and knows when to use each one. A clinician who only does one thing will try to fit your brain into their method, rather than fitting the method to your brain.

If someone tells you their approach is the only one that works, ask them what the alternatives are and why they've ruled them out. If they can't answer that clearly, they may not know enough about the broader field to be making that call.

Your Move:

1. **Reflect:** When you think about "brain training," does the personal training metaphor resonate? Or does it feel too passive, like something is being done *to* you rather than *with* you?

2. **Act:** If you're exploring neurofeedback, ask a prospective provider: "What protocol family would you use for me, and why? How did you decide?" Their answer tells you whether they're matching to your brain or to their method.

3. **Start a conversation:** The next time someone describes neurofeedback as "just biofeedback for brainwaves," you can now explain:

it's operant conditioning of specific electrical patterns, guided by quantitative brain data, using multiple protocol families matched to individual brain profiles. That's a more precise and more accurate description.

Ch 4: The Session Playbook: What Actually Happens (And How to Track Your Progress)

4.1 Before You Begin: The Intake

A good neurofeedback experience starts before any electrodes touch your head.

The first session should be a conversation, a thorough intake where the clinician learns your history, your symptoms, your goals, your medication list, your sleep patterns, and your expectations. This isn't a formality. Everything that follows depends on the clinician understanding your full picture.

You should be asked about:

- **What brought you here:** specific complaints, not just a diagnosis
- **Medical and psychiatric history:** medications, prior treatments, head injuries, seizure history
- **Sleep:** duration, quality, consistency, whether you wake at night, whether you feel rested
- **Lifestyle:** caffeine, alcohol, exercise, screen habits, stress level
- **Goals:** what would "better" look like? Not vague ("less anxiety") but functional ("I want to fall asleep within thirty minutes" or "I want to get through a workday without hitting a wall at 2pm")

If a clinic skips this step and goes straight to selling you a brain map or a training package, slow down. Good clinical work starts with understanding the person, not hooking up the equipment.

4.2 The Brain Map Session

You've been through this in Chapter 1. The brief version of the experience:

You'll sit in a quiet room. A cap with nineteen electrodes goes on your head, with conductive gel at each site to ensure a clean signal. The technician checks impedance, making sure each electrode has good contact, and then you sit still. Ten minutes eyes open, ten minutes eyes closed. You might be asked not to clench your jaw, not to move your eyes around, not to fidget. Muscle activity and eye movements contaminate the recording, so stillness matters.

The recording itself takes less than an hour. Processing and interpretation happen afterward, and you'll typically come back for a separate session to review your results and discuss protocol options. Preparation matters: Appendix I has a full checklist covering medication timing, sleep, and caffeine before your recording.

4.3 What a Training Session Looks Like

What does it actually feel like to do neurofeedback?

You arrive at the clinic. A technician or clinician places one to several electrodes on your scalp at specific locations, determined by your protocol. Gel, tape, good contact. This takes five to ten minutes. Then you sit in front of a screen.

On the screen, you might see a movie, a game, a puzzle, or a simple visual display. As your brain's electrical activity shifts toward the target patterns, the display responds: the movie plays clearly, the game advances, the puzzle reveals a piece. When your brain drifts away from the targets, the feedback stalls, the movie dims, the game pauses, the tone goes quiet.

A typical training session runs twenty to thirty minutes of active feedback. The whole visit, including setup and debrief, is usually forty-five minutes to an hour. You do this two to three times per week.

That's it. You sit. You watch. Your brain does the work. Most people report that the sessions feel mildly engaging but not effortful, like watching a movie that occasionally flickers. Some people feel relaxed during sessions. Others don't feel much at all until they notice changes in their daily life between sessions.

What it actually feels like in the room. The electrodes are cool. The gel is a slight pressure, not uncomfortable. You might notice the faint hum of the equipment or the quiet of a room designed for stillness. The screen becomes the focal point. When SMR training is working, clients often describe a subtle heaviness in the limbs, a settling. One person said it felt like "my body remembered how to be still." When alpha training is active, people report a sense of spaciousness, a slight mental quiet. High-beta reduction can feel like nothing at all during the session, then you notice later that you didn't spiral after a stressful email. The feedback itself varies. Some systems use tones that rise and fall. Others use game elements that advance or stall. The common thread: your brain is getting a signal, hundreds of times per second, about whether it's producing the right pattern. You don't have to interpret that signal consciously. Your nervous system does it for you. The room temperature, the chair, the absence of demands, these all support the brain's ability to relax into the process. We've had clients fall asleep during sessions. We've had others who find it surprisingly alerting. Most land somewhere in between.

The between-session surprises. The real texture often shows up outside the clinic. A client who felt nothing during their first five sessions reports that they fell asleep in twenty minutes instead of ninety. Another notices they didn't snap at their kid over the morning chaos. A third realizes they got through a meeting without checking their phone. These aren't dramatic transformations. They're incremental shifts that the brain has been learning to produce, and they only become visible when life demands them. The session is the practice. The rest of your life is the test.

4.4 What Learning Feels Like: The Timeline

Let's be specific about what to expect.

Sessions 1–3: Nothing, or almost nothing. Most people feel no different after their first few sessions. Some notice a slight shift, a bit calmer, a bit more tired, slightly different sleep, but many feel absolutely nothing. This is normal. Your brain is beginning to respond to the contingency (we can measure changes in the EEG within the first five to ten minutes of the first session), but subjective awareness lags behind.

Sessions 3–5: The first hints. This is when most people start to notice something. Better sleep. A slightly shorter fuse (temporary, we'll get to that). A moment of unexpected calm. One client told us, "I was sitting in traffic and I realized I wasn't angry." These early changes are often subtle and easy to dismiss if you're not tracking them.

Sessions 10–15: Measurable shifts. By this point, most people and their clinicians can point to specific functional changes, better sleep quality, improved focus duration, reduced reactivity, fewer afternoon crashes. These aren't dramatic transformations yet. They're early evidence that the training is engaging the right targets.

Sessions 20-30: Consolidation. This is where the compounding happens. The gains from the first ten sessions have been building, and now they start to feel stable. By this point, a quantitative EEG re-assessment often shows measurable shifts in the trained metrics. In our clinical experience, many clients show visible changes on the heat-map report by this stage, though the magnitude varies by individual and by what is being trained. This has not been quantified in a controlled study with a defined denominator and outcome measure; it is a clinical observation from our practice. This is where the training starts to look like real, durable change rather than a temporary state shift.

Sessions 30–50+: Deep regulatory change. For many presentations, executive function, anxiety, ADHD, sleep, two rounds of roughly twenty-five sessions can produce large behavioral changes. Some people need more, some fewer. The right number depends on what you're training, how complex your brain pattern is, and how your nervous system responds.

The key insight: These session-by-session descriptions are patterns we observe in practice, not published benchmarks with defined response criteria. Some people respond faster. Some respond slower. Some plateau and need a protocol adjustment. The clinician should

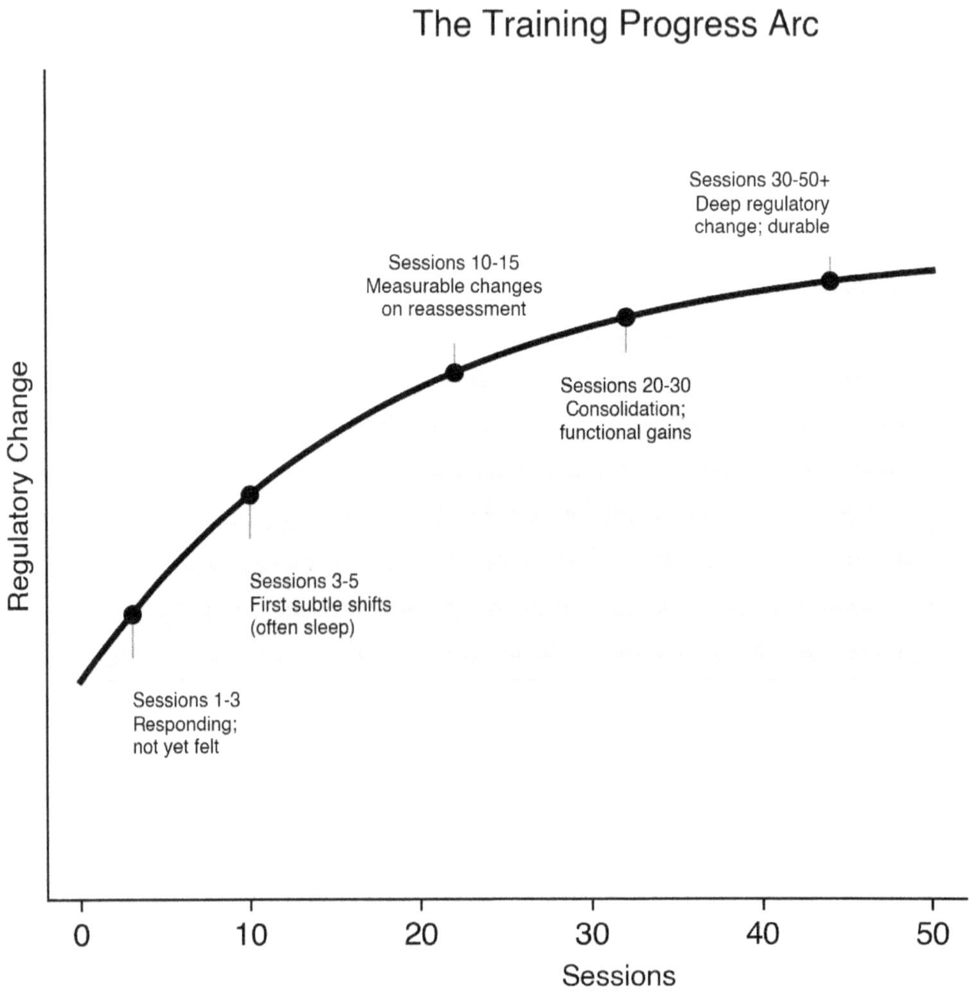

Figure 4.1: The Training Progress Arc

be monitoring your progress with objective measures, not just asking "do you feel better?", and adjusting the plan accordingly.

4.5 The Bumps: What's Normal, What's Not

Neurofeedback is safe (Chapter 6 covers this in detail), but it is not without temporary side effects. Common responses to expect:

Common and usually harmless:

- **Fatigue after sessions:** your brain just did concentrated work. A nap is fine.
- **Irritability:** especially in the first few sessions. It should settle within a day or two. If it persists or worsens across multiple sessions, treat it as a safety signal and tell your clinician promptly. The protocol may need adjustment, and worsening should be assessed, not assumed to be a positive sign.
- **Vivid dreams or sleep changes:** common, especially with protocols targeting arousal or sleep architecture. Usually transient.
- **Headache:** occasionally, usually mild, resolves with hydration and rest.
- **Emotional activation:** old feelings surfacing, brief periods of tearfulness or heightened emotion. More common with alpha-theta and trauma-oriented protocols.

When to speak up:

- Irritability that *increases* over several sessions rather than settling
- Anxiety that gets *worse* rather than better
- Sleep that deteriorates significantly
- Any new symptom that wasn't there before and doesn't resolve between sessions

These are signals that the protocol needs adjusting. Transient effects typically resolve within a day or two. But any new or worsening symptom is a safety signal that deserves assessment, not dismissal. The difference between a minor bump and a genuine problem is whether the clinician recognizes it and acts. Good clinicians expect transient effects and have a plan for them. Bad clinicians don't notice or don't adjust.

Know when to stop and when to call. Use this escalation guide:

RED: Stop training. Obtain urgent assessment. A seizure during or after a session. Loss of consciousness or fainting. New or worsening mania, psychosis, or severely disorganized thinking. Suicidal thoughts, intent, or preparatory behavior (giving away possessions, researching methods, writing final messages) that were not present before training, or worsening of pre-existing suicidal thoughts. Any new focal neurologic symptom (sudden weakness on one side, speech difficulty, vision loss).

YELLOW: Report to your clinician before the next session. Any new symptom that persists beyond two to three sessions (worsening anxiety, new irritability, sleep disruption, headaches). A clear pattern of getting worse rather than better. Emotional activation that feels destabilizing rather than manageable.

GREEN: Expected transient effects. Mild fatigue after a session. Brief irritability that resolves within a day. One or two nights of vivid dreams or lighter sleep. A passing headache that responds to rest and hydration.

When in doubt, report it. Your clinician can only adjust what they know about.

Note: passive EEG neurofeedback (which reads your brain's electrical activity and feeds it back to you) has a different risk profile from brain stimulation methods such as tDCS, tACS, or LENS, which deliver electrical current to the scalp or brain. The escalation guide above applies to passive neurofeedback. If you are receiving any form of brain stimulation, discuss the specific safety considerations with your provider.

The most important thing you can do as a client: Communicate. Tell your clinician what you're noticing between sessions, the good, the bad, and the weird. They can't adjust what they can't see, and what you notice at home is data they don't have.

Fluid, open communication is one of the hallmarks of a good practitioner. If your clinician isn't asking you about your sleep, your mood, and your daily experience at the start of every session, or if they seem rushed past those questions, that's worth noticing. The best clinical outcomes come from a feedback loop that runs in both directions: your brain data tells the clinician what's happening neurologically, and your lived experience tells them whether those neurological changes are landing where they matter.

4.6 How Sleep Tells You If the Protocol Is Right

Your sleep is the first signal that your protocol is working. It's also the first signal that it needs adjustment. A skilled clinician reads your sleep changes the way a mechanic reads engine sounds, and your job is to give them the readout.

Trouble falling asleep that wasn't there before? The training may be pushing activation too hard, leaving the brain revved up at night. Tell your provider. The usual response is to ease off the activating parameters and strengthen the circuits that manage the wake-to-sleep transition.

Waking during the night that wasn't there before? The brain may have been slowed down too much, which often shows up alongside daytime fogginess; a brain that's too slow when awake is also too unstable to maintain sleep. The fix runs the other direction, a bit more daytime activation, so the brain is more awake by day and sleeps more deeply at night.

If alpha or alpha-theta training lightens your sleep, that's a known rebound effect, and the usual response is to rebuild the stabilizing foundation first, then reintroduce the deeper work once sleep is steady. Which sites and bands a clinician adjusts to do all this are protocol decisions on their side. What matters on yours is reporting the change early and precisely. Sleep is the cheapest, fastest readout you have.

4.7 Tracking Your Own Progress

"I feel better" is not a measurement. It's a start, but it's vulnerable to placebo, wishful thinking, and the natural fluctuation of symptoms over time. If you're investing time and money in neurofeedback, you deserve to know, with some precision, whether it's working.

Track these:

Sleep: the single most informative daily metric. Rate your sleep quality each morning on a 1–10 scale. Three things to note: onset (how long it took to fall asleep), maintenance (whether you stayed asleep through the night), and feeling rested when you woke up. Sleep improvements often appear before other changes.

Stress: rate your daily stress on a 1–10 scale. Notice whether you are getting stuck in your head, worrying, over-focusing on problems, or unable to relax even when nothing urgent is happening. Tracking stress alongside sleep reveals how much your nervous system is carrying into each session.

Attention: rate your average daily attention on a 1–10 scale. Three things to watch: Can you sustain alertness through the day without crashing? Can you hold focus on a task without drifting? Are you acting on impulse more than usual, interrupting, clicking, reaching for your phone? Note any patterns: better in the morning? Gone by 2pm? More sustained than last week?

Emotional reactivity: how easily are you triggered? How quickly do you recover? "I got angry but recovered in five minutes instead of two hours" is measurable progress even if the anger still appeared.

Functional outcomes: the things that actually matter in your life. Can you sit through a meeting? Are you snapping at your partner less? Are you finishing tasks you used to abandon? These are harder to quantify but they're the real measures of whether training is translating into life change.

Keep it simple. A daily log with four 1–10 ratings (sleep, stress, attention, mood) takes sixty seconds. Over twenty-five sessions, that log becomes a dataset that can show trends no single session can reveal.

4.7.1 Daily Training Log

Photocopy this page or photograph it on your phone. Fill it out each morning (for sleep) and each evening (for the rest). Sixty seconds a day builds the dataset that makes your progress visible.

Date	Sleep (1–10)	Stress (1–10)	Attention (1–10)	Mood (1–10)	Notes (reactivity, wins, setbacks)

After twenty-five sessions, look for trends: which metrics moved first? Which lagged? That pattern tells you and your clinician something real about how your brain is responding to training.

4.8 When to Re-Map

A good clinic will re-assess your QEEG at planned intervals, typically every twenty to twenty-five sessions. The re-map shows objective changes: has the excessive theta decreased? Has the suppressed alpha strengthened? Have connectivity patterns shifted?

This is where neurofeedback becomes data-driven rather than faith-based. If your subjective experience says "I feel better" but the map shows no change, the clinician needs to investigate, are we targeting the right thing? If the map shows significant change but you don't feel different yet, the question is whether the functional benefits are lagging behind the neural changes (common) or whether the map changes aren't translating to the right brain systems.

Re-mapping also tells you when to stop. If your map has normalized and your symptoms have resolved, continuing to train is like continuing physical therapy after the injury has healed. You're done, or at least ready for maintenance rather than active training.

4.9 Realistic Session Counts

Based on clinical experience and the limited research on dosing, this is what we can say honestly:

20-30 sessions is the minimum meaningful course for most presentations. Below that, consolidated change is unlikely.

25-40 sessions is a common range for regulatory presentations (executive function, anxiety, sleep, attention) in clinical practice. More complex presentations (severe trauma, seizure disorders, nonverbal autism, post-concussion) often run longer, sometimes 40-60+ sessions. These ranges come from clinical experience rather than published dose-response trials; no study has systematically compared different session counts for the same condition and protocol.

Hard promises are a red flag. If a clinic guarantees results in a specific number of sessions, they're selling you a package, not providing clinical care. The right number depends on your brain, your goals, and how you respond. Anyone who claims otherwise is prioritizing their business model over your outcome.

Session frequency matters. We recommend two to four times per week, depending on the client and the setting. In our offices, three times per week is the default. For home training clients, four times per week, unless they're young, fragile, or highly sensitive, in which case we back off.

Experienced practitioners generally prefer three sessions per week over two, and this is a common scheduling preference in the field. No published dose-comparison trial has quantified the difference, so we present this as a practice preference rather than an established dose-response finding. Where more frequent sessions may be most useful is when you're running **multiple protocols:** using the extra sessions to work on different targets rather than repeating the same one.

What we recommend against: three days in a row. People who push too hard, back-to-back-to-back sessions without recovery days, tend to overtrain. Overtraining in neurofeedback looks like getting the adverse effect instead of the desired one: more activation instead of calm, more fatigue instead of energy, increased anxiety or edginess, sleep disruptions, feeling spacey instead of focused, reduced deep sleep. It's the brain equivalent of overtraining at the gym, you're tearing down faster than you can rebuild.

The sweet spot: sessions spaced with at least one rest day between most of them. Monday-Wednesday-Friday works well. Tuesday-Thursday-Saturday works. Monday-Tuesday-Thursday-Saturday works for four-times-a-week clients. Daily training is almost never appropriate outside of intensive clinical programs with close monitoring.

Less than twice per week often means the gains from one session fade before the next one reinforces them, the learning curve flattens and progress stalls.

4.10 When You Train Matters: Circadian Considerations

Your brain at 8 AM is not the same brain at 5 PM. It runs faster and more beta-primed in the morning, dips through a mid-afternoon arousal trough, and shifts toward sleep architecture in the evening. The time of day you train can interact with what you're training, so a few habits help.

Consistency matters more than optimality. If you always train at 9 AM, the brain learns in that state and your session-to-session data is cleaner. If you alternate between early morning and evening, the EEG looks different each time and the learning signal gets noisier.

Be cautious with evening sessions for activating work. Training that revs the brain up, within a few hours of bedtime can interfere with sleep onset, especially if you already run high beta or tend toward insomnia. Calming protocols tolerate any time of day.

Tell your provider if your session time changes. A clinician reviewing your data needs to know whether a noisy session reflects a protocol problem or just a different time of day. The timestamp on the file is one of the first things they check.

If the underlying neuroscience interests you, *Half a Second More* Chapter 13 covers the full day-night oscillatory picture and how it interacts with both meditation and brain training.

4.11 A Note on Stance

For most neurofeedback protocols, your psychological approach to the session doesn't matter much. The brain learns from the contingency regardless of whether you're trying, relaxing, or zoning out. SMR training, beta training, coherence work, Z-score protocols: none of these depend on your attitude in any meaningful way.

The exception is alpha-class and alpha-theta protocols. For these, active cognitive effort can interfere. "Trying harder" to make the feedback respond desynchronizes the very rhythms the training is trying to strengthen. The clients who struggle most with this tend to be high-achievers who approach the session like a test to ace. Their cortex engages effortful processing, and the alpha drops.

The coaching is simple: be present, don't perform. If your provider tells you to close your eyes and let the tones guide you, do that. Don't try to figure out what your brain is doing. Let it work.

4.12 Kids vs. Adults

The fundamentals are the same, but the experience differs.

For kids: Sessions are often shorter (fifteen to twenty minutes of active training). The feedback is more game-oriented, spaceships, puzzles, cartoons. Younger children don't need to understand what's happening. They just need to sit still enough for the electrodes to pick up a clean signal and let the conditioning do its work. Parents often notice changes before the child reports them, better behavior at school, fewer meltdowns, easier bedtimes.

For adults: Sessions run the full twenty to thirty minutes. The feedback can be anything, movies, games, abstract displays. Many adults prefer watching a movie that plays smoothly when their brain is on target and dims when it drifts. Adults are more likely to report subjective changes early but also more likely to overthink the process. The most common question we get from adults: "Am I doing it right?" The answer is always: "Stop trying. Let your brain do its thing."

Your Move:

1. **Reflect:** What would "better" look like for you? Not a vague feeling, a specific, measurable change in your daily life. Write it down. That's your outcome target.

2. **Act:** Start a daily tracking log now, even before you begin neurofeedback. Four ratings each morning: sleep, stress, attention, mood (1–10 each). Two weeks of baseline data before training starts gives you something to compare against.

3. **Start a conversation:** If you're already doing neurofeedback, ask your clinician: "How will we know if this is working? What metrics are you tracking, and when will we re-assess?" If they don't have a clear answer, that's information worth having.

Ch 5: The Evidence: What Works, What Doesn't, and How to Judge for Yourself

---

This is how a careful, scientifically literate person should think about neurofeedback in 2026.

As someone who understands what the evidence shows, where it's strong, where it's weak, and why the gap between published research and clinical experience is both real and explainable.

If you read nothing else in this book, read this.

5.1 The Hierarchy: How Evidence Works

Not all evidence is created equal. The ladder, from weakest to strongest:

Anecdote: "My friend tried neurofeedback and her anxiety disappeared." Interesting. Not evidence.

Case report: A clinician publishes a detailed account of one patient's treatment and outcome. Useful for generating hypotheses. Not proof.

Open-label trial: A group of patients receives neurofeedback and their symptoms are measured before and after. No control group. If they improve, you can't be sure the neurofeedback caused it. Maybe they would have improved anyway. Maybe the attention and structure of regular sessions helped. Maybe expectancy did the work.

Randomized controlled trial (RCT): Patients are randomly assigned to neurofeedback or a control condition. This starts to isolate the effect, but the quality depends entirely on what the control condition is.

Sham-controlled, double-blind RCT: The gold standard. Patients are randomly assigned to real neurofeedback or sham neurofeedback

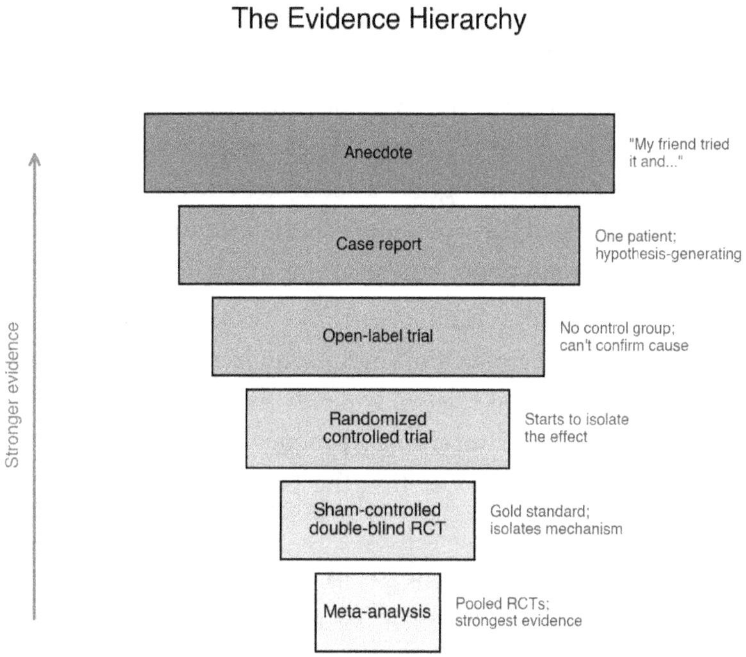

Figure 5.1: The Evidence Hierarchy

that looks and feels identical but doesn't contain the active ingredient (contingent brain feedback). Neither the patient nor the person interacting with them knows which condition they're in. If real neurofeedback beats sham, you can be confident the effect is specific to the brain training.

Meta-analysis: A statistical synthesis of multiple RCTs, pooling results to estimate an overall effect size. The strongest form of evidence, but only as strong as the trials it includes.

Each step up the ladder tells you more. Each step also costs more, takes longer, and is harder to do well for neurofeedback specifically. Understanding why is essential before you look at the condition-by-condition data.

5.2 Five Testable Limitations: What the Current Evidence Can and Cannot Tell Us

Before we show you what the evidence says for each condition, you need to understand what the current trial designs can and cannot tell us. This isn't special pleading. It's a set of structural features that limit the inferential reach of the pooled evidence, and understanding them changes how you read every study summary that follows.

A recent review of the ADHD neurofeedback evidence (Hill, 2026a) identified five testable limitations in the way trials have been designed. Each one constrains what the group-level result can tell us about neurofeedback as delivered in clinical practice. Together, they do not explain the null away; they define the boundaries of what the null means.

Limitation 1: Standardized-for-everyone protocols may dilute subgroup effects. Neurofeedback as practiced clinically is an adaptive, individualized intervention, not a standardized one. The protocol changes based on your brain map. Session targets adjust as your brain responds. A good clinician modifies the approach week to week based on how you're sleeping, what you're reporting, and what the EEG shows. When a trial freezes that into one fixed protocol, the group average erases the subgroup that responded strongly because the protocol matched their brain.

But clinical trials require standardized interventions: the same protocol for every participant, administered the same way, so you can isolate the variable. That's good science, but it systematically tests a version of neurofeedback that no experienced clinician would deliver.

The arithmetic illustrates the problem. To take a hypothetical: if 40 percent of ADHD participants happen to have the theta-excess pattern that the theta-beta protocol targets, and 60 percent have overarousal, connectivity problems, or sleep-driven theta, then even if the protocol produces a large within-responder effect ($d = 0.8$) for the 40 percent, the group average washes out to roughly $d = 0.32$. That's the difference between a clearly positive trial and a borderline one. The phenotype match rate is a plausible hidden variable in standardized neurofeedback studies; the exact subtype proportions are estimated from our clinical observations (see Appendix F) rather than from a published prevalence study.

Limitation 2: The biomarker underlying the most-studied protocol has eroded. The most-studied ADHD protocol targets the theta-beta ratio, once considered a reliable ADHD biomarker. Subsequent research showed the TBR eroding in newer populations, likely because increasing sleep deprivation raised theta levels in everyone, including controls. If the biomarker underlying the most-studied protocol is confounded by a societal shift in sleep behavior, the protocol's results will be too. (Chapter 9 covers this in depth.)

Limitation 3: Trials stop training before clinical practice would. Most trials run twelve to thirty sessions, delivering roughly ten to fifteen total hours of training. Clinical neurofeedback courses commonly run longer, often thirty to sixty sessions in practice, though the optimal dose has not been established in published dose-response trials. Testing whether neurofeedback works by stopping at twenty sessions may be analogous to testing whether physical therapy works by stopping early. RCTs, constrained by budget and participant retention, rarely reach the session counts that clinical practice delivers.

Limitation 4: Sham conditions share procedural ingredients with the active condition, which can compress between-group differences. Creating a convincing placebo for neurofeedback is genuinely difficult. You need a display that looks identical to real training, reward signals at realistic intervals, a brain signal that appears live, all without the rewards being contingent on the participant's actual brain activity.

Some sham designs use pre-recorded EEG from another participant to drive the feedback signal. Others use the person's own EEG but reward the wrong thing, increasing theta in an ADHD study, for instance. Both approaches keep the session experience identical. Both also raise a structural question Sorger and colleagues (2019) characterized in detail: a sham neurofeedback session delivers sustained attention to a brain-computer interface, regular engagement cues, a supportive clinician, and the expectation of improvement. These shared ingredients mean the sham condition controls for more procedural factors than a sugar pill does in a drug trial, which can compress between-group effect sizes (Sorger et al., 2019). This makes the between-group comparison conservative: a positive result would be highly informative, and a null result means the specific mechanism has not demonstrated an added benefit beyond the shared context.

Limitation 5: Questionnaire-based primary outcomes may lack the sensitivity to detect training-specific effects. Most trials measure success using parent-rated or self-rated symptom questionnaires. These are multi-determined instruments: they capture mood, sleep, life events, medication changes, seasonal effects, and reporter bias alongside any treatment effect. EEG measures are more direct. The gap between clear brain-level change and ambiguous symptom-level change partly reflects measurement sensitivity. When the primary outcome is a questionnaire and the brain data are collected as secondary endpoints (or not at all), the study is looking for the signal through the noisiest possible lens.

Does the brain itself change under training?

One part of the evidence debate gets overlooked consistently. If neurofeedback is operant conditioning of the EEG, the trained metrics should move in the expected direction. That claim is testable, and the answer is genuinely mixed.

In ADHD studies, 20 to 40 sessions of theta-beta training do not reliably reduce the trained theta-beta ratio. Some work finds no change in that metric after theta-beta training, while SMR training does modulate its target band; other work finds theta decreases that track clinical improvement. The picture is inconsistent rather than settled (Arns, Heinrich & Strehl, 2014). A randomized controlled trial of QEEG-based neurofeedback in children with dyslexia illustrates the opposite case. Breteler and colleagues found improvement in spelling but not in reading, and found no significant fronto-central power or coherence changes; the authors explicitly linked the absence of coherence normalization to the absence of reading gains (Breteler et al., 2010).

That is a case where the expected EEG shift did not appear and neither did the expected behavioral gain. In a post-concussive sample (N = 26, single-group, uncontrolled), two-thirds of the EEG metrics that changed significantly after live Z-score training were measures of alpha, increasing across frontal and central regions. Theta / alpha ratio reductions predicted improvement in pain intensity and cognitive symptoms, while beta-related power predicted affective symptom improvement. No EEG metric predicted somatic, vestibular, sleep, depressive, or migraine symptoms, and the authors state explicitly that causality cannot be inferred from this exploratory design (Hershaw & Hill-Pearson, 2022). In PTSD, a randomized controlled trial of alpha-rhythm EEG neurofeedback reported decreased PTSD symptoms alongside restored default-mode and salience network connectivity on fMRI (Nicholson et al., 2020).

In some of these studies, pre-post EEG changes reach medium to large effect sizes within the treatment group, but uncontrolled within-group comparisons are exactly the design this chapter teaches you to read with caution. The EEG sometimes changes measurably under training and sometimes does not; where it does change, it sometimes predicts specific symptom shifts. Whether those shifts appear reliably, and whether the changes require contingent feedback rather than structured attention, is not yet established.

Andrew's doctoral research at UCLA added a crucial piece. When he compared real versus sham neurofeedback with identical session environments, both groups showed some EEG change. Sham sessions still produced EEG responses, because structured, attention-demanding sessions change the brain regardless. But only the real feedback group developed frequency-specific and site-specific patterns over time: the trained frequencies at the trained sites showed progressive, learning-like changes in event-related activity that simply didn't appear in the sham arm. That topographic specificity is the brain's signature for genuine operant conditioning. It can't be explained by expectancy, attention, or the general benefits of showing up to regular appointments.

This matters for how you read the condition-by-condition data that follows. Symptom scales are noisy, multi-determined, and often underpowered to show between-group superiority over a credible active control. The EEG metrics are more direct. The brain is clearly learning something. Whether that learning translates into a large, clean symptom advantage over carefully designed sham in short-duration trials is where the picture is more complicated.

With that context in place, the controlled evidence by condition:

5.3 The Evidence by Condition: What the Best Data Shows

A condition-by-condition summary based on meta-analyses and systematic reviews published between 2020 and 2026. The findings are presented straight.

Quick Reference: Evidence by Condition

Condition	Evidence Level	Key Finding	Key Caveat
ADHD	Level 1 (negative)	Does not outperform sham at group level	Standardized protocols on mixed populations; individualized practice may differ
Anxiety	Level 2–3	Large pre-post effects	Weak controls in most studies; effects shrink with better designs
Depression	Level 2–3	Meaningful clinical improvements	Very limited sham-controlled data
PTSD	Level 2	Large effect sizes; SMD ≈ -1.76	Effects decrease as designs improve; VA/DoD CPG (2023) says "insufficient"
Substance Use	Level 2–3	Large pooled effect ($g \approx 0.85$)	Substantial heterogeneity; variable controls

Condition	Evidence Level	Key Finding	Key Caveat
Insomnia	Level 1 (negative)	Controls outperform NF on sleep quality	NF often improves sleep as secondary gain; CBT-I remains first-line
Epilepsy	Level 3	Meta-analytic data, clear direction: most patients had fewer weekly seizures	Tan 2009 pools older, mostly small and uncontrolled studies; no modern sham-controlled replication
Autism	Level 3–4	Small studies, encouraging signals	No ASD-specific meta-analysis
TBI / Concussion	Level 3–4	Supportive case data	No NF-specific meta-analysis
Peak Performance	Level 3	Consumer NF: small distress reduction; cognitive effects ns	Clinical QEEG-guided peak performance not yet meta-analyzed
Chronic Pain	Level 3	Small-moderate effects	High heterogeneity; limited sham control

Evidence levels: 1 = meta-analytic data (clear direction). 2 = multiple RCTs, promising but not definitive. 3 = early/limited data. 4 = case-level only.

5.3.1 ADHD, The Most Studied, Most Debated

ADHD is neurofeedback's flagship condition. More studies have been done here than for any other diagnosis. And the results are complicated.

The 2025 meta-analysis. A 2025 JAMA Psychiatry systematic review and meta-analysis (Westwood et al., 2025) pooled twenty sham-controlled and active-control ADHD trials and found no clinically meaningful benefit of neurofeedback on probably-blinded ADHD symptom ratings: SMD = 0.04 (k = 20; n = 1,214; 95% CI: −0.10 to 0.18). This is a statistically defensible null, consistent with the earlier meta-analysis by Cortese and colleagues (2016), which similarly found that neurofeedback effects on ADHD symptoms did not survive probably-blinded assessment. On the primary symptom endpoint, neurofeedback did not outperform control conditions at the group level.

That finding deserves to be stated plainly, and it has been. What follows are secondary and exploratory findings from the same evidence base and from individual trials within it. These findings do not refute the meta-analysis; they limit its inferential reach.

Standard-protocol subgroup. When Westwood et al. restricted the analysis to trials using standard neurofeedback protocols (theta/beta, SMR, or SCP), the effect on ADHD total symptoms reached significance: SMD = 0.21 (k = 9; n = 681; 95% CI: 0.02 to 0.40). The standard-protocol result for inattention specifically did not reach significance. This is a subgroup analysis and should be read as exploratory.

Processing speed. The same meta-analysis found a significant effect on processing speed: SMD = 0.35 (k = 15; n = 909; 95% CI: 0.01 to 0.69). A domain-specific gain that the pooled symptom endpoint does not capture.

Follow-up divergence. The 2021 Arnold trial (Arnold et al., 2021), a rigorous double-blind study of 144 children at two sites, found no separation between neurofeedback and sham on primary outcomes at treatment end. At thirteen-month follow-up, however, a secondary outcome diverged: 39.7% of the neurofeedback arm met dimensional remission criteria compared with 18.5% in sham (P = .011, unadjusted; attenuating to approximately .06 after baseline adjustment). The neurofeedback arm also required less medication at follow-up (P = .012). These are secondary outcomes and should be read as signals, not proofs.

Temporal pattern. A 2019 meta-analysis (Van Doren et al., 2019) found within-group inattention effects that grew from SMD = 0.64 at post-treatment to SMD = 0.80 at two-to-twelve-month follow-up, while control-group effects faded. The caveat: those comparators were non-active (waitlist, treatment-as-usual), not sham. The temporal pattern is worth noting but does not, on its own, rule out non-specific explanations.

Why these patterns sit alongside the null, not against it. Sham conditions in neurofeedback trials share procedural ingredients with the active condition: sustained attention to a brain-computer interface, structured clinical contact, and the expectation of improvement. Sorger and colleagues (2019) documented how this structural overlap can compress between-group effect sizes more than in drug trials, where the control condition shares fewer procedural elements with the active treatment. This does not invalidate the pooled null. It identifies a design feature worth understanding when interpreting the size of between-group effects.

The honest conclusion. Current trials have not resolved whether standardized, phenotype-informed neurofeedback protocols benefit identifiable ADHD subgroups. The pooled null is real. The standard-protocol subgroup, the follow-up divergence, the processing-speed signal, and the temporal pattern are also real. Individually, each secondary finding is exploratory. Collectively, they suggest that a pooled-endpoint summary may not capture the full picture. Precision-medicine approaches, which Westwood et al. themselves recommend, are the constructive next step. Until those trials are run, guidance to readers should reflect both the pooled null and the protocol-specific, temporal, and domain-specific patterns that sit alongside it.

The brain-level evidence adds another dimension to this picture. But first, the rest of the condition data.

5.3.2 Anxiety and Depression, Promising, Not Proven

Across anxiety-spectrum studies, pre-post effect sizes are consistently large, but most trials used weak controls (waitlist, treatment-as-usual). When restricted to better-designed studies, effects shrink considerably (Russo et al., 2022). For depression, multiple pre-post analyses show similar patterns: meaningful clinical improvements, but very limited sham-controlled data to confirm specificity (Barlas, 2021).

Level of evidence: Level 2–3. Encouraging but not definitive.

5.3.3 PTSD, Growing but Not There Yet

A 2023 systematic review and meta-analysis of both clinical and neurophysiological outcomes (Askovic et al., 2023) found pooled reductions in PTSD symptom severity (SMD ≈ -1.76) and remission rates roughly three times higher in neurofeedback groups than controls. That is an enormous effect, and it is the number you will see quoted.

A 2024 meta-analysis is the better guide (Voigt, Mosier & Tendler, 2024). It was built specifically to correct the earlier reviews, which had pooled non-randomized studies, and it did not reproduce the earlier estimate. Clinician-rated PTSD came out at SMD 0.74, self-rated at 0.47: real, clinically meaningful, and less than half of what Askovic reported. Then the number that decides the question. Split by control condition, neurofeedback beat *passive* controls by 1.30 and beat *active* controls by **0.05**. Against a comparison group that got something, anything, of comparable structure and attention, the clinician-rated advantage disappears.

That is the same pattern as ADHD, arriving a decade later. The VA/DoD Clinical Practice Guideline for PTSD (VA/DoD PTSD CPG, 2023) concludes "insufficient evidence to recommend for or against," and on this evidence that is the correct call.

One bright spot: van der Kolk and colleagues ran the most prominent RCT of neurofeedback for chronic PTSD, reporting significant reductions in PTSD severity versus a wait-list control in adults with treatment-resistant PTSD (van der Kolk et al., 2016). A wait-list is a passive control, which is exactly the comparison the 2024 pooling showed to be flattering. And a double-blind, sham-controlled proof-of-concept trial of real-time fMRI connectivity neurofeedback showed specific reductions in repetitive negative thinking in depression versus sham (Tsuchiyagaito et al., 2023), with a subsequent analysis documenting brain-network changes that tracked symptom improvement (Misaki et al., 2024). This is a narrow but genuine demonstration of mechanism-specific benefit.

Level of evidence: Level 2. Promising, emerging, but not yet Level 1.

5.3.4 Substance Use Disorders, Intriguing

A 2026 meta-analysis of seventeen RCTs of EEG neurofeedback for addiction (Wan et al., 2026) reported a large pooled effect ($g \approx 0.85$), stronger for substance addictions than behavioral ones. Substantial heterogeneity and variable controls limit confidence, but the signal is consistent.

5.3.5 Insomnia: The Clearest Negative

When neurofeedback is compared to strong control conditions specifically for primary insomnia, the findings are sobering: in several rigorous RCTs, control conditions outperformed neurofeedback on subjective sleep quality. The most careful double-blind trial (Schabus et al., 2017) showed both real and sham SMR neurofeedback produced similar subjective improvements, with no differential benefit on polysomnography.

Level of evidence: Level 1, for lack of added benefit. This is the clearest case where high-quality evidence goes against neurofeedback's claims for a specific condition.

This doesn't mean neurofeedback never improves sleep. It often does, as a secondary gain when training targets arousal regulation broadly. But for primary insomnia specifically, CBT-I remains the evidence-based treatment. Chapter 13 addresses this in detail.

5.3.6 Everything Else

Epilepsy: The original neurofeedback application and the deepest evidence base in the field. Level 3 by the standard above. Meta-analytic data exists and points in a clear direction: across the pooled studies most patients had fewer weekly seizures, all of them medication-refractory. The caveat is age and quality, not direction. That meta-analysis is from 2009 and pools older, mostly small and mostly uncontrolled studies, and nothing modern or sham-controlled has revisited it. Neurofeedback is an adjunct here and never a substitute for neurology and antiseizure care.

Autism spectrum: Small studies, no ASD-specific meta-analysis. Level 3–4.

TBI/concussion: Supportive case data, no NF-specific meta-analysis. Level 3–4.

Peak performance in healthy adults: The best available meta-analysis (Treves et al., 2025) covers consumer-grade devices paired with mindfulness meditation, not clinical QEEG-guided training. It found a small reduction in psychological distress but no significant effects on cognitive function or mindfulness after correcting for reporting bias; the authors conclude that consumer-device claims are "not currently supported" and that effects may reflect "neurosuggestion" (placebo). The structural critique from Chapter 5's limitations framework (Hill, 2026a) applies directly: standardized consumer protocols on unselected populations face every design constraint that compresses clinical-NF effect sizes in the research literature. Clinical peak-performance work with individualized, QEEG-guided protocols has not been meta-analyzed. Level 3.

Chronic pain: Small-moderate effects, high heterogeneity, limited sham control. Level 3.

5.4 What the Brain Actually Does Under Training: The Hill 2012 / 2026 Study

For his doctoral research, Andrew worked with Howard Lightstone to build one of the first proper double-blind sham modules. The system blended pre-recorded EEG with the participant's live signal on screen, making it visually indistinguishable from real training, while deriving all training parameters from the stored data rather than the live brain. This let them test whether the brain responds specifically to contingent feedback. It does.

A preliminary 2026 reanalysis of the original dissertation dataset (Hill, 2026b, bioRxiv preprint, not yet peer-reviewed; data from Hill, 2012) applied modern statistical methods (Bayesian mixed models and false-discovery-rate correction) to a small sample and uncovered findings the original analyses could not detect. Because this is a preprint reanalysis of older data from a small study, the numbers below should be read as preliminary. They are worth knowing because they speak to the mechanism question directly, but they are not definitive.

The brain responds to real feedback and not to sham. Across all active neurofeedback groups versus sham, the event-related desynchronization (ERD) in the trained frequency band was large: d = -1.23, FDR-corrected p = 0.001. Sham sessions produced no reward-band ERD at all. Both real and sham sessions produced a theta-band event-related synchronization (a brief 4 to 7 Hz response to the reward tone), confirming that participants in both conditions were processing the feedback signal. The difference: only real neurofeedback produced the frequency-specific power change that operant conditioning predicts.

Different protocols engage different circuits. Beta training at C3 produced the strongest overall ERD (d = -2.38 versus sham), but SMR training at C3 produced the strongest P2 suppression, a cortical signature of altered sensory processing at the trained site (d = -1.33 versus sham). Beta training left P2 intact. This preliminary finding suggests a double dissociation: two protocols, same brain region, different frequency targets, different cortical effects. Different tools, different jobs. If this pattern replicates, the implication is that protocol selection determines not just whether the brain changes, but how it changes.

SMR consolidates. Beta doesn't (in this small sample). At three-to-five-week neural follow-up, only the SMR groups showed lasting resting-state changes. C3 SMR: d = 0.97. C4 SMR: d = 0.78. Beta training: essentially null (d = -0.002). This is a preliminary finding from a small reanalysis and needs replication before it can guide consumer decisions. If it holds, it would suggest that protocol selection influences not just immediate neural change but whether those changes persist at the neural level after training stops.

Training predicts neural follow-up measures. The size of the ERD during training sessions predicted the size of the resting-state change at follow-up: r = 0.54, p = 0.009. In this small dataset, that is a direct link between the brain's real-time learning signal and the neural change observed weeks later. Whether this neural follow-up change translates to clinical or functional outcomes was not measured in this study.

Three independent labs converge. The Hill study is not the only demonstration of contingency-specific operant learning. He, Everest-Phillips, Clouter, Brown, and Tan (2020), published in the *Journal of Neuroscience,* ran a double-blind sham-controlled study of beta-burst suppression training and found specific neural change in the active group, absent in sham, with a behavioral consequence (faster movement initiation) tied to the trained neural feature. Guler and colleagues (2021), using fMRI neurofeedback, showed that reward-related brain circuits were more engaged under contingent than sham feedback, providing anatomical specificity across a different neuroimaging modality. When three independent labs, using different protocols, different imaging modalities, and different populations, all find that the brain distinguishes real from sham feedback, the contingency-specificity argument rests on convergent evidence, not a single study.

This is the strongest evidence that the operant conditioning mechanism is real. The brain produces specific electrical events in response to contingent feedback that it does not produce when the feedback is non-contingent. Different frequency targets produce different cortical effects. And the effects of SMR-class protocols persist after training ends in a way that beta-class protocols do not. Translating that brain-level specificity into consistent group-level symptom superiority is where the research hasn't fully caught up, for all the structural reasons described above.

5.5 The Skeptic's Best Argument

Before putting our clinical experience on the table, the book owes you the strongest version of the counterargument. A rigorous skeptic would say this:

Every practitioner of every therapy believes their clinical results exceed what studies show. Chiropractors say it. Homeopaths say it. Reiki practitioners say it. "The research doesn't capture what I see in my office" is the universal claim of anyone whose method underperforms in controlled trials. Clinical conviction is precisely the bias that randomized controlled trials exist to correct. You can't cite your own uncontrolled observations as evidence that the controlled evidence is wrong. That's circular.

And there's a deeper problem. If neurofeedback's specific mechanism (contingent brain feedback) doesn't outperform sham at the group level, the simplest explanation is that the specific mechanism isn't doing what you think it's doing. The improvement you see may be real, but it may be attributable to structured clinical attention, therapeutic relationship, expectancy, engagement, and the natural trajectory of conditions that fluctuate over time. These aren't "just placebo." They're genuine therapeutic ingredients. But they don't require neurofeedback. They require a good clinician and regular appointments.

That argument is serious. It deserves a serious response, not a defensive one. The honest response:

First, the skeptic is right that clinical observation alone cannot override controlled evidence. We agree. We are not asking you to take our word over the data. We are asking you to hold two things simultaneously: the group-level evidence (which shows limited specificity for standardized protocols) and the brain-level evidence (which shows clear, frequency-specific learning that sham does not produce). Both are real. They point in different directions, and that tension is unresolved.

Second, the "individualization" argument is testable, and the field is beginning to test it. Voetterl et al. (2023) showed that stratifying ADHD patients by individual alpha frequency signatures retrospectively predicted which treatments led to remission, with 29-36% higher remission rates when treatment happened to match the biomarker. That study validated the Brainmarker-I as a predictor of treatment response; it did not prospectively assign patients to QEEG-guided protocols, so it establishes that the biomarker can identify likely responders, not that QEEG-selected individualized neurofeedback outperforms standard protocols in practice. If the next generation of trials uses QEEG-guided protocol selection rather than one-size-fits-all designs, the group-level results may look different. They may not. But the test hasn't been run at scale yet, and dismissing the hypothesis before the data exist is as premature as accepting it.

Third, even if non-specific factors account for a substantial portion of the clinical benefit, that doesn't make neurofeedback worthless. It means the field needs to be honest about what it's selling: a structured, brain-data-informed training program that includes both specific neural learning and powerful non-specific therapeutic elements. The question shifts from "does the specific mechanism work?" to "does the full package, including the specific mechanism, produce better outcomes than alternatives?" That question hasn't been answered yet either.

We don't claim certainty. We claim plausibility, mechanism-level evidence, and clinical consistency that warrants continued investigation and informed use, not faith.

5.6 What We See Clinically

With that epistemic frame in place, our clinical experience for your evaluation:

Most clients show measurable brain changes within the first few sessions; we can see the event-related responses in the session data. Many people notice subjective effects by sessions three to five. By twenty to thirty sessions, quantitative EEG reassessment often shows meaningful shifts in the trained metrics. In our clinical observation, two rounds of training (roughly forty to sixty sessions) frequently produces substantial changes in executive function, anxiety, sleep, and emotional regulation. These are clinical impressions from our practice, not findings from a controlled study with a defined denominator and outcome criteria.

This clinical pattern, which repeats across thousands of clients with individualized, QEEG-guided protocols, looks different from the modest group averages in studies using standardized protocols on mixed populations. We believe this gap reflects a genuine difference between individualized practice and standardized research design. But we hold that belief provisionally, as a hypothesis worth testing, not as a settled fact.

What would disprove the individualization argument. A well-designed RCT of QEEG-guided, individualized neurofeedback versus standardized neurofeedback versus sham, run by independent investigators, adequately powered, with at least forty sessions per participant and protocol blinding verified, that found no significant difference between the individualized and standardized arms would substantially undermine the central clinical argument this book makes. That trial has not been run. The Voetterl et al. biomarker-stratification result supports the direction of the prediction. Until a direct, well-powered test exists, the individualization hypothesis is theoretically well-grounded and clinically consistent, but empirically unconfirmed. We say this not to hedge the book's argument but to name exactly what it would take to defeat it. Science proceeds by testing, not by accumulating supportive cases.

5.7 The Evidence Lens: Your Portable Framework

You're going to encounter neurofeedback claims for the rest of your life, from clinics, websites, well-meaning friends, and this book. A framework for evaluating any of them:

5.7.1 Five questions. Ask every time.

1. Mechanism: Is there a plausible brain-based explanation?

Does the claim connect to known neuroscience? "Neurofeedback trains SMR to stabilize thalamocortical circuits" is plausible. "Neurofeedback raises your vibration" is not. The mechanism doesn't have to be proven, but it has to be biologically coherent.

2. Maps: Does brain data support what's being targeted?

Is there QEEG evidence that the claimed pattern exists in the person being treated? "Your brain map shows elevated high beta frontally, and we're going to train that down" is data-driven. "Everyone with anxiety needs alpha training" is a guess.

3. Outcomes: Are measurable results tracked?

Is the clinic measuring change with standardized instruments, or just asking "do you feel better?" QEEG re-assessment, validated symptom scales, functional outcome measures. These are the minimum. "I feel amazing" after three sessions isn't evidence. Documented change in sleep quality, attention metrics, or brain data over twenty-five sessions is.

4. Trials: What does the controlled evidence show?

For this specific claim, for this specific condition, what do the RCTs and meta-analyses say? Not all conditions have the same evidence level. Use the summary in this chapter as your starting point.

5. Replication: Has it been reproduced?

One clinic's results don't constitute evidence. Has the claim been reproduced across multiple settings, populations, and providers? If it only works at one clinic with one proprietary protocol, be cautious.

This framework reappears in the condition chapters and in Chapter 17. It's your portable tool for evaluating claims, about any brain intervention, neurofeedback included.

5.8 The Bottom Line

Three questions run through this evidence base, and they are worth keeping separate.

Can training change a targeted EEG feature? Multiple independent studies, including Andrew's doctoral research, have found that contingent feedback produces frequency-specific, site-specific brain changes that sham does not. The supporting evidence for this operant conditioning mechanism is strong, though the size and consistency of the effect vary across studies.

Does the intervention improve outcomes that matter to patients beyond a credible control? At the group level, sham-controlled data does not consistently show neurofeedback outperforming credible control conditions on symptom measures, particularly for ADHD and insomnia. This is the central limitation of the current evidence base, and it should be stated plainly.

Is the EEG change what produces the clinical benefit? This question is largely unanswered. Even where brain-level changes are documented, connecting those changes to the symptom improvements patients report has not been cleanly demonstrated for most conditions. It may be that the EEG change, the structured context, the clinical attention, and the expectation of improvement all contribute, and current trial designs cannot fully separate those contributions.

Sham conditions control for shared factors. When both groups improve in a sham-controlled trial, that is the control doing its job, not evidence that sham is a treatment. It means the shared factors (structured sessions, engagement, clinician contact, expectation) are doing real work, and the specific mechanism has not demonstrated an additional benefit beyond them.

Individualized, QEEG-guided clinical practice produces results that look different from group averages. This is our clinical observation across 25,000 maps, not a controlled trial. But it's consistent, reproducible, and we're not the only clinicians who see it. The field is moving toward the personalized approach that could close the gap between clinical experience and published evidence.

Not everyone responds. Even in clinical practice with individualized protocols, a meaningful minority of clients don't show the changes we expect. The proportion varies by condition and by how "response" is defined, and no systematic audit of our own practice outcomes has been published. Good practice means monitoring, adjusting, and knowing when to stop or redirect. Fixed packages sold to everyone are the opposite of that.

5.9 The Mechanism-Outcome Gap: Why Specific Effects Are Hard to Isolate at the Group Level

This is the core intellectual puzzle of the field, and you deserve a clear account of it. The brain data from several controlled studies point in a clear direction: contingent feedback produces frequency-specific, site-specific electrical changes that sham does not. And yet, at the group level, that brain-level specificity often does not translate into clear superiority over a well-designed sham on symptom measures. Why?

Several structural features of trial design contribute. A sham session shares many of the same procedural ingredients as real training: structure, attention, clinician contact, and the expectation of improvement. Those shared factors are exactly what a control condition is supposed to match, and when both groups improve, the control is doing its job. Standardized protocols on mixed populations may wash out individual responders. Trials typically run twenty to thirty sessions, shorter than the courses clinical practice commonly delivers. And symptom questionnaires are noisy, moving with life events and expectations as readily as with treatment.

None of this proves the specific mechanism drives clinical improvement. It explains why the absence of group-level symptom superiority does not, on its own, disprove it either. The honest position is that this remains an open question, and the field needs better-designed trials to resolve it.

5.10 What We Still Don't Know

Scientific honesty requires naming the gaps, not just the strengths. What remains unresolved:

We don't know how much of the clinical benefit is specific to contingent feedback versus the therapeutic context. The brain-level learning is specific. Whether that specificity drives a meaningful share of the symptom improvement hasn't been cleanly demonstrated for most conditions. It may. But we can't yet say with confidence how much.

We don't know whether QEEG-guided individualization produces better outcomes than standardized protocols. Clinical logic strongly suggests it should. Early evidence (Voetterl et al., 2023) supports it for ADHD. But no large RCT has directly compared QEEG-guided neurofeedback against standardized neurofeedback against sham. Until that trial exists, the individualization argument remains theoretically persuasive but empirically unproven.

We don't know the optimal dose for most conditions. Session count recommendations come from clinical experience, not from dose-response trials. We don't know whether 40 sessions is better than 25, or whether diminishing returns set in, or whether the answer varies by condition and phenotype.

We don't know why some people don't respond. A meaningful minority of participants in published trials do not show clear improvement, though the exact rate varies by study design, condition, and response definition. We have hypotheses (wrong protocol, comorbid factors, insufficient plasticity, medication interference), but no validated way to predict who will respond before training starts. The IAF-matching work is promising but preliminary.

We don't know the durability curve. Clinical observation suggests gains persist for years. But no long-term controlled follow-up study has tracked neurofeedback outcomes beyond two years with adequate controls. The durability data are almost entirely observational.

We don't know whether neurofeedback has specific effects on conditions like autism, TBI, and chronic pain, or whether the improvements reflect general regulatory enhancement. For these conditions, the evidence is Level 3-4 at best. Clinical reports are often positive. Controlled data are sparse.

These gaps don't mean neurofeedback is unproven. They mean the field is at a specific stage of scientific development: strong mechanism, promising clinical results, insufficient controlled evidence to make definitive claims about most applications. That's an honest picture, and it's one that should improve substantially over the next decade as trial methodology catches up to clinical practice.

This book isn't going to tell you neurofeedback is a miracle or a sham. The evidence won't support either conclusion.

What it will tell you: neurofeedback is a real intervention with a complicated evidence base, a strong mechanism, and results that depend on protocol selection, session dose, and whether training is individualized to your brain. The rest of this book teaches you to evaluate that, for your condition, your brain, your provider, and your life.

Decision Point: If you've read this far and you're thinking, "OK, this seems real but I need to be careful about who I work with", that's exactly the right reaction. Chapter 6 covers safety. Chapter 17 is your complete buyer's guide. If your reaction is "this sounds like it might help me but I want to see what it looks like for my specific situation", the condition chapters in Section III are written for you.

Your Move:

1. **Reflect:** Where did you start this chapter: skeptical or enthusiastic? Where did you end? If your position shifted, what specifically moved it?
2. **Act:** Pick one claim about neurofeedback you've encountered, from a clinic website, a podcast, a friend. Run it through the Evidence Lens. Does it hold up?
3. **Start a conversation:** The next time someone says neurofeedback "works" or "doesn't work," you can now respond with: "For what condition? Compared to what control? With what protocol, on what population, for how many sessions?" That's not being difficult. That's being literate.

Ch 6: Safety, Side Effects, and What to Watch For

6.1 The Short Answer

Across published reports and clinical experience, serious adverse events from passive EEG neurofeedback appear rare. The professional organizations that oversee the field (ISNR, AAPB, BCIA) converge on the assessment that neurofeedback is low-risk when competently administered. Published trials have not reported seizures in non-epileptic populations or structural harm.

An important distinction runs through this chapter: passive EEG neurofeedback records your brain's own electrical activity and feeds it back to you. It does not deliver current, magnetic pulses, or any external energy to the brain. Methods that deliver energy to the scalp or brain, whether electrical current (tDCS, tACS) or a weak electromagnetic field (LENS), are brain stimulation, not passive recording, and they carry a different risk profile. Unless otherwise noted, the safety discussion in this chapter refers to passive EEG neurofeedback.

That said, formal safety surveillance is limited. No dedicated prospective adverse-event registry exists for neurofeedback, and most trials were not designed to detect rare or delayed harms. The absence of documented serious events partly reflects that gap in surveillance, not only the genuine rarity of harm.

That's the short answer. The longer one matters, because "low-risk" does not mean "no side effects," and there are real scenarios where caution is warranted.

6.2 What You Might Feel: Common Transient Effects

Neurofeedback produces temporary shifts as your brain adjusts to training. These are common, expected, and almost always resolve within hours:

Fatigue. Your brain just did concentrated work. Some people feel tired after sessions, especially early in training. This is normal, not a sign of harm.

Headache. Mild headache after a session is occasional, usually resolves with hydration and rest. If it persists across multiple sessions, tell your clinician.

Irritability. The most common early-training side effect. Some people feel edgy or short-tempered for a day or two after sessions. This usually settles within the first week of training. If it escalates rather than settles, treat that as a safety signal: report it to your clinician before the next session. The protocol likely needs adjustment, and worsening should be assessed rather than assumed to be a positive sign.

Sleep changes. Some people sleep better immediately. Some have vivid dreams. Some have a night or two of disrupted sleep before their sleep improves. All are within normal range.

Emotional activation. Particularly with alpha-theta training or trauma-oriented protocols, old feelings can surface: tearfulness, nostalgia, brief anxiety. This can happen during deep-state work and should be discussed with your clinician so they can calibrate the intensity. If emotional activation feels destabilizing rather than manageable, or persists between sessions, treat it as a safety signal and report it promptly.

The key pattern: These effects are typically acute. They happen during sessions or the same day and usually resolve quickly. Published trials have not documented long-term harm from passive EEG neurofeedback, though few trials were designed to assess long-term safety and no dedicated prospective adverse-event registry exists. Any effect that persists or worsens across sessions is a safety signal that deserves assessment, not an expected bump.

6.3 When to Stop, When to Call, When to Wait

Use this escalation guide throughout your training. Share it with family members or caregivers so someone besides you is watching for these signs.

RED: Stop training. Obtain urgent assessment.

- A seizure during or after a session
- Loss of consciousness or fainting
- New or worsening mania, psychosis, or severely disorganized thinking
- Suicidal thoughts, intent, or preparatory behavior (giving away possessions, researching methods, writing final messages) that were not present before training, or worsening of pre-existing suicidal thoughts
- Any new focal neurologic symptom (sudden weakness on one side, speech difficulty, vision loss)

Do not wait for your next scheduled session, and do not make your neurofeedback provider your first call. For a seizure, a loss of consciousness, or a new focal neurologic symptom, call emergency services or go to the nearest emergency department. For suicidal thoughts, intent, or preparatory behavior, call or text 988 in the United States for the Suicide and Crisis Lifeline, and call 911 if anyone is in immediate danger. For new mania, psychosis, or severely disorganized thinking, get urgent psychiatric assessment. When something needs same-day attention but is not an emergency, urgent care or your primary doctor is the right call.

Tell your neurofeedback provider what happened once you are safe. They need to know, and it changes what should happen to your training. The exception is a provider who is also your primary therapist and part of your immediate mental health care team. In that case they may be the right first call for a psychiatric crisis, though a medical emergency still goes to emergency services.

YELLOW: Report to your clinician before the next session.

- Any new symptom that persists beyond two to three sessions (worsening anxiety, new irritability, sleep disruption, headaches)
- A clear pattern of getting worse rather than better
- Emotional activation that feels destabilizing rather than manageable
- Any change that concerns you, even if you are not sure it is related to training

Do not resume training until your clinician has assessed the change and adjusted the plan if needed.

GREEN: Expected transient effects.

- Mild fatigue after a session
- Brief irritability that resolves within a day
- One or two nights of vivid dreams or lighter sleep
- A passing headache that responds to rest and hydration

Track these in your daily log (Chapter 4) and mention them at your next session. They are common and typically resolve on their own.

When in doubt, report it. Your clinician can only adjust what they know about.

6.4 Who Needs Extra Caution

Two different questions run through this section, and keeping them separate matters. The first is hardware safety: passive EEG neurofeedback records your brain's own electrical activity and does not deliver current, stimulation, or any external energy. The hardware is safe. The second is clinical appropriateness: whether it makes sense to begin or continue training given a person's current clinical state. These are not the same question, and a safe device does not make every clinical situation a good time to train.

When training should wait. Some acute states call for assessment and stabilization before neurofeedback begins or resumes. These are not hardware risks; they are situations where training is not the right clinical priority:

- Current inability to stay safe
- Suicidal intent or preparatory behavior (giving away possessions, researching methods, writing final messages)
- Active psychosis
- Acute mania
- Severe disorganization
- Suspected postpartum psychosis
- Intoxication or medically risky withdrawal
- A new seizure awaiting neurologic evaluation
- A new focal neurologic deficit (sudden weakness on one side, speech difficulty, vision loss)

None of these mean the person can never train. They mean the person needs clinical assessment and appropriate stabilization first. Once they are stable and receiving the care their acute situation requires, neurofeedback can rejoin the plan as an adjunct.

No professional body has published a definitive "do not treat" list, and neurofeedback has few formal contraindications in the hardware-safety sense. But clinical experience and trial exclusion criteria suggest extra care for:

Unstable seizure disorders. Neurofeedback was born from epilepsy research, and SMR training was originally used to raise seizure thresholds. But training without proper assessment, or using protocols that increase excitability rather than stability, can lower thresholds. Seizure-focused training should be done by someone experienced with epilepsy, not a generalist.

Active psychosis or severe mania. These are states where the brain needs stabilization, typically pharmacological, before the kind of regulatory training neurofeedback provides. Neurofeedback has been studied as an adjunct alongside antipsychotic medication with good safety data, but not as a first-line intervention for someone in acute crisis.

A stable bipolar diagnosis does not exclude someone from neurofeedback, but certain protocols carry meaningful risk. Beta up-training and alpha suppression, both designed to increase cortical activation, can push a regulated bipolar brain toward hypomania or a full mood switch, even in clients who have been euthymic (no active mood episode) for months. If you have any history of bipolar disorder (type I or II), disclose this before training begins. Your clinician should select protocols carefully, avoid aggressive beta enhancement, and monitor closely for early signs of mood elevation: reduced sleep need, racing thoughts, or uncharacteristic impulsivity.

Severe suicidality or active self-harm. The priority here is safety-focused intervention. Neurofeedback belongs in the longer-term plan once acute risk is managed.

The postpartum period. Neurofeedback does work with postpartum depression, and we see it help. Two conditions apply. It belongs alongside medical or psychiatric care, not instead of it, so your obstetric provider or a mental health clinician should be involved and know you are training. And it is not the right tool when symptoms are severe. Postpartum psychosis is a medical emergency: confusion, not feeling like yourself in a way that frightens you, hallucinations, or thoughts of harming yourself or your baby all mean emergency care now, not a training appointment. Severe postpartum depression needs psychiatric assessment first. Once you are stable and supported, training is a reasonable adjunct, and the sleep deprivation that comes with a new baby is worth naming to your clinician, since it shapes both how you feel and what the map shows.

Certain medications at high doses. Benzodiazepines and opiates at high levels may interfere with the brain's ability to learn from the feedback signal. The operant conditioning loop depends on the brain being plastic enough to respond to reinforcement. Heavy sedation can blunt that responsiveness. This doesn't mean you can't do neurofeedback on medication. Most people can. But the clinician needs to know what you're taking and may adjust expectations or sequencing accordingly.

Head injuries or implanted devices. Standard EEG recording is safe for people with most implants, but some devices (certain pacemakers, deep brain stimulators) may interact with EEG equipment. Disclose everything.

The hardware is safe for all of these groups. The clinical question is whether the timing, the protocol, and the support structure are right for this person at this point. A good clinician assesses each situation individually rather than applying a blanket rule.

WARNING: Never abruptly reduce or stop benzodiazepines, opioids, alcohol, or any prescribed medication without direct supervision from your prescriber or an addiction-medicine specialist.

Abrupt benzodiazepine discontinuation can cause seizures and other serious withdrawal reactions. The FDA updated benzodiazepine labeling in 2020 with a boxed warning requiring gradual dose reduction under medical supervision (FDA Drug Safety Communication, Sept. 23, 2020). Abrupt opioid discontinuation can cause serious withdrawal symptoms, psychological distress, and in some cases patients seek illicit opioids; the FDA issued a safety communication in 2019 warning against sudden discontinuation (FDA Drug Safety Communication, Apr. 9, 2019). Alcohol withdrawal is potentially life-threatening and can include delirium tremens, seizures, and cardiovascular instability (MedlinePlus / NIH-NLM, "Delirium Tremens").

Neurofeedback is not a substitute for medically supervised withdrawal, detoxification, or medication-assisted treatment. If your substance use or medication regimen changes during training, your prescriber and your neurofeedback clinician both need to know. Dose adjustments should always be directed by the prescribing clinician, never made unilaterally because training "feels like it's working."

6.5 The Potentiation Effect: Medications and Substances

One phenomenon that surprises many people: as neurofeedback training takes effect, your brain's response to certain substances can change.

Stimulant medications (Adderall, Ritalin, methylphenidate, dextroamphetamine) sometimes feel different as training progresses. This is a consistent clinical observation across neurofeedback practices, not a finding from controlled trials: if the brain's regulatory capacity is improving, the same dose of stimulant is now acting on a more responsive system. Perceived changes have many possible causes, including sleep, timing, formulation, adherence, illness, and expectation. Never assume the training caused it, and never change a dose on your own. Record drug, dose, formulation, timing, sleep, and symptoms, and take any concerning change to your prescriber rather than to a protocol adjustment. If you're on stimulants, keep your prescriber informed about your neurofeedback progress.

Cannabis alters the EEG. If you use it, tell your provider how much and how often, because accurate interpretation of your map depends on it.

> **If you use cannabis medically** (for chronic pain, nausea, seizure management, spasticity, or any prescribed or recommended indication): do not modify or discontinue your use based on anything in this book. Consult your prescribing or recommending physician before changing your medical cannabis regimen.

This extends to other substances people use for self-regulation: alcohol for anxiety, cannabis for sleep, caffeine for focus. As neurofeedback addresses the underlying regulatory patterns that drive the use, the need for the substance often decreases.

This is a clinical observation about what happens when regulatory capacity improves: the compensatory strategies become less necessary. It is not a moral argument about substance use.

6.6 The Safety Comparison

Neurofeedback's safety profile compared to other brain interventions, offered for context rather than to argue superiority:

Passive EEG neurofeedback: Non-invasive, non-pharmacological. Reads the brain's own electrical activity; does not deliver current or external energy. Mild transient side effects (headache, fatigue, irritability). Serious adverse events have not been reported in published trials, though systematic surveillance is limited. No neurotoxicity has been documented. Because training involves learning rather than a substance, there is no withdrawal syndrome when training stops, though the durability of gains varies and is not fully established for all conditions.

Psychotropic medication (stimulants, SSRIs, antipsychotics): Well-documented side effect profiles. Stimulants: insomnia, appetite suppression, cardiovascular effects. Antidepressants: GI symptoms, sexual dysfunction, weight changes. Antipsychotics: metabolic syndrome, movement disorders. Effective for many people, but with real trade-offs that must be weighed. The effects are generally present only while you take the medication; stopping typically brings symptoms back.

rTMS (repetitive transcranial magnetic stimulation): Headaches and scalp discomfort are common. Rare seizures have been documented. Requires clinical monitoring and adherence to safety protocols. Considered safe within guidelines.

tDCS (transcranial direct current stimulation): Tingling, burning, itching under electrodes. Rare skin burns with improper contact. Extremely rare seizures. Generally safe when protocols are followed.

The relative picture: These profiles cannot be ranked against each other. Reporting systems, denominators, populations, and follow-up periods differ, and the incidence of serious harm from passive EEG neurofeedback is unknown because capture is inconsistent. The trade-off is that its efficacy evidence is weaker for some conditions. Safety without proven efficacy is not enough. But safety with clinical benefit, even when that benefit has not been fully captured in group-level research, is worth weighing when considering more invasive or pharmacologically burdensome options, in consultation with your clinician.

An important distinction: This comparison applies to passive EEG neurofeedback, which only records brain activity. Methods that deliver energy to the scalp or brain, whether electrical current (tDCS, tACS) or a weak electromagnetic field (LENS), are brain stimulation, not passive recording, and they carry a different risk profile. If you are considering or receiving any form of brain stimulation, discuss its specific safety considerations with your provider.

One limitation of this comparison is worth naming: neurofeedback lacks a centralized adverse-event registry equivalent to the FDA's MedWatch system for medications. The absence of documented serious adverse events partly reflects that absence of systematic surveillance, not only the genuine rarity of harm. A good provider tracks client outcomes and adverse events as a matter of standard practice; ask them how they do it.

6.7 The Real Risks: Bad Providers and Unguided Training

The biggest safety concern with neurofeedback isn't the technology. It's the human.

Poorly trained providers can:

- Train the wrong frequencies at the wrong sites, potentially increasing symptoms
- Fail to notice that a client is getting worse rather than better
- Ignore medication interactions
- Skip assessment and apply generic protocols to complex presentations
- Sell large prepaid packages without built-in reassessment points

Unguided home neurofeedback carries additional risks:

- Training excessive high-beta without monitoring could increase anxiety or insomnia

- Reducing theta without checking whether the theta represents sleep debt rather than ADHD could mask a sleep problem
- Without professional evaluation, serious conditions (major depression, psychosis, epilepsy) might go unaddressed while the person self-treats
- Over-interpretation of noisy consumer-device feedback can fuel health anxiety

Consumer EEG headbands read brain activity passively and do not deliver stimulation, so the risk of lasting neurological harm from passive recording is low. But unguided training can worsen symptoms, and it can waste time, money, and hope. In cases where professional treatment is needed, self-directed training can delay appropriate care.

The bottom line: Passive EEG neurofeedback carries a low risk profile when competently administered, but "low-risk" is not the same as "no risk." The question is whether it is done well. Chapter 17 gives you the tools to evaluate that.

6.8 What Informed Consent Should Look Like

Before you begin neurofeedback, a responsible clinic should tell you:

- What the proposed protocol is and why it was chosen
- What the expected timeline and session count look like (with the caveats described below)
- What the realistic range of outcomes is, including the possibility of non-response
- What side effects to expect and when to report them
- What the reassessment schedule is (when will they re-map and re-evaluate?)
- What the total expected cost is, and whether there are exit points if you're not responding
- That for many conditions, neurofeedback is not yet considered a first-line, evidence-based treatment by major guidelines, even though clinical experience is often more favorable than the published evidence

On timelines: Any clinic giving you a timeline should frame it as an approximation, not a promise. Progress in neurofeedback is individual. Some people respond faster than expected. Some respond slower. A good clinic sets expectations while being transparent that timelines shift, and they discuss this with you openly rather than locking you into a rigid package.

On non-response: This deserves an honest conversation before you start. A meaningful minority of people don't get the kind of response they're hoping for, even in experienced hands. The exact proportion varies by condition, by how "response" is defined, and by the treatment approach. We have not published a systematic audit of our own practice outcomes, so we present this as a clinical observation rather than a measured rate. Even in good conditions, it doesn't work for everyone.

The reasons vary. Sometimes the protocol targeting is off and needs adjustment. Sometimes comorbid factors (sleep disorders, heavy substance use, unaddressed trauma, or a medication regimen that's interfering with neuroplasticity) are blocking progress. Sometimes the brain simply doesn't shift as expected despite appropriate targeting. A responsible clinic monitors for this, adjusts when possible, and knows when to stop or redirect rather than selling you more sessions when the data isn't moving.

Certain baseline features also shift the odds. Individual alpha peak frequency is one of the most promising predictors of who benefits from neurofeedback versus stimulant medication in ADHD (Voetterl et al., 2023): when treatment is matched to the brain's IAF signature, remission rates improve by 29–36 percent compared to unmatched treatment. This is exactly the kind of personalization QEEG-guided practice is designed to support: matching the intervention to the brain, not the brain to the intervention.

6.9 Children: Special Considerations

Parents considering neurofeedback for their children deserve specific reassurance.

Available trials have generally reported mild, transient events in children aged six and up, but systematic harms ascertainment and long-term pediatric safety data are limited. Multiple RCTs and meta-analyses have included children in this age range without reporting serious adverse events. The most common side effect, mild irritability, is the same as in adults and usually transient. However, most of these trials were not specifically designed to detect rare or delayed harms in developing brains, and the longest follow-up periods are typically twelve to eighteen months.

Session modifications for kids are standard: shorter sessions, more engaging feedback (games, cartoons), and less reliance on the child being able to describe what they're experiencing. Progress is often tracked through parent and teacher reports rather than the child's self-assessment.

The sleep question applies doubly to kids. Children who are sleeping poorly look like children with ADHD on both behavior checklists and brain maps. Before assuming your child needs neurofeedback for attention, make sure their sleep has been properly evaluated. A clinician who doesn't ask about sleep before starting ADHD training is missing the most common confounder. Chapter 14 covers the developing brain in detail.

Your Move:

1. **Reflect:** Does the safety profile described here change how you think about neurofeedback relative to other interventions you've tried or considered?
2. **Act:** If you're already in treatment (any kind, not just neurofeedback), check: did your provider explain the potential side effects before you started? Did they give you a framework for recognizing when to report a problem? If not, ask for one.
3. **Start a conversation:** If you're considering neurofeedback for your child, ask the provider: "What will you do if my child gets more irritable after sessions? How do you handle that?" The answer tells you whether they expect bumps and have a plan, or whether they'll just push through.

Ch 7: Your Nervous System, Your Brain, and Why Regulation Matters

If you've spent any time on social media in the last five years, you've heard the phrase "nervous system regulation." It's everywhere: in therapy culture, wellness content, trauma-informed coaching, and podcast conversations about why you feel the way you feel.

But what does it actually mean? Let's start with the basics.

7.1 Your Nervous System in Sixty Seconds

Your nervous system has two major divisions. The **central nervous system (CNS)** (your brain and spinal cord) is the command center. The **peripheral nervous system (PNS)** carries signals between that command center and the rest of your body.

Within the PNS, the **autonomic nervous system** runs the things you don't consciously control: heart rate, digestion, respiration, stress response. It has two branches that work in dynamic tension:

- **Sympathetic:** the accelerator. Fight-or-flight. Mobilizes energy, increases heart rate, sharpens alertness. This is the system that gets you out of danger, meets deadlines, and powers through the workday.
- **Parasympathetic:** the brake. Rest-and-digest. Slows heart rate, promotes recovery, supports sleep and repair. This is the system that rebuilds what the sympathetic branch burned through.

The **hypothalamus**, a small structure at the base of your brain, is the master switch between these two branches. It reads incoming signals about threat, safety, and bodily needs, and tips the balance toward activation or recovery accordingly.

Communication between your brain and your autonomic nervous system runs in both directions. Bottom-up approaches (breathwork, yoga, exercise) send signals from the body to the brain that can shift autonomic balance toward parasympathetic recovery. They work because the body talks to the brain. Top-down approaches like neurofeedback target the brain directly, training the cortical patterns that influence how the hypothalamus and autonomic system respond. Both directions are real. Both are trainable.

Neurofeedback gives you a way to see that brain-level regulation on a QEEG, and then train it directly, rather than approaching it only through the body.

7.2 What Regulation Actually Means

Regulation is measurable. Your brain's electrical patterns, your autonomic balance, and your capacity to shift between states are all quantifiable and trainable. That's what this chapter is about. Not regulation as a feeling or a metaphor, but regulation as a set of measurable capacities that shape everything from your anxiety to your attention to your sleep.

Regulation doesn't mean "always calm." Chapter 3 introduced this as thermostat regulation (stability: maintaining appropriate baselines) and jazz improvisation (flexibility: shifting fluidly between states). This chapter is where those two ideas meet the clinical conditions they govern. Sometimes you need activation: urgency, focus, energy. Sometimes you need recovery: stillness, sleep, repair. Regulation is the ability to do both, at the right time, without getting stuck.

7.3 Stress, Resilience, and Why This Matters

Life is stressful. That's not going to change. What can change is how your nervous system handles the stress.

A well-regulated brain doesn't avoid stress; it processes it and recovers. The sympathetic system fires when you need it, and the parasympathetic system brings you back down when the threat passes. The problem isn't stress itself. The problem is getting stuck: a nervous system that activates and can't deactivate, or one that's been in overdrive so long it collapses into shutdown.

Neurofeedback builds resilience at the source. By training the brain's regulatory circuits, the patterns that govern arousal, recovery, and flexibility, you're not just managing symptoms. You're expanding the brain's capacity to handle whatever comes next without breaking down. Clients consistently report not that their lives became less stressful, but that the same stressors stopped knocking them sideways. That's resilience. And it's measurable on a brain map.

7.4 A Note on Polyvagal Theory

If you've encountered "nervous system regulation" through therapy or wellness content, you've likely heard of polyvagal theory. Stephen Porges' model maps emotional states onto a hierarchy of nervous system responses: safe and social (ventral vagal), fight-or-flight (sympathetic), or shut-down and freeze (dorsal vagal).

There's clinical value in that framework. Therapists use it effectively to help clients understand their stress responses and recognize their own patterns. But the neuroscience is more complicated than the Instagram version suggests. Polyvagal theory has been systematically challenged by autonomic researchers who argue that its core anatomical and evolutionary claims are oversimplified or unsupported. The "ventral vagal = safety" narrative is a useful therapeutic heuristic. It's not a settled mechanistic account of how your nervous system actually works.

What we can measure on a QEEG, on an HRV monitor, through autonomic testing, is more specific and more useful than any theoretical model. That's what the rest of this chapter focuses on.

7.5 What Regulation Looks Like in Your Brain

When we look at a QEEG, we're not looking at a diagnosis. We're looking at regulation: the brain's capacity to manage its own states. And regulation breaks down along specific, measurable dimensions.

7.5.1 Arousal Set-Point

Some brains run chronically hot: too much fast activity, too much beta, a system that can't downshift. These people are anxious, wired, can't sleep, can't stop thinking. Other brains run chronically cool: too much slow activity, too much theta, a system that can't engage. These people are foggy, unmotivated, exhausted despite sleeping ten hours. Your arousal set-point is where your brain defaults when nothing specific is demanding its attention.

What this looks like in real life: The chronically hot person lies down at night and the mental checklists start. They review the day, preview tomorrow, rehearse conversations, calculate risks. Their body is tired but their brain won't release. The chronically cool person can sleep twelve hours and still feel like they're wading through fog. Morning coffee barely dents it. They're not lazy. Their cortex is idling at too slow a frequency.

7.5.2 Stability vs. Volatility

How much does your system swing? Some brains hold a steady state: calm stays calm, focus stays focused. Others oscillate wildly, fine one hour and crashing the next. Emotionally reactive one moment, flat the next. This isn't a personality trait. It's measurable in the variability of your EEG patterns, and it's trainable.

What this looks like in real life: The volatile person has great mornings and terrible afternoons, or they can hold it together at work and fall apart the moment they walk through their front door. Their partner says, "I never know which version of you I'm getting." That unpredictability isn't character; it's a nervous system that can't hold a set-point under changing conditions.

7.5.3 Network Rigidity vs. Flexibility

Your brain needs to coordinate activity across regions, and it needs to shift those coordination patterns depending on what you're doing. Some brains are too rigid: locked into one pattern, unable to shift gears. These people perseverate, stuck on a thought, stuck on an emotion, unable to let go. Other brains are too chaotic: coordination breaks down, processing is disorganized, nothing holds together. The sweet spot is flexible coordination, structured enough to be effective and loose enough to adapt.

What this looks like in real life: The rigid person gets derailed by a change in plans and can't recover. They know they're being unreasonable, and they can't stop. A conversation that should have ended twenty minutes ago keeps circling. The chaotic person starts three tasks, finishes none, and can't explain why. Their desk, their inbox, and their emotional life all have the same quality: nothing quite holds together.

7.5.4 Attentional Control

Can you direct your attention where you want it and keep it there? Can you shift it when needed? Attentional control isn't just about focus. It's about the executive management of where your brain's resources go. Hyperfocused on the wrong thing is as much a regulation problem as scattered and distractible.

What this looks like in real life: The scattered version is obvious: you sit down to write an email and forty-five minutes later you've checked the news, reorganized a drawer, and forgotten the email existed. The hyperfocused version is less obvious but equally costly: you spend four hours perfecting a slide deck that needed thirty minutes, and the three things that actually mattered are now overdue. Both are the same regulatory deficit, just pointed in different directions.

7.5.5 Sensory Gating

How much sensory information gets through to your conscious awareness? Some brains let everything in: noise, light, texture, temperature, social signals. These people are overwhelmed in busy environments. Other brains gate too aggressively; they miss signals, seem disconnected, don't react to things that should register. Gating is a regulatory function, and it varies enormously across people.

What this looks like in real life: The under-gated person can't work in an open office. The hum of the fluorescent lights, the colleague chewing, the conversation three desks over: it all gets in, all the time, and the brain treats each input as equally important. By 3 p.m. they're exhausted, from the effort of filtering. The over-gated person misses their name being called, doesn't notice a friend is upset, seems "in their own world." It's not rudeness. It's a filter set too high.

7.5.6 Sleep Pressure and Circadian Vulnerability

How well does your brain manage the transition from waking to sleeping? How strong is your circadian rhythm? Sleep isn't separate from regulation. It IS regulation. The brain's ability to downshift from waking arousal into the sleep cycle, maintain sleep architecture through the night, and wake rested is one of the most fundamental regulatory capacities. When it's disrupted, everything else downstream gets worse.

What this looks like in real life: The person with poor sleep pressure regulation takes ninety minutes to fall asleep, wakes at 3 a.m. with a racing mind, and drags through the next day on caffeine. Over months, the sleep debt compounds: attention fractures, irritability climbs, and the brain map starts to look like ADHD even though it's exhaustion. Chapter 13 covers this in depth.

Dimension	Too Much	Too Little	Sweet Spot	Train?
Arousal	Wired, can't downshift	Foggy, can't engage	Alert when needed, calm when not	Yes
Stability	(not typical)	Volatile, unpredictable swings	Steady under changing conditions	Yes

Flexibility	Chaotic, disorganized	Rigid, stuck, perseverative	Structured but adaptable	Yes
Attention	Hyperfocused, inflexible	Scattered, distractible	Directed and shiftable	Yes
Sensory Gating	Over-gated, disconnected	Under-gated, overwhelmed	Filters appropriately	Yes
Sleep	(sleep excess rare)	Poor onset, fragmented, non-restorative	Falls asleep easily, sleeps through, wakes rested	Yes

7.6 Why Patterns Matter More Than Diagnoses

Two people walk into our office with the same diagnosis, ADHD, or anxiety, or depression, and their brain maps look completely different. Different regions. Different frequencies. Different connectivity patterns. Same label, different brains.

This isn't a flaw in the brain mapping. It's a flaw in the diagnostic system. The DSM groups people by symptoms. If you have enough symptoms from a checklist, you get the label. But the same symptoms can arise from very different underlying brain patterns. Inattention can come from frontal theta excess (underactivation), or from high-beta overactivation (the brain is so busy scanning for threats it can't focus on anything else), or from connectivity problems between hemispheres, or from chronic sleep deprivation mimicking all of the above.

If you treat all of those the same way (same medication, same neurofeedback protocol, same therapy approach) some people will respond and some won't. Not because the treatment is wrong in general, but because it's wrong for that specific brain.

This is why regulation matters more than diagnosis. When you understand someone's regulatory pattern, where they sit on each of those six dimensions, you can choose interventions that actually match their brain, regardless of what diagnostic label brought them through the door.

Across 25,000 brain maps, these regulatory patterns repeat. Not perfectly; every brain is unique in its details. But certain profiles show up again and again, across different diagnoses, across different demographic groups. We call these **phenotypes**: brain pattern archetypes that tend to cluster together and respond to specific kinds of intervention.

You'll meet these phenotypes in the chapters that follow. Each condition chapter is, at its core, a phenotype deep dive showing you what a particular regulatory pattern looks like, feels like, shows up as on a brain map, and responds to in training.

We want to be transparent about something: **these phenotypes are empirically motivated but not yet a validated taxonomy.** Early cluster-analysis work on large QEEG databases shows that statistical groupings of brain features do cut across DSM categories; the patterns are real. Machine-learning approaches are increasingly able to classify and predict from QEEG data. But no large independent replication has established a fixed set of "brain types" that robustly predict outcomes across multiple datasets and conditions. Maps, not horoscopes. That distinction matters.

The deeper point: **because the brain is the central regulatory hub of your entire nervous system, neurofeedback's effects don't require a diagnosis to be meaningful.** You don't need a DSM label to have a brain that's running too hot, sleeping poorly, or struggling with flexibility. Neurofeedback works because it trains regulatory circuits, and every brain has regulatory circuits. It can help the most clear-cut presentations and the most mysterious ones, because it's targeting what the brain is *doing*, not what the checklist says is *wrong*.

7.7 Regulatory Features vs. Fixed Features

Not everything the brain does is equally trainable. This distinction matters for understanding what neurofeedback can and can't change.

Regulatory features are things the brain actively tunes based on the environment: attention, arousal, stress response, sleep onset and maintenance, sensory gating, social processing speed, energy management (the cycle of deploying energy and recovering it), seizure resistance, migraine resistance. These are dynamic settings, not fixed structures. When they're miscalibrated, you get symptoms. Neurofeedback retrains the calibration.

These regulatory features are the things most visible on a QEEG. They show up as the biggest deviations because they represent the most strained systems, the common pinch points where the brain's resources cramp first under pressure. And counterintuitively, **the worse the regulatory feature, the faster it often responds to training**: there's more room to move, and the system is under more pressure to change.

This is also why regulatory changes are **durable**. You're always using these circuits: always sleeping, always managing arousal, always processing sensory input, always regulating attention. Trained improvements stay online because the circuits are in constant use.

Fixed features are different. Some brain functions have critical periods, developmental windows that close. Fundamental language acquisition has a critical period in childhood. Visual fusion and binocular vision have a critical period in early childhood. Once these windows close, the underlying circuitry is largely set. Neurofeedback can strengthen what's available, but it's not reopening a closed developmental window.

The key framing: **neurofeedback works best on regulatory features, not because it treats diseases, but because regulation is tuning, and tuning is what operant conditioning changes.** Many of the experiences people bring to a neurofeedback clinic, the anxiety that won't quiet, the sleep that won't come, are regulatory settings that can be retrained. And settings can be changed. This does not replace diagnosis and treatment when a genuine psychiatric or medical disorder is present. Generalized anxiety disorder, clinical insomnia, major depression, and other conditions benefit from professional assessment and, often, multiple treatment approaches working together. The regulatory framing is additive: it says your brain has trainable settings, not that those settings are the whole picture.

7.8 Brain Fog as a Cross-Cutting Syndrome

When people say "brain fog," they are rarely naming a single disease in a textbook sense. They are describing a regulatory collapse you can feel: thoughts arrive late, words go missing, reading takes twice the effort, and the day demands more battery than you seem to have. In neurophysiological terms, that experience often lines up with measurable mis-tuning rather than one locked-in label. We often see slow theta climb when cortical engagement falls short. Alpha can sit low when the brain loses the stable "ready" background that keeps processing smooth. Frontal executive networks can stay under-powered when you need them most. None of these are exclusive; many foggy maps show two or three of these strains at once, which is exactly what you would expect when a regulatory system is struggling on several fronts.

The life stories that arrive with that fog vary widely. Inattentive ADHD overlaps with post-COVID cognitive complaints on the intake form. Perimenopause adds heat, sleep fragmentation, and word-finding trouble that look like different conditions until the QEEG shows the same regulatory strain. Chronic fatigue syndromes, side effects from sedating or anticholinergic medications, and plain chronic sleep restriction all deposit people on the same complaint: I am here, but my cognition is not. The diagnosis helps with context and medical triage. It does not always tell you which regulatory loop broke first.

On a QEEG, the signatures often converge anyway. A small handful of phenotypes repeat, even when the intake paperwork lists different conditions. That repetition is one of the clearest lessons large clinical databases teach: symptom categories splinter; electrical profiles cluster. When arousal is wrong, stability wobbles, and frontal control cannot budget attention cleanly, the map lands in a familiar neighborhood regardless of whether the person arrived via infection, hormones, fatigue, or pills.

That overlap is why Chapters 8 through 15 keep returning to shared patterns. The brain does not care what acronym sits on your chart. It cares whether you can raise activation for demand, release it for recovery, gate sensory load, and sleep deeply enough to reset next-day capacity. Where those jobs fail, fog is a common surface report, and the training implications rhyme across ostensibly different conditions.

For a structured tour of those clusters at professional depth, open the *QEEG Field Guide* and read Chapter 6, the phenotype atlas. For the version written for a general reader, use Appendix G in this book: same conceptual spine, less jargon, more translation.

Brain fog is also among the presentations that shift most reliably when neurofeedback targets the right regulatory profile. Individual timelines differ; comorbid medical issues matter; no serious clinician guarantees a calendar from a label alone. Still, the mechanism fits. A large share of what people call brain fog is the felt edge of regulatory strain, not a scar that ignores training. Aim protocols at the patterns the map shows, and you are working on the system that actually generates the symptom. When fog is mostly tuning, training has something concrete to grab.

7.9 What Comes Next

The chapters that follow are organized by the most common presentations we see in clinical practice. Each one opens with a human story, shows you the brain patterns, explains the training approach, and gives you a concrete next step.

You don't have to read them all. Find the one that matches your experience, or read them all and notice where patterns overlap. Because they do overlap. The anxious brain and the trauma brain share features. The ADHD brain and the sleep-deprived brain can look identical on a map. The performer's brain and the burnout brain are sometimes the same brain at different points in time.

Regulation is the thread that connects them all.

Decision Point: Did you recognize a pattern in the dimensions above? The chapters that follow show you what each pattern looks like in detail: the brain data, the lived experience, the training approach, and the next step. Find yours.

7.9.1 Going Deeper

- For the mood axis and the CEO/Lifeguard framework for emotional regulation, see *Half a Second More* Chapters 6–7.
- For the Grumpy Old Man, the CEO, and the Lifeguard archetypes in full, see *Gifted and Tortured.*

Your Move:

1. **Reflect:** Which of the six regulatory dimensions resonated most? Arousal? Stability? Sleep? Where do you feel your nervous system struggles most?

2. **Act:** Rate yourself on each dimension: arousal (too hot / about right / too cool), stability (steady / volatile), flexibility (rigid / flexible / chaotic), attention (scattered / focused / stuck), sensory gating (overwhelmed / balanced / disconnected), sleep (solid / disrupted). This rough self-assessment is the beginning of your regulatory profile.

3. **Start a conversation:** Ask your therapist or doctor: "Have you ever thought about my symptoms in terms of nervous system regulation rather than a diagnosis?" The answer will tell you how they think about what's going on.

Ch 8: The Anxious Brain

8.1 Meet Sarah

Sarah is forty-two, runs a marketing agency, and hasn't slept through the night in four years. She's tried two SSRIs, a benzodiazepine she's afraid of becoming dependent on, meditation apps that make her more anxious because she can't stop thinking about whether she's doing them right, and a therapist who helped her understand her childhood but didn't change the 3am catastrophizing.

She came to us because a friend mentioned brain mapping. She was skeptical ("I've tried everything") but desperate enough to try one more thing.

Her brain map showed what we see in about a third of our anxiety clients: frontal high beta at nearly three standard deviations above the norm. Her brain was running a threat-detection system around the clock, scanning, evaluating, anticipating, never idling. Her alpha rhythm, the brain's natural idle state, was almost entirely suppressed. She had no neutral gear.

"So this is why I can't turn it off," she said.

"This is one reason," we told her. "And now that we can see it, we can train it."

8.2 Anxiety Isn't One Thing

Anxiety is not a single brain pattern. It's a symptom that can arise from at least four different regulatory profiles, and each one responds to different training.

The Ruminator (Frontal High Beta)

This is Sarah's pattern. Excessive fast activity in the frontal lobes, beta and high beta running two to three standard deviations above the norm, especially at rest. The brain is generating threat assessments, what-if scenarios, and worst-case analyses continuously. This person can't stop thinking. Sleep onset is a nightmare because the brain won't downshift. Physically, they're often tense (jaw clenching, tight shoulders, shallow breathing), partly from cortical overdrive. An important caveat from Chapter 1 applies here: frontalis and temporalis muscle tension produces EMG in the same 20-30 Hz range as cortical high beta, so raw-EEG review is required to confirm that the elevated fast activity on the map is cortical rather than muscular artifact, or a mix of both.

The Unprotected Brain (Alpha Suppression)

This person has lost their alpha rhythm, the brain's noise-cancellation system. Without adequate alpha, there's no buffer between the brain and incoming stimulation. Everything gets through: every noise, every emotional signal, every stray thought. They feel raw, exposed, unable to create a quiet internal space. Rest doesn't feel restful because the brain can't idle.

The Vigilant Brain (Right Frontal Overactivation)

In the frontal alpha asymmetry framework, the conventional metric is defined as ln(right alpha power) minus ln(left alpha power). Because alpha is an idling rhythm, lower alpha at a site is read as higher activation. A negative asymmetry score (less right alpha, meaning relatively more right-frontal activation) is associated in population studies with avoidance motivation and vigilance. When this pattern is chronic, the brain defaults to scanning for danger. This person doesn't necessarily have racing thoughts. They have a persistent felt sense that something is wrong, a body-level vigilance that doesn't match their actual circumstances. It's anxiety felt more in the body than the mind.

An important limit: a 2017 meta-analysis (van der Vinne, Vollebregt, van Putten, & Arns, 2017) found that frontal alpha asymmetry has negligible diagnostic value for depression. The same caution extends to anxiety: asymmetry is not a diagnostic marker for any psychiatric condition. Per the framework in Chapter 1, it is a pattern that may inform clinical thinking, an individual difference worth noting, not a diagnosis or a pathology verdict.

The Disconnected Brain (Coherence Disruption)

Sometimes anxiety isn't about excess in a single pattern. It's about regions not coordinating properly. Disrupted coherence (statistical coupling; see the coherence caveat in Chapter 1) between frontal and posterior regions, or between hemispheres, can produce a state where the brain's processing feels fragmented. The person reports feeling "scattered," "unable to think clearly," or "like my brain isn't working right." The anxiety comes from the felt sense of disorganization rather than from a specific worry.

Phenotype	QEEG Signature	Training Approach	First Signs of Change
Ruminator	Elevated frontal high-beta (20–30+ Hz)	Reduce high-beta; enhance SMR	Mind gets quieter; sleep onset improves
Unprotected Brain	Suppressed alpha globally	Alpha enhancement training	Can sit still without needing stimulation
Vigilant Brain	Right frontal overactivation	Alpha asymmetry training (L > R)	Body-level dread lifts; shoulders drop
Disconnected Brain	Coherence disruption (frontal-posterior)	Coherence / connectivity training	Thinking feels less fragmented

These aren't mutually exclusive. Many people show combinations; high beta plus alpha suppression is common. The point is that "anxiety" as a label tells you almost nothing about what the brain is actually doing. The map shows which of these patterns your brain is running, and that difference informs what to try next.

8.3 What We See in QEEG

Across thousands of anxiety presentations, the most common patterns include:

- **Elevated high beta (20-30+ Hz) in frontal regions:** the rumination and threat-scanning signature
- **Suppressed alpha (8-12 Hz) globally or posteriorly:** the brain can't idle
- **Frontal alpha asymmetry:** relatively greater right-frontal activation (lower right alpha) associated in research with avoidance motivation and negative affect, though not diagnostic for any specific condition (van der Vinne et al., 2017)
- **Elevated frontal coherence:** regions locked together too tightly, losing flexibility
- **Beta-to-alpha ratio imbalance:** the "always on" pattern where fast activity dominates at rest

What it might NOT mean: Elevated beta can reflect fast processing, not pathology. Some anxious-seeming patterns are actually sleep deprivation creating a hyperarousal picture. Caffeine elevates beta temporarily. A good clinician checks all of these before concluding the pattern is a trait rather than a state. (To see what these patterns look like on an actual brain map, visit neurofeedbackexplained.com/plates.)

8.4 How Training Addresses It

The protocol depends on the phenotype:

For the Ruminator: Reduce frontal high beta while training SMR (12-15 Hz) for stability. The goal is to teach the brain that it doesn't need to run the threat-detection system at full power during rest. Many clients describe the first shift as "my mind got quieter," less relentlessly busy.

For the Unprotected Brain: Alpha enhancement training, building the brain's capacity to produce alpha rhythm during rest. This restores the idle state. Clients often describe the change as "I can finally just sit without needing to do something."

For the Vigilant Brain: Alpha asymmetry training, shifting the frontal balance from right-dominant (avoidance) toward left-dominant (approach). This changes the emotional default from "something is wrong" toward "I can engage."

For the Disconnected Brain: Coherence and connectivity training, improving the coordination between regions that should be working together. This reduces the fragmented, scattered quality and produces a sense of cognitive clarity.

Most training plans combine elements. High-beta reduction plus alpha enhancement is one of the most common pairings for anxiety presentations.

8.5 What It Feels Like When It Works: The Body Lets Go

People expect the first sign of progress to be a quieter mind. Often it's the body that changes first.

Clients report: the tightness in the chest loosens. The shoulders drop, not because you reminded yourself to relax them, but because the cortical signal that was keeping them clenched finally eased. The jaw unclenches. The shallow breathing deepens without effort. The persistent knot in the stomach, the one you'd forgotten wasn't normal, dissolves.

These aren't downstream reactions to feeling better. They're the body-level cascade of a brain that's finally downshifting. When frontal high beta drops and alpha starts to come online, the entire downstream autonomic response shifts. Less cortical overdrive means less sympathetic activation means less muscular bracing, less adrenaline, less of the physical armor your body has been wearing to match your brain's threat level.

For many clients, this is the moment that makes neurofeedback real: the felt sense that their body has stopped fighting an invisible threat.

8.6 The Obsessive-Compulsive Pattern

OCD sits in a different neighborhood than generalized anxiety, even though they're often treated as close relatives. Where the anxious brain tends to be stuck in a "fast idle" of scanning and catastrophizing, the OCD brain has a specific structural problem: a loop it can't exit.

The neuroscience framework that best explains OCD is the cortico-striato-thalamo-cortical (CSTC) circuit. The orbitofrontal cortex and anterior cingulate keep firing an error signal: "something is wrong, something needs fixing." The striatum and thalamus cycle that signal back to the cortex, which fires it again. The system never updates to "resolved." The brain locks into a correction loop with no exit condition, which is exactly what the compulsion is: a behavioral attempt to satisfy a circuit that can't be satisfied.

On a QEEG, OCD tends to look different from the high-beta ruminator. Research points to increased delta and theta power in frontal regions, reduced alpha connectivity, and disrupted communication in the CSTC loops. The pattern suggests a brain that's rigid rather than hyperactive, locked into a narrow range of states rather than overclocked across all of them.

The protocol approach for OCD reflects this. Rather than simply turning down global arousal (which is the primary target for generalized anxiety), effective OCD training tends to target the rigidity and the connectivity of the error-detection networks. Coherence training at frontal and frontocentral sites is one approach; z-score training that normalizes multiple frontal and cingulate sites simultaneously is another. Some protocols explicitly target the orbitofrontal and anterior cingulate regions, attempting to modulate the activity in the CSTC loop directly.

The evidence base is smaller than for anxiety, but encouraging. Two systematic reviews and meta-analyses (Ferreira, Pêgo & Morgado, 2019; Zafarmand, Farahmand & Otared, 2022) found that neurofeedback reduced OCD symptoms with medium-to-large effect sizes, and in at least one sham-controlled EEG trial outperformed sham on compulsion reduction. Real-time fMRI neurofeedback of the anterior prefrontal cortex produced a small but statistically significant reduction in OCD symptoms compared with yoked sham feedback in a randomized, double-blind trial (Rance et al., 2023).

The honest framing: exposure and response prevention (ERP) combined with SSRIs remains the evidence-based gold standard for OCD. Neurofeedback right now is best framed as a promising adjunct, particularly for people who haven't responded adequately to first-line treatment or who want to reduce the intensity of ERP by calming the underlying circuitry first. We see it used most effectively alongside, not instead of, ERP. The brain calms the loop; therapy rewrites the response to it. We hold this as a working clinical hypothesis, not a settled conclusion; the evidence in Chapter 5's framework applies here.

8.7 What to Measure and How Long

In our clinical experience, anxiety training often shows results in a recognizable sequence. These session ranges are patterns we observe in practice, not published benchmarks:

- **Sessions 3-5:** Sleep begins to improve (often the first change)
- **Sessions 8-12:** Resting tension decreases, reactivity softens
- **Sessions 15-25:** Sustained change in daily anxiety levels, fewer anxious episodes, faster recovery when triggered
- **Sessions 25-40:** Consolidated shift in baseline anxiety

What changes first, and in what order. The progression we observe follows a recognizable arc. The first five sessions often produce almost nothing subjectively, or a slight shift in sleep onset. Clients report falling asleep faster, sometimes without noticing until they're asked. The body often leads the mind. By sessions 8-12, we see resting tension drop. Shoulders that have been elevated for years start to hang differently. The jaw unclenches. Clients describe being able to sit without fidgeting, or noticing that a stressful moment didn't escalate the way it used to. By session 15, the daily anxiety rating typically starts to move.

Lower. Fewer spikes. Faster recovery when something does trigger. "I got anxious about the meeting, but it didn't ruin my whole morning" is a common report. By session 25-30, the baseline has shifted. The person who used to wake at 3am with racing thoughts might still have an occasional bad night, but it's the exception. The person who couldn't sit through a dinner without excusing themselves might still feel some discomfort, but they're staying. The consolidation phase, sessions 30-40, is when these gains become the new normal rather than something you're actively noticing. The brain has learned the new pattern. It's defaulting to it.

Why sleep often leads. High beta and alpha suppression don't just affect waking hours. They prevent the brain from downshifting at night. When training reduces frontal high beta and restores alpha, sleep architecture is often the first downstream improvement (Chapter 13 covers the SMR-spindle mechanism in detail). We track sleep as a leading indicator. If sleep isn't improving by session 10, we're looking at protocol adjustment.

Track: sleep quality, daily anxiety rating (1-10), reactivity (how easily triggered and how fast you recover), physical tension, and any functional measures that matter to you (social situations, work performance, ability to rest).

8.8 The Stack for Anxiety

Neurofeedback alone often produces significant anxiety reduction. But combining it with complementary approaches accelerates results:

- **Sleep optimization:** anxiety and sleep disruption feed each other. Fix sleep and anxiety often improves on its own. See Chapter 13.
- **HRV biofeedback and breathwork:** trains autonomic regulation from the bottom up, complementing neurofeedback's top-down approach.
- **Therapy (CBT, ACT, or somatic):** neurofeedback calms the brain; therapy gives you tools and insight. The combination is more powerful than either alone.

- **Mindfulness practice:** once your alpha rhythm is stronger, meditation actually starts to work. Many clients who "couldn't meditate" before training find it accessible afterward.
- **Exercise:** regular aerobic exercise is one of the strongest anti-anxiety interventions available. It should be part of any anxiety plan.

8.9 What Happened to Sarah

Sarah trained three times a week for twelve weeks. Sleep changed first: by session seven, she was falling asleep in twenty minutes instead of ninety. She didn't connect it to the training at first. "I thought it was the new mattress," she said. It wasn't the mattress.

By session fifteen, her husband noticed before she did. "You're not checking your phone at dinner," he told her. She hadn't realized she'd stopped. The constant low-grade scanning, the threat assessment that had been running in the background of every meal and every conversation, had quieted enough that she could be present without managing it. Her chest still tightened before big meetings, but the tightness would pass in minutes instead of persisting for hours.

At session twenty-five, we re-mapped her. The frontal high beta had dropped from nearly three standard deviations to 1.2. Her alpha, which had been almost absent at baseline, was now visible and sustained. The brain had a neutral gear again.

"I didn't know what calm felt like," she told us. "I thought calm was something other people had. Turns out my brain just didn't know how to get there."

She finished at thirty-six sessions. She still gets anxious. She's a high-performing person with a demanding life. But the anxiety rises and falls now. It doesn't stick. She sleeps through the night. She stopped the benzodiazepine with her psychiatrist's support. And when stress hits, her body doesn't lock up the way it used to.

8.10 Red Flags

- If a clinic promises to "eliminate" your anxiety, walk out. Anxiety is a normal human emotion. The goal is regulation: appropriate anxiety when warranted, recovery when it's not, not elimination.
- If training increases your anxiety consistently across sessions, the protocol needs adjusting. This is a signal, not a reason to push through.
- If you have panic disorder, severe OCD, or anxiety with dissociative features, make sure your provider has experience with complex presentations, not just common, non-clinical anxiety.

Decision Point: If you recognized yourself in this chapter, the most useful next step is a QEEG brain map from a qualified provider. A map won't tell you what's wrong with you, but it will show you which of these patterns your brain is running. That information changes everything about what to try next. Chapter 17 shows you exactly how to find a good provider and what questions to ask.

Your Move:

1. **Identify before you book:** Before your first conversation with a provider, write down which anxiety description fits your experience: the frontal high-beta Ruminator, the alpha-suppressed Unprotected Brain, the threat-scanning Vigilant Brain, or the coherence-disrupted Disconnected Brain. Bring that to the intake session. A good provider will cross-check your description against your map.

2. **Act:** Track your anxiety for one week before taking any next step. Three times a day (morning, midday, evening) rate your anxiety 1-10. Note what was happening when it spiked. Patterns will emerge.

3. **Start a conversation:** Tell your therapist or doctor: "I've been reading about how different anxiety brain patterns respond to different approaches. Can we talk about whether my current treatment matches my specific pattern?" That question opens a door.

This chapter is educational only and does not constitute medical advice. Discuss any decision to begin, modify, or stop neurofeedback or any other treatment with a licensed clinician.

Ch 9: The Distracted Brain: ADHD and Attention

The most frustrating version of this story starts with the same sentence: "You're so smart. Why can't you just focus?" This chapter is for the people who've heard that sentence too many times to count, and the parents saying it who suspect it's the wrong question.

9.1 Meet David

David is thirty-four. Diagnosed with ADHD at eight, medicated through college, now working in software engineering and wondering if there's another way. He's functional, but the stimulants make him feel flat, he crashes every afternoon, and he's not sure the medication is doing what it used to.

His brain map showed excess theta frontally, the classic "underaroused" pattern that's been the textbook ADHD signature for decades. But it also showed something nobody had mentioned before: a coherence asymmetry between hemispheres. His left and right frontal lobes weren't coordinating efficiently. The stimulant was addressing the arousal problem while completely ignoring the connectivity problem.

"So there's more going on than just attention," he said. He paused. "It's like I've been patching one thread without knowing the whole process was misscheduled."

"Exactly like that," we told him. "ADHD is never one type of brain."

9.2 ADHD Is Not One Type of Brain

The same diagnosis can come from completely different brain patterns. Treat them all the same way and you'll help some people and miss others entirely.

Structural brain imaging is beginning to line up with what individualized EEG work has been arguing for a long time. Pan, Long, Qin and colleagues (2026), in JAMA Psychiatry, used morphometric similarity network analysis on structural MRI data and reported at least three neurobiological subtypes within ADHD. One subtype was organized more around emotional dysregulation than around classic inattention. That is not a small footnote. If the label "ADHD" hides multiple biologies, the default playbook for medication and for neurofeedback will help some people, bore others, and occasionally push the brain in the wrong direction.

EEG subtyping research has been making a parallel case for roughly two decades (Clarke et al., 2001; Clarke et al., 2011; Slater et al., 2022). Different ADHD presentations often map onto different electrical signatures at the scalp. MRI and QEEG do not measure the same thing. When independent methods keep finding splits inside one diagnosis, the old single-mechanism picture stops working as a treatment guide. We see the downstream version of that problem every week: bright, motivated people who have cycled through the usual medication and training menus without anyone asking which pattern they are actually carrying.

For you, the practical read stays simple. ADHD is an umbrella. The same stimulant choice or the same neurofeedback protocol will not fit every subtype. That is why the phenotype-matching frame from Chapter 1 is not abstract theory for attention problems. It is the difference between aiming at the pattern you actually have and guessing from a label.

Across thousands of ADHD presentations, we see:

The Underaroused Brain

Excess frontal theta, low beta, the brain that can't engage. This is the classic pattern Lubar identified in the 1970s and the one most ADHD research has targeted. The brain defaults to an idle state even during tasks that require engagement. These people zone out, lose track, miss deadlines: the cortex isn't activating.

What this feels like in real life: the brain is at the mercy of whatever stimulation is most salient in the moment. The next shiny stimulus is always more appealing than the task you're supposed to be doing, and the frontal cortex, which should function as the CEO telling the rest of the brain "no, stay focused on this," has a compromised ability to override those pulls. The brain's executive override is underpowered.

Clinically, we see this person arrive late, forget the second half of the sentence they started, lose their keys three times before noon. They describe a fog, a sense that they're watching themselves from a distance. Parents report that getting the child out the door in the morning is a daily battle of redirects. The underaroused brain needs external structure because it can't generate enough internal structure on its own. Deadlines create urgency. Body doubling helps. Caffeine and stimulants work because they supply the activation the cortex isn't producing.

The Overaroused Brain

The opposite pattern, too much fast activity, especially high beta. This person isn't zoned out; they're overwhelmed. Too much information processing, too many simultaneous streams, inability to prioritize. They look "scattered" but the mechanism is overload, not underactivation. Giving this person a stimulant can make them worse. You're accelerating a brain that's already running too fast. (The EMG caveat from Chapter 1 applies: elevated 20-30+ Hz readings must be checked against the raw EEG to separate cortical fast activity from scalp-muscle artifact before building a protocol around them.)

What we see in the clinic: the person who talks fast, interrupts, can't sit still during the brain map. They describe their mind as "a browser with fifty tabs open." They're exhausted by the end of the day from the cognitive load of processing everything at once. They often have a history of being told they have anxiety when the real issue is cortical overactivation. The overaroused brain needs calming protocols, not activation. Alpha enhancement, high-beta reduction. Stimulants can produce agitation, insomnia, or a paradoxical sense of being "wired and tired."

The Connectivity-Disrupted Brain

Normal power levels at individual sites, but the coordination between regions is off. Hemispheres not talking efficiently. Frontal-posterior connections weak. These people can focus on individual tasks but struggle with complex executive demands, planning, sequencing, switching between tasks, integrating information from different sources. Their ADHD is a network problem, not a power problem.

In practice, this shows up as the person who can hyperfocus for hours on something engaging but falls apart when the task requires multiple steps, multiple sources of information, or frequent switching. They might ace a test on a single topic and fail a project that requires planning across weeks. They describe feeling "scattered" or "like my brain has too many departments that don't talk to each other." Medication response is variable. Coherence training and Z-score normalization often produce the most dramatic shifts, because you're addressing the actual bottleneck.

The Sleep-Confounded Brain

This is the pattern we check for first and the one most often missed. Chronic sleep deprivation elevates theta, reduces beta, impairs executive function, and destroys sustained attention, producing a brain map and a symptom profile that looks identical to "real" ADHD. The relationship runs deeper than co-occurrence: in ADHD, when SMR neurofeedback normalizes sleep-onset latency mid-treatment, those sleep improvements statistically mediate the later gains in inattention, but not hyperactivity or impulsivity (Arns et al., 2014). A substantial portion of what presents as ADHD attention problems may be exhaustion-driven vigilance instability, not a standalone attentional disorder.

Clinically, the sleep-confounded presentation has telltale signs. The theta is diffuse, not focal. The person reports that their symptoms are worse when they're tired and better after a good night. They might have a history of sleep onset delay, frequent night waking, or simply never feeling rested. We have seen individual clients whose attention complaints improved substantially with sleep treatment alone; others continued to meet ADHD criteria. Others needed both: fix the sleep, then train what remains. The key is not to assume. A diffuse slow pattern on the map can prompt a closer look at sleep, but it is nonspecific; clinical sleep history and standard diagnostic assessment are required to distinguish a sleep-driven picture from a primary attentional one.

Before we train anyone's "ADHD," we check their sleep. If sleep is devastated, we start there, but the good news is that neurofeedback often improves sleep rapidly through SMR training, even when the primary target is attention. Many clients find their sleep and attention improving in parallel, because the same regulatory circuits are involved.

Phenotype	**QEEG Pattern**	**Protocol Direction**	**Medication Note**
Underaroused	Excess frontal theta, low beta	Theta down, beta/SMR up	Stimulants often effective
Overaroused	Elevated high-beta, fast processing	High-beta down, alpha up	Stimulants can worsen
Connectivity-Disrupted	Normal power, poor inter-regional coherence	Coherence training, Z-score normalization	Variable response
Sleep-Confounded	Diffuse theta elevation, low alpha	Fix sleep first (SMR training)	Sleep and circadian work may help first

(To see what these ADHD phenotype patterns look like on an actual brain map, visit neurofeedbackexplained.com/plates.)

9.3 The TBR Controversy

The theta-beta ratio (TBR) was once considered the gold-standard ADHD biomarker: theta power divided by beta power, measured at

Cz or frontal sites. Monastra's early work showed clear separation between ADHD and typical children on this metric. The FDA cleared a device (NEBA) based on TBR as a diagnostic aid in 2013.

Then the signal eroded.

When researchers retested TBR in newer populations, the effect sizes shrank dramatically. By 2024, multiple analyses had concluded that TBR alone cannot reliably differentiate children with and without ADHD (Arns, Conners & Kraemer, 2013; Ogrim, Kropotov & Hestad, 2012; Lansbergen et al., 2011; Gloss et al., 2016; Boxum et al., 2025). What happened?

The most likely explanation: population-level sleep deprivation. As children and adolescents slept less over the 2000s and 2010s, their theta levels rose, from exhaustion rather than from ADHD. The control groups started looking more "ADHD-like" on TBR, shrinking the between-group difference. The biomarker was real in Monastra's era but confounded by a societal shift in sleep behavior.

This has a direct consequence for the research: when studies enrolled children with attention problems and elevated TBR, some of those children were genuinely ADHD, and some were chronically sleep-deprived. Treating the sleep-deprived kids with theta-beta training meant targeting a theta elevation that was a symptom of exhaustion, not a trait of ADHD. The real issue was sleep, and the protocol couldn't fix what it wasn't designed to address. This is one reason why group-level ADHD neurofeedback studies show mixed results: they were often targeting a confounded metric in heterogeneous populations, and some of those "non-responders" were never going to respond because they needed sleep.

It's also why QEEG-guided individualization matters more for ADHD than for almost any other condition. If your ADHD comes from high theta, theta-beta training makes sense. If it comes from overarousal, connectivity problems, or sleep debt, it doesn't.

9.4 The Evidence Reality for ADHD

We covered this in Chapter 5, but it bears repeating here because ADHD is the most contested neurofeedback application:

The 2025 JAMA Psychiatry meta-analysis (Westwood et al., 2025) found neurofeedback does not outperform sham or active controls at the group level for core ADHD symptoms. The 2021 Arnold double-blind trial (Arnold et al., 2021) found the same.

Both groups improved. Neurofeedback had effects, it just didn't clearly outperform credible placebo at the group level, with standardized protocols, on heterogeneous populations.

Our clinical experience, across thousands of ADHD maps with individualized, QEEG-guided protocols, looks different. We typically see measurable changes in brain data within the first few sessions and functional improvements by session fifteen. But as we discussed in Chapter 5: clinical conviction isn't evidence, and every practitioner believes their results exceed what trials show. The gap between our clinical observations and the group-level data could reflect a genuine advantage of individualization, or it could reflect the same selection and expectancy biases that affect every uncontrolled clinical setting. The individualization hypothesis is testable (matching protocols to brain signatures, as in Voetterl et al., 2023), and early results are encouraging. But the large-scale test hasn't been run yet. We hold our clinical experience provisionally, not as proof.

9.5 The Medication Question

We're not anti-medication. Stimulants work, they produce rapid, reliable symptom improvement for many people with ADHD. If medication is working for you and you're satisfied with it, nothing in this book says you have to change course.

Medication has real limitations worth weighing alongside its strengths:

- Stimulant effects are generally present while you take the medication and diminish when you stop, though some evidence suggests

that long-term treatment may have lasting functional and neurobiological effects in some individuals.
- Not everyone responds. About 20 to 30 percent of people don't get adequate benefit from initial stimulant trials.
- Side effects are real: appetite suppression, sleep disruption, emotional blunting, cardiovascular effects.

Neurofeedback, when it works, aims to change the brain's regulatory patterns directly. Follow-up data suggest that gains may persist after training ends. A 2019 meta-analysis (Van Doren et al., 2019) found within-group inattention effects that grew from post-treatment to follow-up, though the comparators were non-active (waitlist, treatment-as-usual), not sham. In the Arnold et al. (2021) trial, both neurofeedback and sham groups maintained gains at thirteen-month follow-up with no significant between-group difference on the primary outcome ($p = .41$), so the persistence was not NF-specific. Long-term controlled durability data are limited, and whether neurofeedback produces more durable improvement than medication for ADHD has not been established in a head-to-head comparison. Medication works in hours; neurofeedback takes months. The trade-off involves onset speed, side-effect profile, cost, evidence base, and uncertainty about long-term durability on both sides.

Many families and adults use both, medication for immediate function, neurofeedback to build long-term capacity, with the goal of reducing medication dependence over time. That's a reasonable, evidence-informed approach. The key is that someone is looking at the brain data and making individualized decisions, not applying a one-size-fits-all formula.

9.6 Training for ADHD

In our clinical framework, the phenotype observed on the QEEG informs which protocol approach we consider:

- **Underaroused:** Theta reduction, beta enhancement frontally, SMR enhancement centrally

- **Overaroused:** High-beta reduction, alpha enhancement
- **Connectivity-disrupted:** Coherence training, Z-score normalization across sites
- **Sleep-confounded:** Fix sleep first (see Chapter 13), then reassess

Session counts for ADHD training vary. In our clinical experience, most people begin to see measurable improvement within twenty to forty sessions, with some complex presentations needing longer courses. These numbers come from clinical practice, not from published dose-response trials; no study has established the optimal session count for individualized ADHD neurofeedback. Track: sustained attention (can you get through tasks?), executive function (planning, prioritizing, switching), impulsivity, afternoon energy, and sleep quality.

Decision Point: If you're a parent reading this: you don't have to choose between medication and neurofeedback. Many families use both, starting with a brain map to understand what they're actually working with. If you're an adult: the same applies. A map doesn't commit you to anything, it shows you what's there.

9.6.1 Going Deeper

- For the Stabilizer, the Supervisor, and the Fog archetypes in full, see *Gifted and Tortured*.
- For attention systems and the Fog character in depth, see *Half a Second More* Chapters 4–5.
- For the four ADHD phenotypes at clinical depth, see *QEEG Field Guide* Chapter 6.

Your Move:

1. **Ask this one question at your next appointment:** "Which ADHD pattern does my presentation match: underarousal, overarousal,

connectivity, or sleep-driven theta?" If your current clinician can't answer that without looking at brain data, ask what it would take to get that data. Most ADHD presentations haven't been phenotyped; the answer to that question could change the treatment plan.

2. **Act:** If you're considering neurofeedback for ADHD, track sleep for two weeks first. If sleep is poor, address it before assuming the attention issue is purely ADHD.

3. **Start a conversation:** Ask your prescriber or clinician: "Has anyone ever looked at my brain data to see which type of ADHD pattern I have?" If the answer is no, a QEEG might change the conversation.

This chapter is educational only and does not constitute medical advice. Discuss any decision to begin, modify, or stop neurofeedback or any other treatment with a licensed clinician.

Ch 10: The Trauma Brain

By session twenty, the most significant thing Elena said was the hardest to name.

She's a therapist herself: successful practice, loving family, good life by any external measure. She came to us because EMDR had given her understanding without relief. She could narrate her childhood trauma without crying now. She understood it, had mapped its origins, traced its contours. But in a safe room, on an ordinary Tuesday afternoon, her body still scanned the exits.

"The scanning stopped," she told us. Not as an announcement. More like reporting an absence she'd only just noticed, the way you notice a sound has stopped when a refrigerator shuts off. She turned her head toward the window. "I didn't even check the door when you walked in."

Eight months earlier, her brain map had shown what we see in hundreds of trauma survivors: alpha suppression so severe that her brain had lost its resting state. Always on, no resting state, no recovery mode, no neutral gear. The high-frequency activity in her right hemisphere running a continuous threat scan that no amount of cognitive insight could override.

"Therapy helped me understand what happened," she had told us at intake. "But my nervous system didn't get the memo."

That's the trauma brain in one sentence. And that brain, it turns out, shows a recognizable pattern on a map, one we treat as a working clinical hypothesis, not a diagnosis. And the pattern can change.

10.1 How Trauma Reshapes Brain Patterns

Trauma doesn't just create bad memories. It appears to reshape the brain's regulatory patterns, and those changes can show up on a

QEEG. The patterns we describe below are working clinical hypotheses, not diagnostic markers.

Alpha suppression. The most consistent finding in trauma survivors. The brain's resting rhythm (the alpha "off switch") gets suppressed, sometimes dramatically. Without alpha, the brain can't idle. It's always processing, always scanning, always reactive. This is the neurological basis of hypervigilance: a cortical pattern operating below the level of choice or habit.

Coherence disruption. Trauma often disrupts the coordination between brain regions. Frontal-posterior connections weaken (the planning brain loses its link to sensory processing). Interhemispheric coherence can be disrupted (the two halves of the brain stop communicating efficiently). The result is a fragmented processing experience: feeling "scattered," "not in my body," or "unable to think clearly" under stress.

High-beta hypervigilance. Similar to anxiety, many trauma survivors show elevated high beta in frontal regions: a threat-detection system stuck on high alert. (The EMG caveat from Chapter 1 applies here as well: scalp-muscle artifact in the 20-30 Hz range must be ruled out through raw-EEG review before attributing frontal fast activity to cortical hypervigilance.) But in trauma, this pattern is often more severe, more treatment-resistant, and more tightly linked to specific triggers. In some cases, we also see elevated activation at the temporoparietal junction (TPJ), the region where sensory integration, self-other processing, and threat assessment converge. In our clinical experience, when this pattern is present, clients often report amplified sensory input: sounds seem louder, touch is more startling, social cues feel more intense. We treat this as a clinical hypothesis linking the TPJ pattern to sensory hypervigilance; the relationship between resting TPJ activation on scalp EEG and lived sensory experience has not been validated in controlled research. When this pattern appears alongside cognitive hypervigilance, the person may be overwhelmed from both directions.

The locked nervous system. Many trauma survivors show a combination of all three: suppressed alpha, disrupted coherence, and elevated fast activity. The system is stuck, locked in a defensive posture, unable to return to baseline after activation. You can see it in the room before you look at the EEG: the person sits with their back straight, feet flat, scanning. Their breathing is shallow and high in the chest. Their hands are still but not relaxed, held in a kind of readiness. If a door closes in the hallway, their head turns before they can decide to turn it. The body is on sentry duty, and it has been for years. This is what clinicians mean by "a dysregulated nervous system," and it's what neurofeedback directly addresses.

Pattern	QEEG Signature	Training Target	What Changes First
Alpha suppression	Low alpha globally; no resting idle	Alpha enhancement (posterior, then global)	Sleep onset; ability to "just sit"
Coherence disruption	Weak frontal-posterior / interhemispheric links	Coherence training; Z-score normalization	Thinking feels less fragmented
High-beta hypervigilance	Elevated frontal high-beta (20–30+ Hz)	High-beta down; SMR up	Startle response softens
TPJ hyperactivation	Overactive temporoparietal junction	Site-specific amplitude training	Sensory overwhelm decreases
Locked system (combined)	All of the above	Stabilization sequence (clinical hypothesis): SMR → alpha → coherence	Sleep improvement is often the first reported change

(To see what these trauma patterns look like on an actual brain map, visit neurofeedbackexplained.com/plates.)

10.2 Why Insight Isn't Enough

Elena's experience is common: therapy provides understanding, and good trauma therapy can also produce regulatory change, through somatic processing, EMDR, and other approaches that engage the body and the nervous system alongside cognition. But in some cases, cognitive and meaning-making progress outpaces the nervous system's shift. Neurofeedback works at the regulatory level directly. Both are real, both produce measurable change, and the most consistent clinical outcomes come from coordination rather than substitution. The evidence that neurofeedback uniquely addresses what talk therapy cannot reach is suggestive but not yet established; the evidence that neurofeedback complements first-line trauma treatments productively is the more defensible claim.

Neurofeedback doesn't replace evidence-based trauma treatments. It addresses regulatory patterns that may be limiting how fully those treatments can take hold. The goal is coordination: NF builds the regulatory substrate; therapy does the processing work that requires that substrate.

If you are currently receiving evidence-based treatment for PTSD or complex trauma (including Prolonged Exposure, CPT, EMDR, or IFS): do not discontinue or substitute that treatment with neurofeedback. Talk to your treating clinician before adding any new intervention to your care plan.

The following sequence reflects our clinical approach. We treat it as a working framework, not a validated protocol; the specific ordering has not been tested against alternatives in controlled trauma-neurofeedback research:

1. **Stabilize:** train SMR or alpha to build basic regulatory capacity. Sleep often improves first.
2. **Build tolerance:** as the nervous system stabilizes, the window of tolerance expands. Emotional material becomes more manageable.

3. **Process:** for clients who choose deeper work, alpha-theta training (Chapter 12) accesses the theta-dominant twilight state. The working hypothesis (see Chapter 12) is that traumatic material activated in this regulated state may be reconsolidated with reduced emotional charge, though direct evidence for reconsolidation during alpha-theta has not been established. A caution: the hypnagogic state is suggestible, and memories that surface in it are not reliably accurate. This work requires a clinician experienced in both alpha-theta and trauma.
4. **Integrate:** combine with trauma therapy (EMDR, IFS, somatic experiencing) once the brain has the regulatory capacity to handle the processing.

The key principle: **stabilization before processing.** If you dive into deep trauma work with a nervous system that can't regulate itself, you risk destabilization. If you stabilize first, the processing work is safer and more effective.

What the timeline has looked like in our clinical experience (individual responses vary widely; these are observations, not predictions):

Phase	Sessions	What Changes
Early stabilization	1–10	Sleep onset improves; startle intensity drops; the body starts to unclench between sessions
Window of tolerance expands	10–25	Triggers still fire, but recovery is faster; emotional flooding lasts minutes instead of hours
Regulatory capacity builds	25–40	Baseline shifts: calmer mornings, less hypervigilance, more capacity for difficult conversations
Deep processing (if chosen)	30–50+	Alpha-theta or trauma therapy integration; material that was overwhelming becomes workable

What it feels like when it works:

Elena's experience was typical. The first change wasn't emotional relief. It was physical. After about eight sessions, she realized she'd stopped clenching her jaw at night. Her neck, which had been locked for years, loosened enough that she turned her head without thinking about it for the first time she could remember. Sleep came next: she started falling asleep within twenty minutes instead of the usual ninety, and the 3 a.m. waking dropped from nightly to once or twice a week.

By session twenty, Elena described a shift harder to name: "The scanning stopped." The constant background hum of threat assessment, the feeling that something bad was about to happen, had quieted. Not gone. But quiet enough that she could sit in a room without mapping the exits. Quiet enough that a loud noise startled her and she recovered in seconds instead of being flooded for the next hour.

Around session thirty, she went back to her EMDR therapist. "I could go to places in the work I couldn't go before," she said. "The memories hadn't changed, but I could hold them without my body detonating." That's the stabilization principle in practice: the brain builds the capacity first, and then the processing work becomes possible.

10.3 Elena: A Longer Look

What follows is a more detailed account of one case, not because it's representative of every trauma presentation, but because a single case followed closely over time shows what the numbers can't. Consider it a companion reading to the tables above.

Elena had been a therapist for nine years when she came to us. She specialized in perinatal loss: she sat with women whose pregnancies had ended badly, whose bodies had failed them, who were trying to find a way back to themselves in the aftermath of grief they couldn't explain to people who hadn't lived it. She was very good at this work. Her clients described her as steady, attuned, present in a manner her clients called rare. What they didn't know was that the steadiness was calibrated and costing her.

She had grown up in a house where emotional climate was volatile and unpredictable. Her father moved between charm and rage on a schedule she could never quite decode. She had learned, early, to read the room the way a pilot reads weather: scanning for signals, adjusting her altitude before the storm arrived. By the time she was nine, she could tell from the sound of her father's car in the driveway whether the evening would require hiding in her room or performing cheerfulness at the dinner table. The skill kept her safe. It never turned off.

She carried this into her adult life so smoothly that for a long time she mistook it for ordinary attentiveness. She was good at reading people. She was good at anticipating needs. Her marriage was stable, her friendships affectionate, her children (two daughters, ten and seven) secure and funny and opinionated in ways that clearly came from somewhere secure. Nothing in her biography signaled distress. She had done years of her own therapy, had worked with three different EMDR practitioners over the course of a decade, understood the architecture of her childhood as well as she understood anything, could name the patterns, trace the origins, see where the wiring had come from. She was in her mid-forties and she could not sleep through the night.

The insomnia had been with her for as long as she could remember. Not the falling-asleep part; that was manageable. The waking part. The 2 a.m. or 3 a.m. return to full alert: heart rate elevated, a sense of threat with no object, the body ready for a threat that wasn't there. She would breathe carefully, as she'd been taught, and often drift back after an hour. Sometimes she wouldn't, and she'd sit with tea in the quiet of a sleeping house and wait for morning. She had done this so many times it had become part of her, like a chronic pain the self eventually incorporates. She didn't present it as a problem when she came to see us. She presented an EMDR plateau: she had done the processing work, she understood her history, and she still woke at 3 a.m. with her heart in her throat. She was calm about trying neurofeedback. Not desperate; methodical.

The first session was the brain map. She sat with the cap on, eyes open and then closed without comment, as clinicians learn to sit still for procedures. Nineteen minutes of clean data. Afterward she studied the topographic displays as she studied everything: attentively, without urgency, absorbing difficult information without letting it show.

The map showed, in severe form, the pattern we associate with trauma. The posterior regions that should have been humming with relaxed alpha were largely quiet; her brain, eyes closed in a comfortable chair in a quiet room, was not resting. The right hemisphere ran continuous fast-frequency activity, and the thalamocortical pathways showed a pattern we associate, in our clinical framework, with poor sleep consolidation. Nothing in the map said "this person had a difficult childhood." The pattern was consistent with a nervous system that could not settle to rest.

She asked good questions. She understood the frequency band terminology from having read about it. She wanted to know what the alpha suppression meant clinically, specifically. We talked through the relationship between posterior alpha and what clinicians mean when they say "resting state," the brain's ability to idle, to downshift, to not be scanning. She was quiet for a moment and then said: "So my brain never learned to rest." Not as a question.

"Or it learned and then was interrupted," we said. "Either way, the pattern is there, and it's trainable."

She asked what the training would feel like. We explained: you will sit in the chair, you will watch the screen, the feedback signal will respond to your brain's activity, you won't feel yourself doing anything. Your brain will learn from the contingency without your conscious participation. It's involuntary in the best sense. This reassured her, though she didn't say why.

She was a punctual, reliable client. She came three times a week for the first two months, a schedule she maintained by building it into her calendar as she built in supervision hours, non-negotiable professional infrastructure. The early sessions were uneventful as early sessions often are: the brain is learning the contingency, the changes are happening below the level of subjective experience, and the person sitting in the chair mostly reports feeling slightly drowsy afterward. Elena reported this. She described the early sessions as "neutral." She was watching carefully for effects and was careful not to overinterpret absence of change as failure.

Around session eight, it was her jaw.

She had clenched her jaw for so long that she no longer experienced it as clenching. It was simply the set of her face. A physical therapist had mentioned it years earlier; she had done some targeted stretching and forgotten about it. The morning after session eight, she woke and realized that her jaw had not been clenched during the night. The muscles of her face felt unfamiliar, loose for the first time in years. She noted this in the monitoring journal we ask clients to keep during training. She wrote it with the deliberate understatement of someone who didn't want to read too much into a single morning.

She kept noticing it. On many mornings. Around session twelve, she mentioned her neck. She had been experiencing low-grade neck tension for so long that it had become definitional, part of her physical texture. She turned to look at something during a session and something moved differently. "Like a gear I'd forgotten was stuck," she said. She turned her head again, experimenting. She laughed, short and surprised. "When did that happen?"

Sleep came next, more slowly. The sleep onset had always been manageable, but she was falling asleep faster, within fifteen or twenty minutes of lying down instead of the usual forty-five. And the middle-of-the-night waking, while it did not disappear, changed in character. She still woke. But recovery was faster, ten or fifteen minutes instead of an hour or more. The waking itself felt different, less urgent. Still alert; not alarmed. The distinction mattered to her. She knew the neurological difference and knew what it meant.

Around session eighteen, she brought material to the session that she hadn't planned to bring.

She had been in the car, driving to pick up her daughters from school, when another car cut across her lane without signaling. Standard traffic annoyance. She startled sharply, as she always did; her startle reflex had always been elevated. But this time, something different happened. She recovered. Not gradually, not through conscious effort or breath work, just: the threat resolved and her nervous system let it go. Within thirty seconds she was simply driving again, registering mild irritation and then not even that. She sat with this afterward, parked in the school pickup line, trying to understand what had been absent. The aftershock, she said. The residue that lingers when a startle doesn't quite resolve, where a piece of the threat-response keeps running even after the trigger has passed, where the next hour carries a residue of activation she'd have to work through. Gone. Or significantly diminished.

She was careful, in reporting this, not to overstate it. She had learned through years of clinical training not to mistake early improvement for completion, not to declare victory based on one good week. We appreciated this caution. We also pointed at her monitoring data, the incidence rates from the training sessions, the threshold-crossing patterns, the session-to-session learning metrics. The brain data showed what she was reporting from the inside: the regulation patterns were shifting. The shifts came unevenly, and the trend was clear.

Session twenty was the session where she said "the scanning stopped."

She described it the way you describe a sound you hadn't known was playing until it was gone. There was a quality to her habitual attentiveness, she said, that she now recognized as vigilance, a particular flavor of watching that was different from ordinary curiosity or presence. She was always watching for information that would tell her whether the emotional climate was safe. She had built her clinical career in part on this capacity and had never been able to fully separate the skill from its origins. During the previous week, the watching had changed. It was still there, but it was thinner, less urgent, less effortful. She sat in her intake sessions with clients and noticed that she was tracking their emotional state because she was interested in them, not because she was managing against threat. The distinction seemed important to her.

She said this plainly, without drama. She was looking at the floor when she said it, which for Elena, who maintained careful eye contact, was a tell. A feeling was being handled.

Around session twenty-five, she began to speak about her father.

This was notable because she had not, in three sessions a week for two months, mentioned him except in passing. She had the kind of clinical sophistication about trauma that can sometimes make the material feel theoretical, well-mapped and managed rather than alive. But around session twenty-five, the character of what she brought shifted. She started telling stories that had specific physical texture, the smell of his aftershave, the particular quality of the silence that preceded an explosion, the way she had learned to go still when she heard certain footsteps on the stairs. Stories she'd told before, in previous therapy, but differently. Not narrated; experienced. We noted the change. She noted it too. "I couldn't access this before," she said. "It wasn't that I hadn't tried. It was that my body wasn't ready to go there and stay there."

We referred her back to her EMDR therapist at session thirty.

Her EMDR therapist, whom she saw monthly for maintenance, reported back through the coordination channels we'd established: the work was different. She could go to places the work had not previously reached. The material that had been processed cognitively but not somatically was becoming available. She and her therapist began working specifically with some of the body-level memory that had been inaccessible before. This was not comfortable work. Elena described some sessions as hard in ways she hadn't expected, old activation patterns returning temporarily as the processing opened things that had been contained. We adjusted the training during this period, moving back toward stabilization protocols when the somatic work was particularly intense, building the regulatory floor before the processing pushed further. This coordination, between the neurofeedback and the trauma therapy, was what made the work coherent. Neither could have done what both together did.

She completed forty sessions over about eight months.

The last time we reviewed her map against the baseline, the changes were visible and consistent: posterior alpha recovering toward normal range, the right-hemisphere fast-frequency activity reduced, the thalamocortical signatures showing better organization than at intake. This was not a map of a different brain; it was a map of the same brain differently configured. The wiring was the same. The regulation was better.

She still wakes occasionally at 3 a.m. She said this without apparent distress. When she does, she falls back asleep. The waking doesn't have a hook in it anymore, doesn't catch and pull her into alertness. It's a body shifting. Sometimes she lies in the quiet and thinks about something, the day ahead, a client, what her daughters are learning. And then she sleeps. "That's enough," she said. "That's enough to change everything about the next day."

She was right that it was enough. She was also right that it had changed what was available to her afterward. The EMDR work she had done before this had been real, had been valuable, had accomplished what cognitive processing can accomplish. What the neurofeedback had given her was different: not insight, not language, not understanding. A different substrate. A nervous system that had room to work with what she already knew.

When she left our practice, she was considering whether to add QEEG literacy to the professional development she recommended to her clinical colleagues. She thought it might be worth more of them knowing what their clients' brains were doing underneath the words.

10.4 The Evidence for Trauma

PTSD is one of the more promising areas for neurofeedback, though the evidence is still developing:

- A 2024 meta-analysis (Voigt, Mosier & Tendler, 2024) found moderate effects on PTSD symptoms overall (clinician-rated SMD 0.74, self-rated 0.47). Split by comparison group, the clinician-rated advantage over passive controls was 1.30 and the advantage over active controls was 0.05. The effect lives almost entirely in the contrast with people who got nothing
- A multicenter prospective study of amygdala-derived EEG-fMRI-pattern neurofeedback for chronic PTSD showed clinically meaningful symptom reductions across sites (Fruchter et al., 2024)
- The VA / DoD Clinical Practice Guideline for PTSD (VA / DoD PTSD CPG, 2023) still classifies neurofeedback as "insufficient evidence to recommend for or against," though clinical momentum is strong

The strongest clinical tradition for trauma neurofeedback comes from Sebern Fisher's work with developmental trauma (Fisher, 2014) and Bessel van der Kolk's advocacy (van der Kolk, 2014). Fisher's approach emphasizes that trauma disrupts the brain's capacity for self-regulation, and that neurofeedback restores that capacity directly at the level of the circuits, not the narrative.

If the trauma patterns in this chapter resonate with your experience but you're looking for a longer treatment of the framework (including the phenotype-to-experience translation, the composite case model, and the clinician's perspective on what healing looks like over time), *Your Brain on Trauma* covers this terrain from a consumer-clinical perspective, written for the same informed reader. The books are designed to be complementary: this chapter introduces the brain-map view; *Your Brain on Trauma* develops the full clinical picture.

What would disprove the trauma-neurofeedback argument. If a well-designed RCT found that QEEG-guided neurofeedback added no symptom reduction beyond evidence-based first-line PTSD treatments (Prolonged Exposure, CPT, EMDR) in a trauma population, even when used as an adjunct to those treatments and with adequate session dose, this book's central clinical claim for this chapter would be substantially weakened. That test has arguably already run in miniature. In the Voigt et al. meta-analysis, neurofeedback's clinician-rated advantage over *active* control conditions was 0.05, which is to say: nothing. The evidence base is methodologically limited in the ways that keep this from being settled: most studies lack sham controls, few compare directly to first-line treatments, and the multicenter open-label studies cannot control for non-specific treatment factors. The evidence is enough to warrant informed clinical use. It is not enough to establish NF as a first-line trauma intervention, and we do not claim it is.

10.5 Combining NF with Trauma Therapy

Neurofeedback works best for trauma when it's coordinated with a therapist who understands the process:

- **NF + EMDR:** NF stabilizes arousal and builds regulatory capacity; EMDR processes specific traumatic memories. Many clinicians describe NF as the "platform" that makes EMDR safer and more effective. No RCTs test this combination, but it's widely used and clinically reported as powerful.
- **NF + IFS (Internal Family Systems):** NF calms the system; IFS works with the parts. Similar complementary logic.
- **NF + Somatic Experiencing:** Both work at the body/nervous system level. NF provides the measurable brain component.

If you're currently in therapy for trauma: talk to your therapist before adding neurofeedback. The best outcomes come from coordination, not from two practitioners working in isolation.

10.6 Red Flags

- **Pushing alpha-theta too early.** Alpha-theta training accesses deep emotional states. In clients with severe trauma, dissociative disorders, or fragile reality testing, this can trigger destabilizing experiences. A responsible provider does stabilization work first (sometimes for many sessions) before any deep-state protocols. Ask whether your provider screens for dissociation using the DES-II (Dissociative Experiences Scale-II) before beginning alpha-theta. It is a brief, validated questionnaire that asks about experiences like feeling detached from your body or having no memory of important events. Scores above 20 to 30 signal the need for thorough clinical assessment before any deep-state work begins.

- **No therapeutic support.** Neurofeedback for trauma should not be done in isolation from psychological support. Emotional material surfaces during training. Someone should be available to help process it.
- **Promising to "cure" PTSD.** Trauma work is not linear and doesn't have a guaranteed endpoint. Be cautious of providers who offer certainty.

Decision Point: If you're currently in therapy for trauma and considering adding neurofeedback: talk to your therapist first. The best outcomes come from coordination. A QEEG can help your therapist and your neurofeedback clinician build a shared picture of what's happening in your brain: a shared map that both can work from.

Your Move:

1. **Reflect:** Has your understanding of your trauma moved further than your nervous system's response to it? If cognitive progress has outpaced the body-level shift, the regulatory patterns described in this chapter may be part of the picture. Neurofeedback may complement your existing care by addressing the regulatory layer alongside whatever cognitive and processing work you're already doing.

2. **Act:** If you're considering NF for trauma, ask potential providers: "What stabilization work do you do before any deep-state proto-

cols?" and "How do you coordinate with my therapist?" The answers tell you whether they understand trauma-informed practice.

3. **Start a conversation:** Share this chapter with your therapist. Ask: "Could my nervous system be stuck in a pattern that therapy alone isn't changing? What would you think about adding brain-level regulation work?"

This chapter is educational only and does not constitute medical advice. Discuss any decision to begin, modify, or stop neurofeedback or any other treatment with a licensed clinician.

Ch 11: The Autistic Brain: Neurofeedback and Autism Spectrum

The parents had been told their son lacked empathy.

Kai is eleven. Verbal, bright, intensely interested in marine biology. He can describe cephalopod camouflage for forty-five minutes without losing the thread. He cannot handle the school cafeteria. He cannot handle loud, unpredictable spaces, and his parents had come to understand that as a social processing problem: Kai was disconnected from other people, unable to read the room, indifferent to the emotional weather around him.

His brain map said something different.

His right temporoparietal junction, the region where sensory integration and self-other processing converge, was running at high activation. Present and processing. Showing a pattern that differed markedly from the age norm, one we often see in people who report sensory overload in busy environments.

"He's not disconnected from other people," we told his parents. "His brain is showing a sensory-processing pattern consistent with overload, not absence. What looks like withdrawal may be the nervous system pulling back from more input than it can handle."

That reframe changed the conversation more than anything that had come before it. And it changed what we trained.

Kai had been through ABA, which produced some behavioral compliance but required him to suppress responses that were, from his brain's perspective, necessary regulation. He'd tried occupational therapy and social skills groups. His pediatrician had suggested increasing his stimulant dose. Nobody had looked at what his brain was actually doing. The map turned on a different light entirely.

A note on ABA: behavioral approaches that focus on eliminating autistic behaviors without understanding their regulatory function may increase distress even when outward behavior changes, and undermine the regulation neurofeedback is trying to build. If your child is in an ABA program, the question worth asking is not only "is the behavior changing?" but "is the underlying stress load increasing or decreasing?" A brain map can show arousal and regulatory patterns that may inform that question, but it cannot determine behavioral cause on its own. Clinical observation and the child's own responses remain essential.

11.1 No Single Autism Signature

There is no single "autism pattern" on a QEEG. Two people with autism can have completely different brain maps, different power profiles, different connectivity patterns, different regulatory challenges.

What we see across hundreds of presentations is heterogeneity organized around common themes:

Connectivity abnormalities: the most consistent finding. Some networks show hyper-connectivity (rigidly locked together), others show hypo-connectivity (not coordinating enough). The specific pattern varies enormously between individuals, which is why a one-size-fits-all "autism protocol" makes no sense.

Right temporoparietal junction (rTPJ) activation: we see this frequently. The rTPJ is where social cognition, self-other distinction, and sensory integration converge. In people with autism, this region often shows atypical activation, differently tuned rather than absent. This creates an interesting clinical puzzle: the same rTPJ patterns that show up in autism also show up in highly empathic, highly sensitive presentations. The line between "difficulty reading others" and "overwhelmed by reading others too intensely" is thinner than most people realize. (For a deeper exploration of this overlap, and what it means for adults living with both giftedness and sensory sensitivity, see *Gifted & Tortured*, which examines these patterns across the lifespan.)

Atypical power patterns: elevated theta, altered alpha, unusual gamma activity in various regions. But these vary so widely between individuals with autism that they're useful for individualized treatment planning, not for diagnosis.

Sensory gating differences: many brains with autism show patterns consistent with too much sensory information getting through the filters. This is a measurable cortical pattern, and it's trainable.

11.2 What We Train (And What We Don't)

We don't "treat autism." That framing is wrong on multiple levels: it pathologizes a neurotype, implies a cure, and sets up expectations neurofeedback can't meet.

What we do is train the specific regulatory challenges that cause suffering in many people with autism:

Sensory gating. Reducing cortical overwhelm so noisy environments, bright lights, and social demands are less flooding. This is one of the most reliable training targets. Parents typically notice their child tolerating previously intolerable environments within fifteen to twenty sessions.

Emotional regulation. Meltdowns, shutdowns, and extreme emotional volatility often improve as the brain's regulatory circuits strengthen. Not eliminating emotional intensity, building the capacity to recover faster. It's worth understanding what a meltdown often is: the nervous system's attempt to discharge an overload it cannot process any other way. When the sensory and emotional input exceeds the brain's regulatory capacity, the system breaks down. It's a communication of overwhelm, not defiance. Training that builds regulatory capacity gives the nervous system more room before it hits that breaking point.

Flexibility. Rigidity in transitions, routines, and expectations is partly a connectivity pattern, networks locked too tightly. Connectivity training improves the brain's capacity to shift between states, which produces more tolerance for changes in routine.

Sleep. Severely disrupted in many children and adults with autism. SMR training and arousal regulation protocols improve sleep onset, night wakings, and morning regulation, and when sleep improves, almost everything else follows.

Attention and executive function. When the map shows specific patterns overlapping with ADHD-like underactivation, which it often does, given that ADHD and autism co-occur frequently, standard attention-oriented protocols can help.

The protocol is always individualized to the QEEG. We don't run an "autism protocol." We look at what this brain shows and we train what's trainable.

11.3 What the Research Shows

Autism neurofeedback research is active but early-stage:

- A systematic review (Rezaee et al., 2025) found that 83% of included studies reported positive cognitive effects, attention, memory, executive function, speech, but most studies were small with variable controls.
- Among the better sham-controlled autism NF studies is a 2018 RCT of the Mente Autism device, a clinical/prescription home-use auditory neurofeedback system (distinct from consumer wellness headbands). Of 83 children randomized, only 34 completed the trial, a dropout rate near 60%. Results were mixed: QEEG patterns normalized and some behavioral measures improved versus sham, but other outcomes (social responsiveness, posturography) showed no significant group differences. The study was funded by the device manufacturer's parent company, a conflict of interest worth noting (Carrick et al., 2018).
- Connectivity/coherence training (Coben's work) has shown improvements in social withdrawal and communication versus wait-list controls, but without sham conditions.
- Mu rhythm neurofeedback, which some researchers hypothesize indexes the mirror neuron system (a link that remains contested; see Hobson & Bishop, 2017), has generated promising results in

small studies (Friedrich et al., 2015). It hasn't translated into standard clinical practice; it's a research model, not something you'll find in most clinics.

Evidence level: Level 3-4. Promising and active, with no definitive large-scale RCTs yet. Clinical reports are strongly positive, particularly for regulation and sleep, which matches what we see. The formal evidence is catching up to clinical practice. We hold the observations in this chapter as working hypotheses: the evidence supports informed, individualized use, not certainty.

11.4 What Changes, and What Doesn't

What can improve: Reduced distress and faster emotional recovery, communication access, sleep quality and duration, sensory tolerance, pain tolerance, autonomy in daily routines, energy and stamina, and chosen participation in activities that matter to the person. These are the most consistent gains we see.

What doesn't change: Your child's fundamental neurotype. Autism isn't a disease to cure; it's a way of being in the world. What causes suffering is the regulatory challenges that accompany the neurotype. The goal is more capacity, more range, better sleep, more flexibility, so they can be more fully themselves. Deep social communication differences show more variable improvement. Sensory preferences and processing style stay stable; what shifts is how overwhelmed your child gets.

The honest expectation: Modest to moderate improvements in regulation, attention, and behavior for many children, within a broader support plan. Not everyone responds, and the children who do respond still need their other supports. Neurofeedback builds a regulatory foundation; it doesn't replace the therapies that build on it.

11.5 Practical Considerations

Session modifications for autism:

- Sensory sensitivity to the cap and gel can be a real barrier. Some children need gradual desensitization over several visits before full sessions are possible. Flexible setups with fewer electrodes may be necessary initially.
- Sessions are typically shorter (fifteen to twenty minutes) with highly engaging, individualized feedback.
- Children who can't sit still or can't tolerate the setup may benefit from ILF or other approaches that require less electrode coverage.

Timeline: In our clinical experience, twenty-five to forty sessions is a common range, with some complex presentations needing more. These numbers come from practice, not from published dose-response data for autism-specific neurofeedback. Progress is often behavioral before verbal; parents and teachers notice changes before the child reports them.

What to watch for: If irritability or meltdowns *increase* during training, the protocol needs adjustment. Because many children with autism have difficulty reporting internal states, clinicians need to rely on parent observation and behavioral data more heavily than with neurotypical clients. For children who are nonspeaking or minimally speaking, verbal self-report is not available, and structured behavioral observation becomes the primary safety tool. Track concrete markers between sessions: changes in sleep, appetite, meltdown frequency and intensity, self-injurious behavior, stimming patterns, toileting, and engagement with preferred activities. A note on stimming specifically: stimming that signals activation or stress is not the same thing as stimming that is enjoyable, and some enjoyable stimming is also a tic. It is the stress-driven kind, and tics, that often ease during or shortly after a protocol. Enjoyable stimming is not a treatment target and its absence is not a goal. A simple log (date, session number, brief notes on each marker) gives the clinician data to adjust protocols, and gives you as a parent a clear record when something feels off.

11.6 For Adults with Autism Reading This Chapter

Most neurofeedback-and-autism literature is written about children and addressed to parents. If you're an adult with autism reading this, a few direct points.

The regulatory challenges described in this chapter, sensory overwhelm, emotional flooding, sleep disruption, difficulty with transitions, don't stop at age eighteen. Neither does the potential for training-based improvement. Adult brains with autism are differently plastic. Many of the most striking cases we see are adults with autism in their thirties and forties who arrive having spent decades developing elaborate compensatory strategies around regulatory challenges nobody had named. When the map shows them what their nervous system has been doing, the reframe is often more significant than the training itself.

What changes as an adult: you have full agency over your own training. You don't need a parent to advocate for sensory-friendly session modifications. You can describe your own internal state more precisely than a child can, which makes the feedback loop between session experience and protocol adjustment faster and more accurate. You are often better at identifying the specific situations that trigger overwhelm, which helps narrow the training targets.

What to look for in a provider as an adult with autism: someone who has worked with adults with autism, not just children; someone who understands that autism is a neurotype with specific regulatory patterns that respond to training; and someone who modifies session setup for sensory sensitivities without requiring you to justify the need. If a provider is dismissive of your self-knowledge, find a different provider.

The autism community has legitimate critiques of some neurofeedback practice, particularly protocols aimed at "normalizing" behaviors that are adaptive rather than dysfunctional. Those critiques are right. The goal of neurofeedback for adults with autism is not to make you less autistic. It is to build the regulatory capacity that gives you more range, more flexibility, more energy reserves, and a better sleep foundation, so you can be more fully yourself.

11.7 When NF Isn't the First Lever

Before neurofeedback for your child with autism, check:

- **Sleep.** Is sleep adequately assessed? Sleep disruption can worsen attention and regulation whether or not those difficulties are also related to autism.
- **Sensory environment.** Are there environmental changes (school, home, routines) that could reduce overwhelm without brain training?
- **Core therapies.** Are speech, OT, and educational supports in place? NF is an adjunct, it builds the regulatory foundation that makes other therapies more effective, but it doesn't replace them.
- **Medical factors.** GI issues, pain, medication side effects, all common in autism, all capable of driving dysregulation that looks like a "brain problem" but has a medical cause.

11.8 The Overclaiming Problem

A direct word to parents: **be cautious of any provider who tells you neurofeedback will "recover" or "cure" your child's autism.** This claim has no evidence behind it. It exploits parental desperation. And it misunderstands what neurofeedback actually does.

The goal is to give their nervous system more range, better sleep, calmer processing, more flexibility, so they can be more comfortable in the world as they are. That's a meaningful, achievable, and honest goal.

Decision Point: If your child has autism and you're considering neurofeedback: find a provider experienced with autism specifically (not just ADHD). Ask what pediatric normative databases they use, how many children with autism they've worked with, and what they consider realistic outcomes. A QEEG can show you what's trainable, and that information is valuable regardless of what you decide to do with it.

Your Move:

1. **List the three biggest problems:** Before you talk to a neurofeedback provider, write down the three behaviors or situations causing the most suffering for your child right now. Sensory overwhelm in specific environments? Meltdown frequency? Sleep onset? Bring that list and ask the provider: "Which of these does the QEEG address directly, and which does it address indirectly through broader regulation?" The specificity of the answer tells you whether this provider knows what they're doing.

2. **Act:** If your child has had evaluations from multiple providers, collect them in one place. OT reports, psychological evaluations, school assessments. A good neurofeedback clinician will want to see the whole picture, not just the brain map.

3. **Start a conversation:** Ask your child's team (OT, therapist, pediatrician): "Would adding brain-level regulation training help the other work we're doing?" Frame NF as a foundation for their existing interventions, not a replacement.

This chapter is educational only and does not constitute medical advice. Discuss any decision to begin, modify, or stop neurofeedback or any other treatment with a licensed clinician.

Ch 12: The Addicted Brain: Neurofeedback, Addiction, and Alpha-Theta Training

12.1 Meet Rachel

Rachel is a forty-eight-year-old social worker who's been sober for three years. She did the work, residential treatment, AA, ongoing therapy, naltrexone for the first year. She's functional. She's also miserable. The anxiety that drove her drinking is still there. The trauma underneath the anxiety is still there. She describes it as "white-knuckling sobriety", she's sober, and still searching for peace.

Her brain map showed the pattern we see in many post-addiction clients: residual high-beta hyperarousal (the anxiety engine that drove the drinking), suppressed alpha (no ability to rest or feel calm naturally), and disrupted connectivity patterns consistent with both the trauma history and years of alcohol's impact on brain function.

"I stopped the substance," she said. "But I didn't fix the reason I needed it."

That's the gap alpha-theta neurofeedback was designed to fill.

12.2 The Peniston Protocol: Where This Started

In the late 1980s, Eugene Peniston at a VA hospital developed a protocol for Vietnam veterans with chronic alcoholism that was unlike anything else in neurofeedback.

The Peniston protocol has three components:

Temperature biofeedback: training to warm the hands, a direct measure of parasympathetic activation. This comes first, establishing the body's capacity for deep relaxation before the brain work begins.

Alpha-theta crossover training: eyes closed, electrodes at O1 (a site over the left occipital cortex). The brain is rewarded for producing theta that exceeds alpha, the "crossover" point where the brain shifts from relaxed wakefulness into the hypnagogic "twilight" between waking and sleep. Sessions last thirty to forty minutes in this deep state.

Guided imagery: during the theta-dominant state, structured scripts address trauma, addiction patterns, and recovery identity. The imagery isn't passive, it's therapeutic work conducted while the brain is in a state of heightened plasticity and emotional accessibility.

Peniston's early VA trials reported high sustained abstinence rates. In the original 1989 alcohol study, about 80 percent (8 of 10) of the experimental group sustained abstinence at thirteen-month follow-up, far exceeding standard addiction treatment. Depression scores dropped. Personality measures shifted. Beta-endorphin levels (a stress marker) normalized in the alpha-theta group but not in controls.

These results were dramatic. They were also methodologically fragile, small samples, no sham control, no blinding, and heavy co-treatment in the VA residential setting. The field has debated them ever since. Replications (Saxby & Peniston 1995, Callaway & Bodenhamer-Davis 2008) showed consistent patterns, depression reduction, personality change, high abstinence, but shared the same methodological limitations.

The clinical signal is strong and consistent, but the research rigor hasn't matched it. Alpha-theta for addiction is "probably efficacious" by AAPB/ISNR criteria, not "definitely efficacious" by modern RCT standards.

12.3 How Alpha-Theta Works (Best Current Understanding)

Alpha-theta doesn't work like standard neurofeedback. It's not training a specific frequency up or down to normalize a Z-score. It's accessing a specific brain state, the hypnagogic twilight, and using that state as a platform for deep processing.

The twilight state is the transition zone between waking and sleep. Theta dominates. Imagery is vivid and spontaneous. Emotional material surfaces without the usual defenses. It's the state you're in during that moment before sleep when your mind wanders freely, except in alpha-theta training, you stay there for thirty to forty minutes while a feedback system keeps you from falling fully asleep.

What the crossover actually feels like. Clients describe the alpha-theta crossover in consistent terms. There's a moment when alpha, the relaxed waking rhythm, gives way to theta, the deeper twilight state. Some say it feels like "sinking" or "dropping through." Others describe it as the boundary between watching your thoughts and being inside them. Imagery becomes vivid and often unexpected. Old memories surface. Emotions that have been walled off appear without the usual cognitive filters. One client said, "It was like my brain finally had permission to show me things I'd been too busy to look at." Another described the crossover as "the moment the noise stopped and something else could come through." The experience can be profound, even spiritual for some. It can also be unsettling. This is why alpha-theta requires therapeutic support. The clinician isn't just running equipment. They're holding space for whatever emerges. The feedback tone, which shifts as alpha and theta cross, becomes an anchor. You're not lost in the state. You're in it, with a tether.

Why this state matters: Multiple mechanisms likely converge:

- **Memory reconsolidation (working hypothesis):** traumatic and addiction-linked memories activated in a relaxed, safe context may be re-stored with reduced emotional charge. This hypothesis draws on the same reconsolidation framework invoked in EMDR and psychedelic-assisted therapy research; direct evidence that alpha-theta training triggers reconsolidation specifically has not been established.
- **Parasympathetic conditioning:** the combination of hand-warming and deep alpha-theta states conditions the nervous system toward parasympathetic dominance. The body learns that deep relaxation is safe.

- **State-dependent learning:** new associations formed in the theta state (sobriety imagery, self-efficacy, trauma resolution) may be more accessible later when similar states are entered naturally.

Alpha-theta functions, in our clinical analogy, as **instrumented hypnosis with EEG verification:** the feedback confirms and maintains the brain state while the therapeutic imagery does the processing work. The analogy is clinically useful, though alpha-theta and formal hypnosis have not been directly compared in controlled trials.

12.4 What a Real Alpha-Theta Crossover Looks Like

The state that makes alpha-theta work is not the same as "so relaxed you might fall asleep," even though the two can feel similar from the inside. Within-session theta/alpha ratios reliably increase during alpha-theta training, and these changes do not represent falling asleep (Raymond et al., 2005). In clinical practice, the therapeutic crossover is described as a specific state: theta rising into the foreground while alpha stays in play and the cortex keeps quietly processing, rather than simply powering down toward sleep. At true sleep onset the waking rhythms just fade out. In a useful crossover they stay in a particular interplay, and the EEG is clear enough about the difference that trained eyes can distinguish a productive session from a pleasant nap.

That distinction should change how you shop for alpha-theta. Good practice doesn't start with alpha-theta. It builds a regulatory foundation first, stabilization protocols that give the nervous system resilience before you open anything up. When the clinician determines you're ready, the protocol is introduced carefully, with post-session check-ins that track how you respond. A session that drifts into sleep without the crossover may feel deep, but you may not be in the window the work depends on. The safeguard isn't necessarily a clinician watching the trace in real time; it's a structured approach: readiness criteria, careful dosing, and close follow-up that catches problems early and adjusts before the next session.

For the wider meditation and attention science that sits behind these rhythms, including how alpha, theta, and executive control trade off in practice, see Chapter 14 of *Half a Second More.*

12.5 How the Protocol Evolved

Peniston bundled three things: temperature biofeedback, alpha-theta EEG training, and guided imagery scripts delivered during the theta state. For years the field treated the bundle as indivisible. Two questions eventually surfaced: does the imagery actually matter, and what happens after you open someone up?

The imagery question. Scott, Kaiser, Othmer and Sideroff (2005) ran the largest alpha-theta addiction study to date: 121 participants randomized in an inpatient substance abuse program. Their protocol used beta / SMR training followed by alpha-theta, with no guided imagery scripts and no temperature biofeedback. Pure EEG training. At twelve-month follow-up, 77 percent of the treatment group maintained abstinence versus 44 percent of controls. This was a larger sample than any Peniston-protocol study, and it achieved comparable outcomes without the autosuggestion component.

Supporting evidence points the same way. Egner, Strawson and Gruzelier (2002) showed in a sham-controlled study that real alpha-theta feedback produces genuine theta / alpha ratio changes that mock feedback does not, even without imagery scripts. Moore et al. (2000) found that visualization during neurofeedback occurs across all feedback types, not just alpha-theta, and is actually inversely related to theta dominance: you get less spontaneous imagery, not more, in deep theta.

The most defensible reading: the EEG state change is the active ingredient. The guided imagery may enhance the clinical experience, particularly in trauma and addiction work where the scripted content carries therapeutic weight, but it is not what drives the neurophysiological shift. No head-to-head comparison of scripts versus no scripts in the same population has been published, so the question is not fully closed. But the weight of evidence points to the training, not the scripting.

The stabilization step. The second evolution addressed what happens after the deep work. Many clinicians now follow alpha-theta sessions with **SMR training** (see Chapter 3) to stabilize the nervous system. The clinical rationale uses a metaphor: alpha-theta "opens" the nervous system to deep processing, and SMR "closes" it back to stable waking regulation. The metaphor tracks clinical observation well, though the neurophysiological mechanism behind the sequencing has not been isolated in a controlled comparison. Without the stabilization step, some clients leave sessions destabilized, emotionally raw, dissociated, or dysregulated.

This SMR-follow approach (associated with Jay Gunkelman and David Kaiser, among others) is widely used in addiction and trauma clinics. There is no RCT comparing SMR + alpha-theta versus alpha-theta alone, but the clinical logic is sound: you do not leave someone in a deep state without helping their nervous system return to baseline.

12.6 Why People Use Substances (The Regulatory Driver Model)

Neurofeedback addresses addiction by targeting the regulatory drivers underneath the substance use, but you can't understand those drivers without first asking why people use substances in the first place, not through a moral or disease model, but through a regulatory one.

An important frame before we continue. The regulatory driver model is one clinical lens for understanding substance use, and it is the lens most relevant to neurofeedback. It is not the whole story. Substance use disorders involve neurobiological changes (tolerance, sensitization, withdrawal physiology), genetic vulnerability, social and environmental factors, and often co-occurring psychiatric conditions that require their own treatment. A brain map does not replace a substance-use-disorder assessment by a qualified addiction specialist. If you or someone you care about is actively struggling with substance use, the first step is a clinical evaluation by a provider trained in addiction medicine or addiction psychiatry, not a QEEG. Medication-assisted treatment (MAT), including medications like naltrexone, buprenorphine, and acamprosate, has strong evidence for specific substance use disorders and should be discussed with a prescriber as part of any comprehensive plan. Neurofeedback may complement these approaches; it does not substitute for them.

> **Cross-reference:** The withdrawal warning later in this chapter (see Safety section) applies here too: never abruptly reduce or stop any substance, prescribed or otherwise, without medical supervision.

People use substances to regulate states their nervous system can't manage on its own:

- **Anxiety** → alcohol, cannabis, benzodiazepines for calming
- **Pain** → opiates, cannabis for pain relief
- **Sleep** → alcohol, cannabis, sedatives for sleep onset
- **Emotional overwhelm** → alcohol, cannabis for emotional blunting
- **Understimulation** → stimulants, nicotine, caffeine for activation
- **Social discomfort** → alcohol for disinhibition

The substance works, temporarily. It addresses the regulatory gap. But it creates its own problems: tolerance, dependence, withdrawal, and the progressive erosion of the brain's own regulatory capacity.

When the anxiety calms through training, the need for the anxiolytic substance decreases. When sleep improves, the need for the sedative substance decreases. When emotional regulation strengthens, the need for the numbing substance decreases.

This is a consistent clinical observation across neurofeedback practices, not a finding from controlled trials: as training progresses and the brain's regulatory capacity improves, substances start hitting differently. Stimulant medications work more strongly (often requiring dose reduction). Cannabis effects intensify. And many regular cannabis users who complete neurofeedback moderate or stop their use, not because anyone told them to, but because they prefer how they feel with a regulated brain.

> **If you use cannabis medically** (for chronic pain, nausea, seizure management, spasticity, or any prescribed or recommended indication): do not modify or discontinue your use based on anything in this chapter. Consult your prescribing or recommending physician before making any changes to your medical cannabis regimen.

The substance use doesn't stop because of willpower. It stops because the need changes.

12.7 Beyond Addiction: Alpha-Theta for Trauma and Creativity

The Peniston protocol started with addiction, but the alpha-theta approach has expanded:

Trauma processing. Many trauma clinicians use alpha-theta as the deep-processing phase of a longer treatment arc, after initial stabilization with SMR or other protocols (see Chapter 10). The twilight state accesses emotional material that standard training doesn't reach, making it a powerful tool for clients whose trauma has been intellectually processed but not neurologically resolved.

Creativity and flow. The theta-dominant state is associated with loose, associative thinking, the kind that produces creative insight, novel connections, and "aha" moments. Some practitioners use alpha-theta with artists, musicians, and writers seeking creative access. The evidence is thin (small pilot studies, clinical reports), but the experiential reports are consistent: alpha-theta opens something that focused, beta-dominant work can't reach.

The immune connection. Alpha training may engage the vagal-cholinergic anti-inflammatory pathway, a well-established neuroimmunological circuit in which vagal efferent activity reduces inflammatory cytokines. Preliminary evidence suggests alpha neurofeedback can improve heart rate variability (a proxy for vagal tone), but the direct link from cortical alpha uptraining through vagal efferents to cytokine reduction has not been experimentally confirmed. Alpha-theta could activate the same pathway through extended periods of high alpha and theta with deep parasympathetic activation. The mechanistic logic is sound, but the full chain from cortical alpha training to immune function remains a plausible hypothesis rather than a demonstrated effect.

12.8 Safety: When Alpha-Theta Is Not Appropriate

Alpha-theta is not a beginner protocol. It intentionally induces altered states with heightened emotional accessibility. This means:

- **Not for active psychosis or severe dissociative disorders:** the deep state can trigger destabilizing experiences in fragile clients
- **Not without therapeutic support:** emotional material surfaces during sessions and needs professional containment
- **Not before stabilization:** clients should have solid regulatory capacity (often built through SMR or standard training) before alpha-theta work begins
- **Not during active substance withdrawal:** the brain needs to be stable enough to learn from the feedback
- **Not for early stimulant recovery without specialized assessment.** The alpha-theta tradition grew out of work with alcohol and opioid populations, and those protocols assumed that neurochemical landscape. Stimulant-class substances (cocaine, methamphetamine, prescription amphetamines) produce a distinct recovery profile: lowered seizure thresholds, elevated psychosis risk, and prolonged mood instability that can persist months into abstinence. The deep altered states of alpha-theta can destabilize a nervous system still recalibrating from chronic stimulant use. If you are in recovery from stimulant use, work with a clinician experienced in both neurofeedback and stimulant recovery to determine when, and whether, alpha-theta is appropriate

WARNING: Never abruptly reduce or stop benzodiazepines, opioids, alcohol, or any prescribed medication without direct supervision from your prescriber or an addiction-medicine specialist.

Abrupt benzodiazepine discontinuation can cause seizures and other serious withdrawal reactions (FDA boxed-warning update, Sept. 23, 2020). Abrupt opioid discontinuation can cause serious withdrawal symptoms and psychological distress (FDA Drug Safety Communication, Apr. 9, 2019). Alcohol withdrawal is potentially life-threatening and can include delirium tremens and seizures (MedlinePlus / NIH-NLM). Neurofeedback is not a substitute for medically supervised withdrawal, detoxification, or medication-assisted treatment. If your substance use changes during training, both your prescriber and your neurofeedback clinician need to know.

In the right hands, with the right preparation, alpha-theta is one of the most powerful tools in neurofeedback. In the wrong hands or at the wrong time, it can be destabilizing. This is why clinician skill and sequencing matter more for alpha-theta than for any other protocol.

Decision Point: If substance use is part of your picture, whether it's the primary concern or a coping strategy alongside anxiety, trauma, or sleep problems, the regulatory driver framework in this chapter can help you understand what you're actually trying to fix. A brain map can show whether the underlying regulatory patterns are trainable, and alpha-theta with proper clinical support may address what standard approaches haven't reached. The evidence base for this work is promising but not definitive; Chapter 5's framework for evaluating any neurofeedback claim applies here too, and we hold our clinical observations provisionally.

If the regulatory driver model introduced here resonates and you want to go deeper into the psychology of the patterns underneath substance use, *Borrowed Peace* (Andrew Hill, Peak Brain Press) addresses regulatory dysregulation, self-medication, and the path toward stable self-regulation from a consumer-clinical perspective. The books are complementary: this chapter provides the brain-map view; *Borrowed Peace* develops the human story behind what those maps mean.

12.8.1 Going Deeper

- For the meditation-neuroscience context in which alpha-theta sits, see *Half a Second More* Chapter 14.
- For alpha-theta clinical protocols and Peniston methodology, see *QEEG Field Guide* Chapter 7.

Your Move:

1. **Name the driver:** Before your first session with a neurofeedback provider, write down one sentence: "I use [substance] primarily because it helps me with [calming / sleep / pain / emotional management / social situations / focus]." That named regulatory need is the target. A good neurofeedback clinician will look for that exact pattern on your brain map. If they don't ask about it, ask them.

2. **Act:** If you're in recovery and still struggling with the underlying anxiety, sleep disruption, or emotional dysregulation that drove your use, consider a brain map. The patterns that drove the substance use are often still visible, and trainable.

3. **Start a conversation:** If you're working with an addiction counselor or therapist, ask: "Could we look at the brain patterns underneath my substance use? There might be regulatory targets that training could address." Not every provider will know about this approach, but the question opens a door.

This chapter is educational only and does not constitute medical advice. Discuss any decision to begin, modify, or stop neurofeedback or any other treatment with a licensed clinician.

Ch 13: The Brain Asleep: Sleep, Waking Signatures, and Why It All Starts Here

Before we started neurofeedback, we stopped and did something different.

Priya had come to us for ADHD. Thirty-one years old, struggling to focus at work, losing track of conversations, missing deadlines. Her primary care doctor had started her on a low-dose stimulant. It helped for a few hours each morning, then she crashed.

Her brain map showed excess frontal theta, the pattern that looks like ADHD. But it also showed diffuse slowing and alpha suppression that didn't fit a straightforward attentional picture. It looked like a brain running on empty.

We asked about her sleep. She said it was fine. We pushed. How long to fall asleep? About forty-five minutes. Wake during the night? Usually once or twice. Feel rested in the morning? She paused. "I can't remember the last time I felt rested."

So we did not start neurofeedback. We started with sleep hygiene: consistent bedtime, no screens after 9pm, blackout curtains, magnesium. Six weeks later, without a single training session, half her "ADHD symptoms" were gone. Her frontal theta had dropped on re-assessment. Her focus had improved. Her stimulant was finally working because her brain had the resources to respond to it.

Then we trained what remained: the patterns that weren't sleep-driven. Those responded quickly. The foundation was solid.

That story is why this chapter comes before the chapter on when things don't work. If there is one variable that silently undermines every other intervention, it is sleep. This chapter is about what your waking brain tells us about your sleeping brain, and why it all starts here.

13.1 The Most Common Finding

Across thousands of brain maps, the single most common finding is this: **sleep is dysregulated in the majority of presentations.**

This reaches beyond insomnia clients, beyond people who mention sleep at intake. The majority of people who walk through the door for anxiety, ADHD, depression, trauma, cognitive decline, or performance optimization show evidence of disrupted sleep in their waking EEG: elevated theta from sleep debt, high beta from hyperarousal that prevents downshifting, suppressed alpha from a brain that can't idle.

Sleep debt doesn't just make you tired. It distorts your brain map. It mimics ADHD. It amplifies anxiety. It deepens depression. It impairs every regulatory function your brain performs. And it's the single most addressable factor in most people's brain health.

Sleep is foundational, and neurofeedback directly improves it. This isn't a "fix sleep before you start training" situation. Priya's story showed how disruptive sleep dysregulation can be, so much so that it makes a non-ADHD brain look and feel like one. We highlighted her hygiene changes to show how powerful that foundation is. But SMR training, which is part of most neurofeedback protocols, strengthens the same thalamocortical circuits that produce sleep spindles. Many clients see sleep improvement as one of the first changes, sometimes within the first five to ten sessions. The worse the sleep disruption, the more room there is to improve, and often the faster the change.

What we do recommend: if basic sleep hygiene is a disaster (screens until midnight, no consistent bedtime, six cups of coffee), fix the obvious stuff first. But you don't need perfect sleep to start neurofeedback. In fact, neurofeedback is one of the best tools for getting there.

13.2 What a Waking QEEG May Show About Sleep

Your waking brain map carries signatures of your sleep quality:

Elevated theta during waking: excess slow activity when you're supposed to be alert. This is the hallmark of sleep debt. It looks like

ADHD on a brain map, and in many cases, it IS the functional equivalent of ADHD. The brain simply doesn't have the energy to sustain focused engagement. The theta-beta ratio controversy we covered in Chapter 9 is partly a sleep story: as population sleep worsened, "ADHD-like" theta increased in everyone.

High beta at rest: a brain that can't downshift. This person may fall asleep eventually, but only after hours of lying in bed with a racing mind. Their waking brain map shows the same pattern, fast activity that won't quiet. This is cortical hyperarousal, and it's one of the most reliable QEEG signatures of insomnia.

Suppressed alpha: the brain's idle rhythm is offline. Without alpha, there's no transition between waking engagement and sleep onset. The brain goes from "on" to "on" to "on" until it crashes rather than gently downshifting through the alpha → theta → delta transition that healthy sleep requires.

Alpha intrusions (a sleep-study finding, not a waking-map finding): alpha activity appearing during sleep stages where it shouldn't be (particularly in N2 and N3). This is associated with non-restorative sleep and conditions like fibromyalgia. The person sleeps but doesn't recover. Alpha intrusions are identified through polysomnography (overnight sleep recording), not through a waking QEEG. On a waking map, the clue is often suppressed alpha power; but confirming alpha intrusions during sleep requires a sleep study. (To see what these sleep-related patterns look like on an actual brain map, visit neurofeedbackexplained.com/plates.)

13.3 How Neurofeedback Actually Helps Sleep

Sleep improvement is one of the most consistent and earliest changes we see across all neurofeedback protocols, and understanding *how* it happens clarifies what to expect.

The indirect path (and why it's powerful). When we train someone for anxiety and their frontal high-beta calms down, their sleep improves, not because we targeted sleep, but because the brain's arousal regulation improved and the system can finally downshift at night. When we train for ADHD and SMR strengthens, sleep consolidation improves, because SMR is the waking echo of the sleep spindle rhythm, and stronger thalamocortical circuits mean better sleep architecture. When we train for trauma and alpha comes back online, the brain regains its ability to idle, and idling is the gateway to sleep.

This is the most common clinical pathway: neurofeedback improves sleep *as a consequence of improving the regulatory systems that sleep depends on.* The anxiety client whose high-beta drops sleeps better. The ADHD client whose SMR strengthens sleeps deeper. The trauma client whose alpha recovers can actually rest.

The complementary path. When good sleep hygiene is in place (consistent timing, managed light, no caffeine after noon) the brain training can focus on the true bottlenecks that remain. Sleep hygiene handles the environmental factors. Neurofeedback handles the neurological ones. Together, they're more effective than either alone.

The caveat: direct insomnia treatment. When researchers specifically test neurofeedback as a primary insomnia treatment, targeting sleep directly rather than addressing it as part of broader regulation, the results are sobering. The most rigorous double-blind trial (Schabus et al., 2017) showed both real and sham SMR neurofeedback produced similar subjective improvements, with no differential benefit on polysomnography. Meta-analytic data suggest that when neurofeedback is compared to strong control conditions for insomnia specifically, the effect sizes are modest at best.

This is Level 1 evidence that neurofeedback, on its own, is not a proven insomnia-specific treatment. For primary insomnia (when sleep is the only problem, with no underlying anxiety or arousal dysregulation) CBT-I (cognitive behavioral therapy for insomnia) remains the gold-standard treatment. We take this finding seriously: we hold our observations about sleep improvement during broader training as clinically consistent but not established as specific effects, and Chapter 5's standards for evaluating neurofeedback claims apply here.

A fair question: If the specific mechanism doesn't beat sham for insomnia when tested directly, why should we trust that sleep improvements during other training are genuinely caused by the neurofeedback rather than by the non-specific elements of treatment? We can't be certain in every case. Some of the sleep improvement may reflect the general benefits of regular clinical attention and structured self-monitoring. But the SMR-spindle mechanism provides a plausible, testable pathway that goes beyond non-specific effects, and the Hoedlmoser polysomnography data (increased spindle number and reduced sleep onset latency versus an active control trained on randomized frequencies) demonstrate that this pathway is real. The most defensible position: neurofeedback reliably improves sleep through a combination of specific thalamocortical training and the broader regulatory benefits of the clinical context. Disentangling how much of each is contributing, for each person, remains an open question.

The practical takeaway: If your sleep is bad *and* you have anxiety, ADHD, trauma, or other regulatory challenges, neurofeedback targeting the broader pattern will very likely improve your sleep along the way. If sleep is truly your only problem with no other regulatory issues, CBT-I first. Most people who walk through our doors have both: disrupted sleep and something driving the disruption, and the training addresses the full picture.

There are hints of it in the trial literature. In an open-label PTSD study of amygdala-targeted neurofeedback, a different modality from the SMR training this section is about, roughly 64% of the fifty-eight completers showed clinically meaningful reductions in sleep disturbance by three-month follow-up, and sleep improvement tracked overall symptom reduction (Tendler et al., 2025). With no control arm, that number cannot separate the training from time, attention, or regression to the mean. Across our own clinical datasets, sleep improvement is among the first changes during SMR-based protocols, often within the first ten to twenty sessions, before primary symptom targets have fully shifted. That is an observation from a clinic, not a controlled finding. Neurofeedback reliably improves sleep when it's

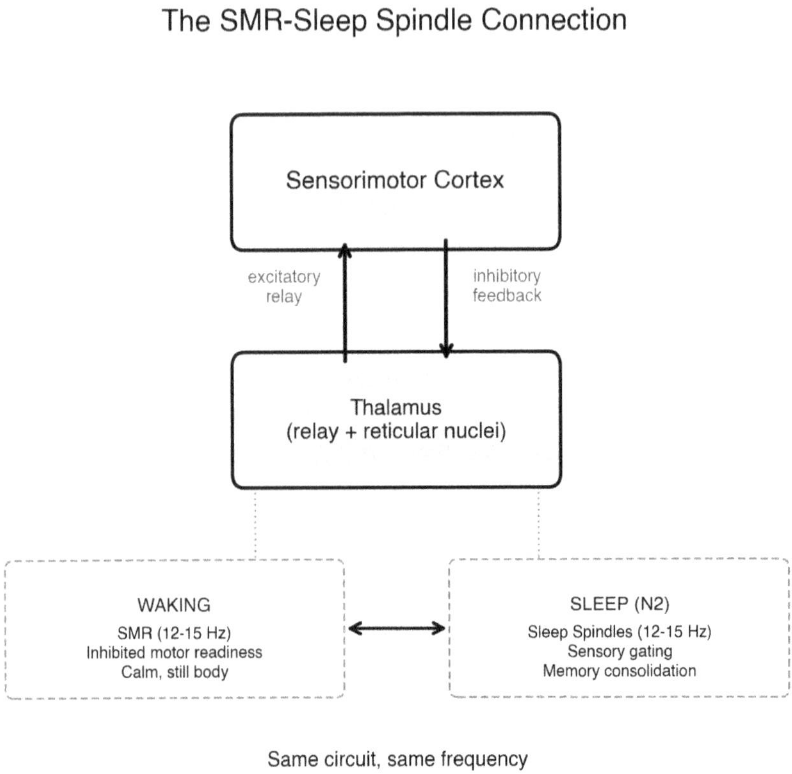

Figure 13.1: The SMR-Sleep Spindle Connection

working. The question, which the next section takes up, is whether it's doing so through the front door or the back.

13.4 The SMR-Sleep Spindle Connection: Why Brain Training Improves Sleep

The mechanistic connection between SMR training and sleep is unusually direct.

The sensorimotor rhythm (SMR, 12-15 Hz) is generated by thalamocortical circuits: thalamic relay and reticular neurons projecting to the sensorimotor cortex. During waking, SMR reflects a state of **inhibited**

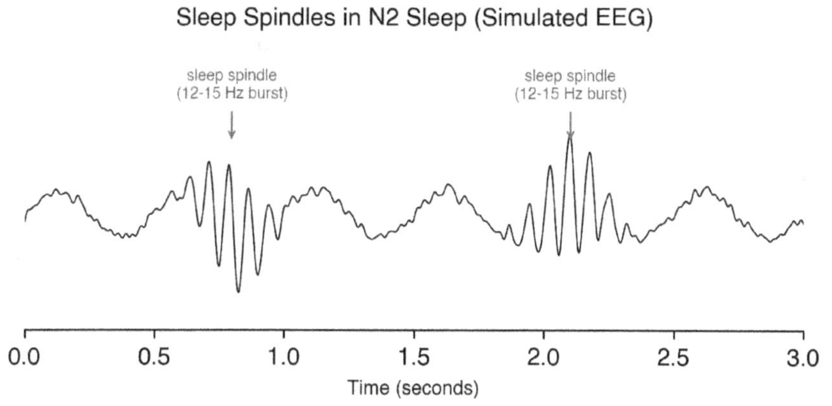

Figure 13.2: Sleep Spindles in N2 Sleep

movement with preserved readiness: the motor system is quiet but available. It's your brain's "idle but ready" mode.

Sleep spindles, the brief bursts of 12-15 Hz activity that occur during N2 sleep, are generated by the **same thalamocortical circuits**. They're the nighttime version of the same rhythm. Spindles serve critical functions: they protect sleep continuity by suppressing arousals, gate sensory input so sounds don't wake you, and support memory consolidation by replaying recently learned information.

Training SMR during waking hours strengthens the thalamocortical machinery that produces spindles at night, and the mechanism is unusually direct. This isn't theoretical. A small randomized study in healthy adults trained one group on SMR and the other on randomized frequencies, then measured what happened that night with polysomnography rather than a questionnaire (Hoedlmoser et al., 2008). The SMR group's sleep spindles went up, from 444 to 651 per night. They fell asleep faster, dropping from about fifteen minutes to eight. And they remembered more of what they had learned before bed. Note what the control group did: real feedback on a real signal, just the wrong frequency. That is the comparison that matters, because it isolates the frequency rather than the ritual.

Be precise about the limits. Slow-wave sleep did not reliably increase, and neither did the number of awakenings; both moved in the right direction and neither reached significance in twenty-seven people. The spindles moved. That is the claim the study supports.

The same mechanism explains why SMR training raises seizure thresholds, making the brain more seizure-resistant (Sterman's original finding), calms motor restlessness in ADHD, and improves sleep in anxiety clients. The common thread is **inhibitory tone**: the brain's ability to suppress unwanted activity. Stronger thalamocortical inhibition means fewer seizures, less motor noise, fewer nocturnal awakenings, and more stable sleep architecture. One mechanism, broad impact.

In ADHD specifically, an open-label pilot in adults (Arns et al., 2014) found sleep onset latency falling from roughly forty minutes to nineteen after SMR training, but not after theta-beta training, with the sleep improvement tracking the attention gains. Thirty-seven people, no control group, no randomization: this is a before-and-after in a clinic, not a trial, and the honest weight it carries is that it points somewhere worth testing properly.

This is why sleep improvement is often the first change clients notice during neurofeedback, even when sleep wasn't the training target. When you train SMR for any reason, ADHD, anxiety, performance, general regulation, you're strengthening the same circuits that produce sleep spindles. Better spindles, better sleep. Better sleep, better everything.

13.5 When the Braking System Fails: What Weak Thalamocortical Inhibition Actually Looks Like

Understanding the SMR-spindle connection changes how you read a long list of sleep complaints that most people treat as separate problems. They're not separate. They're the same braking system failing at different points in the sleep cycle.

Restless legs and periodic limb movements. Restless legs has a medical workup that comes first. Iron deficiency is one of the most common and treatable causes, and the treatment threshold is higher than for ordinary anemia: a ferritin level that looks normal on a standard lab report may still be low enough to drive restless legs. Serum ferritin and iron studies are the starting point. Several common medications can also worsen it, including certain antidepressants, antihistamines, and antinausea drugs, and both pregnancy and kidney disease are relevant. See your physician for this evaluation before assuming the problem is purely neurological.

The thalamocortical mechanism is also real. This is inhibitory failure in its most literal form, the motor system not quieting down when it's supposed to. The circuits that SMR training strengthens are specifically tasked with suppressing unwanted movement during rest. When they're weak, the legs need to move, the arms twitch, the body can't settle. Restless leg syndrome and periodic limb movement disorder involve, at their neurological core, a failure of the same inhibitory machinery that SMR addresses. This is one of the most direct clinical illustrations of why SMR training helps sleep: you're rebuilding the circuitry that produces stillness.

Sleep onset as a body problem, not just a mind problem. The cultural narrative around sleep onset difficulty is almost entirely cognitive, racing thoughts, worrying, can't turn off the mental chatter. But for many people the problem is more physical than that: muscle tension that won't release, a jaw that won't unclench, a heart rate that stays elevated despite nothing happening, legs that feel restless before they get all the way to RLS territory. The motor cortex isn't inhibiting. The body is still in "available" mode. SMR training teaches the motor cortex to produce the inhibitory signal that settles the body, and the body settling is often what finally allows the mind to follow.

Sleep maintenance and the spindle protection mechanism. Sleep spindles don't just mark light sleep, they actively protect sleep continuity. Their primary function is to gate incoming sensory signals during N2 sleep: sounds, temperature shifts, light changes, the movement of a partner in the bed. A spindle fires, the thalamus blocks the signal from reaching the cortex, and you stay asleep. When spindle density is low, when the thalamocortical circuits are undertrained, sensory signals get through. Every noise is a potential awakening. Every temperature shift registers. Sleep becomes light and fragmented not because anything is wrong with the stimuli, but because the brain's noise gates aren't working. This is why clients who "sleep through the night" but still feel exhausted often show poor spindle density on polysomnography. They're technically sleeping but not protected.

What SMR training feels like in the body. Something clients almost universally report once their SMR starts to strengthen is worth naming because it is the clearest evidence that the training is working, and because it connects directly to what happens at bedtime. During sessions where SMR is building, the body gets heavy. The jaw unclenches. Limbs settle with a kind of involuntary weight. Breathing deepens and slows without any intention to breathe differently. This isn't the relaxation response from meditation, it's not something you're directing. It's the motor cortex learning to produce the inhibitory signal it's supposed to produce. The brain is generating real thalamocortical inhibition during the session, and the body is responding accordingly.

That settling, which clients often describe as "I've never felt my body do that before", is the same state the brain is supposed to produce every night at bedtime. The motor cortex quiets, the thalamus shifts into inhibitory mode, the body stops being "available" for movement, and sleep onset becomes possible. SMR training is, in a meaningful sense, practicing the neurological transition into sleep while you're awake, and as those circuits strengthen, they produce that transition more reliably at night, in your bed, when you actually need it. (Controlled studies targeting RLS or PLMD with SMR neurofeedback specifically have not yet been published; the mechanistic rationale is direct, and clinical reports consistently describe motor quieting as an early training response.)

13.6 The Brain Asleep Shows Up When You're Awake

This is one of the most clinically important insights in this chapter: **your waking brain carries signatures of poor sleep quality.**

Your daytime brain map can show state patterns consistent with sleep disruption, such as excess theta from sleep debt or high beta from hyperarousal, and those patterns show up as changes in processing speed, executive function, impulsivity, and emotional regulation that affect every waking hour.

An important boundary: A waking QEEG can suggest that sleep is disrupted, but it cannot tell you *why*. It cannot rule in or rule out obstructive sleep apnea, periodic limb movement disorder, narcolepsy, or parasomnias. Those conditions require overnight sleep testing. The American Academy of Sleep Medicine (AASM) treats polysomnography (in-lab sleep study) as the standard diagnostic test for suspected obstructive sleep apnea (Kapur et al., 2017). A waking brain map and a sleep study answer different questions, and one does not replace the other.

When to seek a sleep-medicine evaluation: If you or your bed partner notice loud snoring or witnessed breathing pauses during sleep, if you experience severe daytime sleepiness despite adequate sleep time, if you have episodes of sudden muscle weakness triggered by emotion (cataplexy), if you act out dreams physically (dream-enactment behavior), or if you have uncomfortable leg sensations that worsen at rest and improve with movement (restless legs), these are red flags for conditions that require a sleep-medicine referral and often a formal sleep study. Do not assume a waking brain map addresses these concerns.

Sleep Problem	What You Feel	What the Waking QEEG Shows
Sleep debt	Foggy, flat, slow processing	Elevated theta globally, slowed alpha peak frequency

Sleep Problem	What You Feel	What the Waking QEEG Shows
Cortical hyper-arousal	Racing mind at bedtime, can't wind down	Elevated frontal high-beta at rest
Non-restorative sleep	Sleep 8 hours, wake exhausted	Waking map may show low alpha power. (Note: alpha intrusions during sleep are a polysomnographic finding seen on overnight sleep study, not on a waking QEEG.)
Suspected low spindle density	Light sleeper, every noise wakes you	Low central SMR (12–15 Hz) on waking map is a plausible *proxy* for weak thalamocortical circuits; actual spindle density can only be measured by polysomnography during sleep.
Fragmented sleep	Wake multiple times, can't stay asleep	Diffuse theta elevation, reduced frontal beta

Processing speed drops. When sleep is inadequate, the brain's background rhythms slow down. Alpha peak frequency, a reliable marker of processing speed, decreases. The brain is literally running slower. Tasks that should be automatic require effort. Conversations feel laggy. Reaction time suffers. On a QEEG, this shows up as slower individual alpha frequency and elevated theta / alpha ratios, the brain is dragging.

Executive function collapses. The frontal lobes are disproportionately affected by sleep loss. Frontal theta increases, frontal beta decreases, and the circuits responsible for planning, decision-making, task-switching, and impulse control go offline. A sleep-deprived adult's frontal EEG can look nearly identical to an ADHD pattern, because the functional impairment is the same, even though the cause is different.

Impulsivity rises. When the frontal inhibitory circuits are underpowered from sleep loss, the brain's ability to say "no" to itself degrades. Impulse control, emotional reactivity, and risk-taking all increase. On a QEEG, this often shows up as decreased SMR and increased fast-wave activity, the braking system weakens while the accelerator stays on.

Emotional regulation destabilizes. Sleep debt amplifies the amygdala's threat response while weakening prefrontal control over it. Cortisol rises. Emotional reactivity increases. High-beta worsens. A sleep-deprived brain is functionally an anxious brain, and a brain map will show the arousal pattern to prove it. Most people have experienced being overwhelmed by a problem, getting a good night's rest, and finding that problem feels half as big in the morning. That is the anxiety-sleep relationship made visible in a single night.

The numbers are stark:

- In ADHD, normalized sleep-onset latency mid-treatment specifically mediates inattention improvements but not hyperactivity, suggesting sleep dysregulation is a primary driver of attentional symptoms, not just a comorbidity (Arns et al., 2014)
- Two weeks of six-hour nights produces sustained-attention impairment equivalent to **approximately one full night of total sleep deprivation**; four-hour nights produce impairment equivalent to two nights (Van Dongen et al., 2003)
- Sleep disruption and depression feed each other in a vicious cycle, with alpha asymmetry shifting and motivation circuits going offline

Before concluding that your brain has a problem, rule out the possibility that your brain is just exhausted. A brain map may show patterns consistent with sleep debt, a diffuse quality that trained clinicians learn to recognize as a prompt to investigate sleep further. But the pattern is nonspecific; clinical sleep history and standard diagnostic assessment are required to separate a sleep-driven picture from a primary attentional or regulatory one. The theta is everywhere, not localized. The slowing is global. And it often resolves, sometimes dramatically, once sleep is restored.

13.7 What You Can Do Now

Sleep support does not require neurofeedback. These are the interventions that matter, in order of impact:

Consistent timing. Same bedtime and wake time within thirty minutes, every day including weekends. Your circadian rhythm needs consistency more than it needs any supplement.

Light management. Bright light (ideally sunlight) within the first hour of waking. Dim light in the evening. No bright screens within an hour of bed, or use blue-light filtering if you must.

Temperature. Cool bedroom (65-68°F). Warm shower or bath before bed (the subsequent cooling promotes sleep onset).

Caffeine cutoff. No caffeine after noon. Half-life of caffeine is five to six hours, the afternoon coffee is still in your system at midnight.

Alcohol reality. Alcohol is a sedative that destroys sleep architecture. You fall asleep faster but sleep worse. If you're drinking to sleep, you're making the problem worse.

A note on sleep trackers and what to actually monitor:

Consumer sleep trackers (Oura, Whoop, Apple Watch, Fitbit) give you useful trend data, but you need to understand what they measure well and what they don't.

What they measure well: Total sleep time and overall sleep-wake patterns. Oura is the best-validated consumer device against polysomnography, with high overall sleep-wake detection accuracy but lower per-stage agreement, in the range of 51 to 65 percent depending on the sleep stage (de Zambotti et al., 2019). All devices are good enough for trend tracking: is my sleep getting better or worse week to week?

What they don't measure well: Sleep onset latency and wake-after-sleep-onset are often underestimated, especially in insomnia, quiet wakefulness gets misclassified as light sleep. Stage-by-stage accuracy varies by device and is never lab-grade.

The metric most worth tracking: deep sleep. Deep sleep (N3, slow-wave sleep) is the garden you can tend. It responds to interventions:

exercise, alcohol reduction, temperature management, sleep scheduling, and SMR training. It declines with age, and that decline is meaningful and modifiable. Track your deep sleep as a trend over weeks, not as a nightly target.

The metric NOT worth chasing: REM. REM sleep is self-regulating, like blood pH. Your body maintains it through homeostatic mechanisms. If it changes dramatically, you're dealing with a medical issue (medication effects, severe sleep disruption) that warrants clinical attention, not self-optimization. Trying to "optimize REM" is like trying to optimize your blood oxygen, the system handles it. If it's seriously disrupted, see a doctor.

The simplest tracking method: Rate your sleep quality 1-10 every morning. After about two weeks of consistent rating, you're calibrated, and research suggests your subjective ratings track intervention benefits about as accurately as consumer devices. It's free, takes ten seconds, and gives you trend data you can trust.

What to actually track daily:

- Subjective sleep quality (1-10)
- Approximate time to fall asleep
- Number of times you woke during the night
- How rested you feel in the morning (1-10)

What to track weekly (if using a device):

- Average deep sleep duration (track the trend)
- Average total sleep time
- Sleep efficiency (time asleep / time in bed)

What to ignore:

- Night-to-night REM fluctuations
- "Sleep score" algorithms (proprietary, opaque, often misleading)
- Fine-grained stage percentages (too noisy to act on)

If these basics don't resolve the problem within two to three weeks of consistent implementation, that's when a brain map and potentially CBT-I or neurofeedback enter the conversation.

Decision Point: If you're considering neurofeedback for any reason and you're sleeping poorly, fix the obvious sleep-hygiene problems first: screens until midnight, no consistent bedtime, six cups of coffee. You don't need perfect sleep to begin, though. Many brain patterns that look like pathology are really sleep debt, and a brain map can often show the difference. Sleep improvement is one of the most consistent early changes our clients report during SMR-based training, so for most people sleep becomes one of the earliest things that shifts rather than a prerequisite they have to solve alone. If you also have symptoms suggesting a primary sleep disorder (loud snoring, witnessed apneas, severe daytime sleepiness, restless legs, dream-enactment), see a sleep-medicine specialist. A waking brain map does not substitute for a proper sleep evaluation when those red flags are present.

13.7.1 Going Deeper

- For circadian rhythms and the oscillatory architecture of sleep, see *Half a Second More* Chapter 13.
- For sleep-related phenotypes at clinical depth, see *QEEG Field Guide* Chapter 6.

Your Move:

1. **Score your sleep honestly:** Answer these four questions: (a) How long to fall asleep? (b) How many times do you wake? (c) Do you feel rested in the morning, or just not-asleep? (d) Has your clinician ever asked these questions, or just "how many hours?" If your honest answers to (a)-(c) are concerning and your clinician has never asked, bring them to the next appointment. Sleep is the first lever. It may be the whole story.

2. **Act:** Implement the sleep basics above for two weeks, consistently. Track sleep quality daily (1-10 scale). If it doesn't improve, that's data worth bringing to a clinician.

3. **Start a conversation:** Tell your doctor, therapist, or neurofeedback provider: "Before we address anything else, can we make sure my sleep isn't driving the rest of my symptoms?" That question could save you months of misdirected treatment.

This chapter is educational only and does not constitute medical advice. Discuss any decision to begin, modify, or stop neurofeedback or any other treatment with a licensed clinician.

Ch 14: The Developing Brain: Neurofeedback for Kids and Adolescents

---

Parents arrive at our clinic with binders. Not always literally, though Marcus's mom had a two-inch binder with color-coded tabs. More often it's a mental binder: every evaluation, every diagnosis, every medication trial, every professional's opinion stacked up with no shared picture underneath. This chapter is for them.

14.1 Meet Marcus

Marcus is nine years old. He has two ADHD diagnoses, one autism evaluation that was "inconclusive," and a mother who's exhausted. "Nobody's looked at all of it in the same room," she told us.

He can hyperfocus on Legos for three hours. He can't follow a two-step instruction at school. His teacher says he's defiant. His pediatrician says he needs a higher dose of stimulant. His occupational therapist says he's sensory-seeking. Nobody agrees, and his mother is drowning in conflicting advice.

His brain map showed something none of the previous clinicians had measured: a developmental lag in frontal connectivity. His frontal lobes were producing age-appropriate power at individual sites, but the coordination between regions was behind where it should be for his age. He could focus on one thing (single-site engagement) but couldn't integrate complex instructions (network coordination).

"His brain isn't broken," we told his mom. "It's still building the wiring."

14.2 Kids' Brains Are Not Small Adult Brains

Children's brains are developing systems, not static ones. The patterns you see on a brain map at age eight may look very different at age twelve, often through normal maturation alone, independent of any intervention.

This means:

Developmental norms matter. An adult normative database will flag patterns as "abnormal" in children that are actually developmentally appropriate, the frontal lobes mature last, so frontal theta that's excessive in a thirty-year-old might be normal in an eight-year-old. Responsible pediatric brain mapping uses age-matched developmental databases, not adult norms.

Plasticity is higher. The developing brain is more malleable than the adult brain. This is good news, children often respond to neurofeedback faster and more completely than adults. But it also means the brain is changing anyway, which makes it harder to attribute change specifically to the training.

Patience is required. Children's progress in neurofeedback is often visible in behavior before the child can articulate it. Parents and teachers may notice calmer mornings, fewer meltdowns, easier transitions, better sleep, before the child says "I feel different."

14.3 The Developing Brain Phenotypes

The regulatory phenotypes from Chapter 7 show up differently in kids:

The Explosive Brain. Emotional dysregulation, meltdowns, low frustration tolerance: this child goes from zero to one hundred over what looks like a minor trigger. Explosive presentations differ widely in their underlying brain pattern, and treating them identically is one of the most common clinical errors.

What we most often see is right frontal disinhibition. In our clinical framework, the right sensorimotor strip more often serves an inhibitory, supervisory role: it monitors, adjusts, and brakes reactivity. When it underperforms, the right frontal circuits associated with avoidance and threat-detection run without adequate braking. The result is a brain that reads ambiguous situations as threatening, generates strong fear or anger, and has very little capacity to pause between impulse and action. The left sensorimotor strip, in our experience, more often serves a stabilizing role, providing the activating resources that help hold things together; when both the inhibitory side (right) and the stabilizing side (left) are underperforming, the accelerator runs with nothing to counter it. These lateralization tendencies are patterns we observe clinically, not fixed rules, and individual variation is real.

The underlying cause varies more than the surface behavior suggests. This pattern can arise from reactive attachment, complex or single-incident trauma, chronic sleep disruption, and in some cases subclinical temporal lobe activity. That possibility is a referral, not a protocol. Abrupt behavioral arrest, unresponsive staring, mid-sentence blanking, automatisms, episodic fear or déjà vu, confusion after an event, developmental or language regression, stereotyped nocturnal events, or a first suspected seizure all need pediatric medical and neurologic assessment. A QEEG is not a seizure workup, and neurofeedback must never delay a standard EEG or a specialist referral. It also appears in kids who carry significant inflexibility: when expectations are violated and there's no tolerance for things going differently than anticipated, the explosion is the nervous system's only available response. Getting the right clinical picture matters enormously before choosing a protocol.

The Non-Expressive Brain. Flat affect, poor social engagement, processing delays. This child seems "checked out," not defiant, just absent. Their brain shows underactivation in regions associated with social processing and emotional expression. This pattern is often confused with autism spectrum features, though the QEEG picture is usually quite different from the autistic brain.

Parents describe these kids as "easy" when they're young, the baby who never fussed, the toddler who played alone for hours. The concern starts at school when teachers notice the child doesn't raise their hand, doesn't engage in group work, doesn't light up when praised. It's not that they don't want connection. The circuits that generate expressive social signaling are underperforming, and the child often has rich inner experience they simply can't get out. Training typically focuses on activation and connectivity in regions associated with social engagement and emotional expression. Progress shows up as more spontaneous communication, more initiated interaction, and more energy for social engagement, often noticed by teachers before parents.

The Scattered Brain. ADHD-spectrum presentation, executive function lags, working memory gaps, difficulty sustaining attention. This is the most common pediatric referral for neurofeedback, and the one where phenotype subtyping matters most (see Chapter 9 for the different ADHD patterns).

The critical detail for kids: many children referred as "ADHD" are actually sleep-deprived, sensory-overwhelmed, anxious, or some combination. A brain map can show patterns that prompt a closer look at sleep, sensory processing, or anxiety alongside the attention picture, adding information that behavioral checklists alone may miss. We regularly see children whose attention problems resolve entirely when sleep is addressed, with no direct attention training required. That information can help inform where to start.

The Sensitive Brain. Sensory overwhelm, anxiety, avoidance patterns. This child is easily flooded by noise, light, social demands, or new environments. Their brain often shows gating problems, too much information getting through the sensory filters, and may show alpha suppression similar to anxious adult patterns.

This child covers their ears at assemblies, refuses certain fabrics, melts down at birthday parties, and has a short list of acceptable foods. Parents often hear "sensory processing disorder" from OTs and "anxiety" from therapists, and neither label quite captures the full picture. What the brain map often shows is a gating deficit: the thalamic relay that should filter sensory input before it reaches cortex is letting too much through. Everything is too loud, too bright, too much. Training targets sensory gating directly through SMR and coherence protocols. We typically see changes in daily life within the first ten to fifteen sessions: the child tolerates more, avoids less, and recovers faster from overwhelm.

These are labels children commonly arrive with, not conditions a brain map can identify. A QEEG cannot diagnose or subtype any of them. Standard pediatric, developmental, and mental-health assessment comes first, and the map informs the training plan rather than the diagnosis.

Phenotype	Looks Like	Labels these children often receive	What We Observe	NF Approach
Explosive	Zero-to-100 meltdowns, low frustration tolerance	ODD, bipolar, DMDD	Right sensorimotor disinhibition; left sensorimotor underactivation	SMR, right-side stabilization
Non-Expressive	Flat affect, checked out, poor social engagement	Autism, depression	Underactivation in social processing regions	Activation training, connectivity
Scattered	Can't sustain attention, executive function gaps	ADHD (all subtypes lumped)	See Chapter 9 phenotypes (varies widely)	Matched to specific ADHD phenotype

Sensitive	Sensory overwhelm, avoidance, anxiety	Anxiety disorder, SPD	Gating problems; alpha suppression	Alpha enhancement, sensory gating

14.4 What QEEG Looks Like in Kids vs. Adults

Several important differences:

- **Higher theta is normal in young children.** Don't let anyone tell you your seven-year-old's theta is "abnormal" without checking it against pediatric norms.
- **Frontal maturity lags.** The prefrontal cortex is the last region to mature, into the mid-twenties. Frontal metrics should be interpreted cautiously in children and adolescents.
- **Connectivity is developing.** Interhemispheric coherence and frontal-posterior connectivity increase with age. Low coherence in a child may be a developmental lag, not a fixed deficit.
- **Medications change the picture.** Stimulants, in particular, alter the EEG profile significantly. If your child is mapped on medication, the map shows the brain on that medication, not the brain at baseline.

14.5 The Adolescent Brain: A Different Clinical Animal

Teenagers are not big children. The clinical picture shifts in ways that change both the training targets and the therapeutic relationship.

The prefrontal cortex is still under construction through the mid-twenties. In adolescence, the limbic system (emotional reactivity, reward sensitivity, social evaluation) is running at full power while the frontal circuits that regulate it are still wiring up. This creates a specific regulatory mismatch: strong drives, limited braking. A brain map of a sixteen-year-old often shows connectivity patterns that would concern us in an adult but are developmentally normal in a teen. The clinical question is whether the pattern reflects normal maturation in progress or a pattern that needs training now.

What brings adolescents in. School failure that wasn't there in elementary school (frontal demand spikes in middle and high school). Anxiety that intensifies with social complexity. Sleep that has drifted catastrophically late (the biological circadian shift of adolescence colliding with early school start times). Mood instability that doesn't fit a clean diagnostic box. Gaming or phone use that has become the primary regulatory strategy because nothing else works. Many arrive already on a stimulant or SSRI, prescribed in childhood, that nobody has reassessed against the current brain.

What's different from younger kids. Teens can report internal states, which makes the feedback loop faster and more precise. They also have opinions about whether they want to be in the chair, and forcing a resistant teenager through forty sessions produces compliance without learning. Engagement matters more here than at any other age. We're direct with adolescents: "This is what your brain is doing. This is what the training targets. You decide if you want to do it." Framing neurofeedback as something they're choosing, not a procedure being done to them, changes outcomes.

Common adolescent patterns. Sleep-phase delay creating downstream attention and mood problems (the most under-recognized pattern in this age group). Frontal connectivity still catching up to demand. High-beta anxiety patterns that emerged with puberty and social pressure. Reward-circuit dysregulation in teens who game or scroll as their primary regulation strategy. These respond well to targeted training when the teen is on board.

Timeline and expectations. In our practice, adolescents often begin showing improvement within twenty to thirty sessions, though these are clinical impressions rather than published benchmarks. Progress may be harder for parents to observe because teenagers don't always share internal changes. Academic metrics, sleep data, and self-report scales often tell the story before behavior in the house does. We check in with the teen directly, not just the parents.

14.6 What Parents Should Expect

Timelines: In our experience, children often begin showing behavioral changes within fifteen to twenty-five sessions, though some respond faster and complex presentations (autism spectrum, developmental delays, combined diagnoses) may need more. These are practice observations, not published session-count benchmarks.

Session modifications: Sessions are shorter (fifteen to twenty minutes of active training), more game-oriented (spaceships, cartoons, puzzles), and less reliant on the child's ability to describe what they're feeling. The child does not need to understand the process for it to work. Most neurofeedback is passive operant conditioning, so the brain learns whether or not the person sitting in the chair knows what is happening. Your child cannot fail at it. That said, it is good to teach a child about their own brain. You do not have to, but explaining what the training does and why gives them something valuable in itself, a vocabulary for their own internal experience.

The child's ability to stop. One thing is not optional. Before the first session, offer a simple explanation at the child's level of what will happen and why. Practice a pause or stop signal together, a word, a gesture, or a card, so the child knows how to say "I need a break" or "I want to stop." For children who are nonspeaking or who communicate through AAC, the signal should fit their communication system, and clinicians should watch for behavioral dissent (pulling away, covering ears, increasing distress) as seriously as a spoken "stop." Build in breaks, offer sensory adaptations for the cap and setup, and honor the signal every time. A child who cannot opt out is not receiving training; they are being subjected to it.

What clinicians watch in session: Because young children are not good at reporting how they feel, the body reports for them. Clinicians observe posture, activation level, energy, and eye contact during and right after a session to read whether the training is landing. These are proxy readouts, not goals in themselves, and not a compliance checklist.

What "progress" looks like: Often behavioral before subjective. Better mornings. Fewer meltdowns. Easier homework time. Teachers noticing improved focus. These changes may appear before the child says anything is different, because kids don't always have the vocabulary for internal state changes.

School coordination: Do not bring a brain map to a school meeting on its own. A map by itself is not the kind of evidence a school works from, and it does not establish eligibility for anything. What travels well is an executive function report, including continuous performance testing, which measures what your child actually does on sustained attention and impulse control. Bring that, with the map as context, and only after your provider has walked you through what the data show and what they do not. If you cannot explain a finding in your own words, it is not ready to take into a meeting. Some neurofeedback providers are experienced in communicating with schools; others are not. Ask.

The reverse holds too. A map that looks better is not grounds for removing support. Accommodations are set by how a child is functioning at school, so functional evidence is what adds them and functional evidence is what removes them.

14.7 The Medication Question for Kids

This is sensitive territory.

Stimulant medications work for many children with ADHD. They're fast-acting, well-studied, and can be life-changing, especially when a child is struggling in school and needs immediate support.

Neurofeedback is slower. It takes months, not hours. For a child who's failing classes right now, "wait for the brain training to kick in" may not be practical.

Many families use both: medication for immediate function while neurofeedback builds long-term regulatory capacity. The goal, for families who choose this path, is often to reduce medication dependence over time as the brain's own capacity improves.

> **Any decision to start, change, or stop psychiatric medication for a child (including any reduction in stimulant dosage) must be made in close coordination with the prescribing physician.** A child's response to medication can change during a course of training for many reasons. Report these changes to your prescriber; do not adjust dosing on your own. Medical supervision of medication is not optional.

We don't push either option. We present the brain data and let families make informed decisions based on their child's specific pattern, their values, and their circumstances. What we recommend: get a brain map before starting neurofeedback training. The map informs the training plan rather than the diagnosis or the prescription. Standard pediatric, developmental, and medical assessment comes first; the map adds a layer of information about regulatory patterns that those assessments do not capture. Treating all ADHD-diagnosed children identically ignores everything we know about phenotype diversity.

14.8 When NF Isn't the First Lever for Kids

Before neurofeedback, check:

- **Sleep.** Is this child sleeping enough? Screen time before bed? Consistent bedtime? Sleep-deprived children look exactly like ADHD children on both behavior checklists and brain maps. Screen for sleep disorders, not just sleep habits. Habitual snoring, mouth breathing, gasping or choking, witnessed breathing pauses, restless sleep or restless legs, unexplained daytime neurobehavioral change, sudden loss of muscle tone with emotion, sleepwalking or night terrors, and stereotyped nocturnal events all need a pediatric sleep-medicine referral. Sleep apnea in children can present as behavior and attention problems without obvious sleepiness.

- **Nutrition.** Is the child eating regularly? Blood sugar crashes mimic attention problems.
- **Sensory environment.** Is the classroom overwhelmingly stimulating? Is home chaotic?
- **Family dynamics.** High-conflict homes produce stress responses that look like ADHD or anxiety on a brain map. This isn't neurofeedback territory, it's family therapy territory.

Screen and address these in parallel, according to urgency. Do not wait to perfect home routines before seeking evaluation. If attention and behavior issues persist after sleep, nutrition, and environment are sorted out, the brain data becomes much more interpretable and the training much more targeted.

Decision Point: If you're a parent considering neurofeedback for your child: start with a QEEG from a provider experienced with kids. Ask them what pediatric normative database they use and how many children they've worked with. A brain map gives you and your child's team a shared picture, a starting point. Chapter 17 shows you exactly how to find the right provider.

Your Move:

1. **Pick the lead pattern:** Look at the four phenotypes (explosive, nonexpressive, scattered, sensitive) and identify which one describes your child's biggest daily challenge. Then ask your pediatrician or next specialist: "Could a brain map show us which pattern is primary here? I want to make sure the interventions are targeting the right thing." Most providers will not volunteer this question; you have to bring it.

2. **Act:** Before pursuing neurofeedback, audit the basics. Sleep, nutrition, screen time, sensory environment. Address what you can, and do not delay an evaluation while you work on them.

3. **Start a conversation:** Bring this chapter to your child's next appointment, whether that's the pediatrician, the school psychologist, or the occupational therapist. Ask: "Has anyone looked at the brain-level patterns underneath these behaviors?" The answer may surprise you.

This chapter is educational only and does not constitute medical advice. Discuss any decision to begin, modify, or stop neurofeedback or any other treatment with a licensed clinician.

Ch 15: The Performer's Brain: Optimization, Flow, and Cognitive Resilience

15.1 What Happens to Your Brain After Thirty

Your brain at forty is not your brain at twenty. Processing speed slows. Individual alpha frequency drops. Connectivity between regions becomes less efficient. These are not signs of disease. They are the normal trajectory of a brain that has been used hard for decades.

But the trajectory is not fixed. And how much of it is aging, versus sleep debt, versus chronic stress, versus a regulatory pattern that's been running inefficiently for years, is often impossible to tell without looking at the brain. That is the central argument of this chapter.

One measurable handle on that slowing is the P300, an event-related potential (ERP). Unlike the resting QEEG discussed throughout this book, the P300 is not part of a standard resting brain map. It requires a separate test: an active "oddball" paradigm in which you sit at a screen and respond to infrequent target stimuli among frequent non-targets. When a stimulus is rare, meaningful, or otherwise worth updating your beliefs about, cortex generates a positive-going response peaking around three hundred milliseconds after the event in healthy young adults. Latency reflects the pace of stimulus evaluation and context updating. In plain performance terms, a later peak means a brain that needs more time to register that something important changed.

The aging trajectory is consistent. After roughly thirty, P300 peak latency drifts later by one to two milliseconds per year in many samples. By sixty, peaks near three hundred thirty to three hundred fifty milliseconds are common. Alongside that, amplitude typically declines. Less capacity to tag each salient event with neural emphasis. The shift is reliable enough that researchers use P300 timing as a processing-speed yardstick: it tells you how fast the brain is working, not just what you scored on a questionnaire.

Older brains compensate. They recruit additional cortical territory to hold performance steady on tasks younger brains solve with leaner activation, a pattern described by CRUNCH, the Compensation-Related Utilization of Neural Circuits Hypothesis. Extra circuits buy you runway. The strategy works until demand outruns what the expanded network can supply, and then scores and reaction times fall together.

This is where neurofeedback enters the picture, as a tool for training the brain toward faster, cleaner event-related responses when the task demands them.

15.2 The Optimization Distinction

Most of this book addresses neurofeedback for conditions, anxiety, ADHD, trauma, autism. This chapter is different. It's for people whose brains work fine and who want them to work better.

The distinction matters because the training approach is different:

- **Remediation** targets deviations from the norm, bringing outlier patterns back into range.
- **Optimization** targets efficiency, taking a brain that's already in range and improving its coordination, flexibility, and resilience.

Both are valid uses of neurofeedback. Both produce measurable changes. But the expectations are different. Optimization clients aren't looking for dramatic symptom relief, they're looking for marginal gains that compound over time. Sharper decision-making. Faster recovery from cognitive load. Better sustained performance under pressure. An extra five percent that, in their world, translates to millions.

15.3 What High-Performing Brains Look Like on QEEG

Across hundreds of optimization clients, executives, athletes, surgeons, musicians, founders, we see common patterns in high performers:

Strong alpha. High performers typically have well-developed alpha rhythms; their brains can idle efficiently and recover quickly between bouts of focused work. Weak alpha often correlates with the "always on" pattern that leads to burnout.

Efficient coherence. The coordination between brain regions is clean, not too rigid, not too loose. Information flows efficiently between frontal executive regions and posterior processing areas. Decisions are fast because the network is well-organized.

Flexible state transitions. The ability to shift from deep focus to creative exploration to recovery to sleep, smoothly, without getting stuck in any one gear. Rigidity here is what eventually leads to burnout.

What we also see: Many high performers have subtle inefficiencies they've been compensating for through sheer effort. A slight connectivity asymmetry. A sleep pattern that's functional but not restorative. High beta that they've channeled into productivity but that's also keeping them wired at night. The compensation works, until it doesn't. And the crash, when it comes, looks like burnout.

Protocols we use for optimization. For the high performer whose map is already in range, we're not remediating. We're tuning. Coherence training to smooth communication between frontal and posterior regions. Alpha enhancement to strengthen recovery capacity and idling. SMR at Cz to stabilize sleep onset, which many optimization clients discover has been fragile for years. Alpha asymmetry training when the map shows right-frontal dominance, shifting the default from avoidance to approach. The targets are subtle. A Z-score that's 0.8 above norm might not be "abnormal," but bringing it to 0.3 can produce noticeable gains in decision clarity and stress resilience. We typically run twenty to thirty sessions, then reassess. The aim is to remove the small inefficiencies that compound.

What optimization clients report. The changes are often described in performance terms. Faster decisions. Less second-guessing. Quicker recovery from demanding stretches. Sleep improvements, even when sleep wasn't the stated goal. Energy resiliency, the ability to bounce back to optimal levels even after a rough night. A sense that the brain has more headroom: capacity that wasn't there before.

15.4 James

James runs a hedge fund. Nothing is clinically wrong with him: no diagnosis, no medication, no complaints that would land him in a clinician's office. He came in because he wanted an edge. "I want to know what my brain is doing and whether I can make it do it better."

His brain map was good. Good, with room to tune. We saw subtle coherence inefficiencies between frontal regions, a slight alpha asymmetry suggesting his brain defaulted slightly toward avoidance rather than approach, and a sleep architecture issue he'd been compensating for with caffeine for fifteen years. None of this would qualify as "abnormal." All of it was trainable.

Twenty sessions later, he wasn't performing better through effort. He'd stopped needing the caffeine. His sleep had improved without targeting it. He described a shift we hear about often from optimization clients: "I didn't know I was operating with the parking brake on until someone released it."

That phrase captures what this chapter is about. Not remediation. Removing the drag that high-functioning brains accumulate and learn to work around.

15.5 The Burnout Brain

The crash, when it comes, doesn't look like what most people expect. It mimics both depression and ADHD. It's specific, it's common among high performers, and it's consistently misidentified.

The burnout/shutdown phenotype is distinct from depression, distinct from ADHD, and overlapping with both. It's the high performer who hit a wall, post-COVID crash, caregiver depletion, years of sleep debt finally catching up, the executive who pushed through one too many quarters.

What we see on QEEG:

- **Theta intrusion:** slow-wave activity creeping into waking states, because the brain is exhausted
- **Alpha collapse:** the recovery rhythm is suppressed, meaning the brain can't rest even when work stops
- **High beta coexisting with high theta:** the brain is simultaneously wired and tired, pushing hard while running empty

This is not the same as depression, though it can look similar on symptom checklists. Depression often shows frontal alpha asymmetry (right-dominant) and pervasive slowing. Burnout shows a brain that's still trying to perform but has depleted its regulatory resources. The training approach is different: depression protocols target mood circuits; burnout protocols target recovery capacity.

The first intervention for burnout is almost always sleep. Chapter 13 explains why. The critical distinction for anyone in recovery from burnout: neurofeedback doesn't push you harder. It builds back the regulatory capacity that let you push in the first place.

15.6 Cognitive Resilience: What the Data Shows

The rate of cognitive decline varies enormously, and more of it is modifiable than most people believe. What we see in brain maps of healthy aging adults:

- **Individual alpha frequency (IAF) decline:** the speed of your brain's dominant rhythm slows gradually with age (the developmental trajectory described in Chapter 3). Lower IAF is associated with slower processing and, in extreme cases, cognitive impairment. Some neurofeedback studies report modest shifts in IAF with training, though the size and durability of those shifts are still debated in the literature. IAF is highly heritable (~0.81; Smit et al., 2006) and stable in the short term, so expectations for large frequency shifts should be tempered. What training may do more reliably is improve how efficiently the brain uses the alpha rhythm it has.

- **Theta increases:** within normal range unless excessive, when they track cognitive fog and early cognitive decline.
- **Connectivity changes:** some networks become less efficient. Targeted connectivity training can strengthen them.

The clinical principle: **a brain map in midlife is as valuable as a blood panel.** Not because it screens for disease, but because it gives you a baseline you can track. Alpha slows as sleep quality drops or anxiety rises. Connectivity shifts under chronic stress. A map at fifty gives you a reference point at sixty. The value is the same as tracking triglycerides: the number is not deterministic, but watching it change over time tells you something real about the direction things are moving. This is the same logic behind the sleep tracking Chapter 13 asks you to do. Sleep quality, deep-sleep trends, subjective morning ratings, and a periodic brain map are all signals in the same feedback loop: each one tells you whether what you are doing is landing.

Neurofeedback for aging is not about "anti-aging" hype. It is about maintaining the brain's regulatory capacity as it naturally shifts, keeping alpha strong, keeping connectivity efficient, keeping processing speed in a healthy range. The evidence is emerging (Level 3), but the clinical logic is sound and the intervention is low-risk.

Without that baseline, you have no way to see gradual change for what it is. That is the tracking argument, and it holds even if you never have a clinical symptom.

15.7 Athletes, Creatives, and the Flow Question

Neurofeedback has been used with athletes and performers for decades, often quietly, because competitive advantage isn't advertised.

Sports applications: Reaction time, focus under pressure, recovery between bouts of effort, and the ability to maintain performance during fatigue. SMR training and alpha training are the most common approaches. We've worked with athletes across sports, and the maps often show the same pattern: strong baseline, but subtle coherence inefficiencies or alpha asymmetry that limit peak performance. The training targets those gaps. Athletes report faster recovery between competitions, less performance anxiety, and the ability to "get in the zone" more reliably. The evidence base is small (Level 3) but consistent with the mechanism, building regulatory stability lets the brain perform closer to its ceiling for longer.

Creative applications: Alpha-theta training (Chapter 12) has been explored for accessing flow states and enhancing associative thinking. Musicians and writers describe it as "opening a channel" that focused work can't reach. One composer said the training gave him "access to the part of my brain that used to only show up at 3am." The controlled research here is small and largely unblinded, so how much of that effect is specific to the training remains an open question.

The flow question: Can neurofeedback reliably produce flow states? No, not on demand. What it can do is improve the regulatory conditions that make flow more accessible: better arousal control, stronger alpha for idling between creative bursts, more flexible state transitions. Flow emerges when the conditions are right. Neurofeedback trains the conditions.

15.8 The Stack for Performance

For optimization clients, neurofeedback sits within a broader protocol:

1. **Sleep:** always first. No amount of brain training compensates for chronic sleep debt.

2. **Exercise:** aerobic fitness is among the strongest neuroprotective interventions available. A year of aerobic training increased anterior hippocampal volume by about two percent and raised serum BDNF, reversing one to two years of age-related loss (Erickson et al., 2011).
3. **Brain map:** establish a baseline, identify subtle inefficiencies.
4. **Neurofeedback:** target specific patterns: coherence training, alpha strengthening, sleep architecture improvement.
5. **HRV training:** autonomic regulation complements cortical training.
6. **Nutritional and metabolic optimization:** fuel for the hardware.

The order matters. Sleep and exercise are foundational. Brain training is more effective when the foundation is solid.

Decision Point: You don't need a diagnosis to benefit from a brain map. If you're interested in cognitive performance or long-term brain health, a QEEG baseline is the most useful data you can have, and it gives you a baseline to compare against over time.

Your Move:

1. **Measure your baseline:** Ask a neurofeedback provider for a brain map as a baseline assessment, not as a treatment plan. You're not buying sessions; you're getting data. What you learn from the map determines whether neurofeedback is the right tool, the right protocol, and whether there's anything worth addressing at all.

2. **Act:** Get a brain map. You don't need a problem to justify one. Knowing your current baseline is how you track change over time.

3. **Start a conversation:** If you're a high performer who's noticed a decline, less sharp, more fatigued, harder to recover, that's not "just getting older." It might be a trainable pattern. A brain map would tell you.

This chapter is educational only and does not constitute medical advice. Discuss any decision to begin, modify, or stop neurofeedback or any other treatment with a licensed clinician.

Ch 16: Beyond Brainwaves: Blood Flow, Heart Rate, and the Full Regulation Toolkit

---

Chapter 3 covered how neurofeedback trains your brain's electrical patterns through operant conditioning. But electrical patterns aren't the only thing worth training. Your brain runs on blood flow. Your nervous system runs on autonomic balance. And some of the most powerful clinical tools work on these systems directly, not instead of EEG neurofeedback, but alongside it.

If EEG neurofeedback trains the **signal**, the tools in this chapter train the **infrastructure** that supports it.

16.1 HEG Neurofeedback: Training Prefrontal Metabolic Activity

While EEG neurofeedback trains electrical rhythms, HEG (hemoencephalography) trains something different: **prefrontal vascular and metabolic activity**, measured indirectly through optical or thermal proxies.

A small sensor sits on your forehead, no gel, no cap. It measures a proxy of local blood oxygenation or thermal output in real time. A movie or game responds: when the proxy signal increases, the feedback rewards you. Over sessions, you learn to increase prefrontal metabolic activity on demand.

Two lineages exist, and the measurement distinction matters. **nirHEG** (near-infrared, developed by Hershel Toomim) shines near-infrared light through the scalp and skull and measures the ratio of oxygenated to deoxygenated hemoglobin in the tissue beneath the sensor. It is an optical blood-oxygenation proxy, not a direct blood-flow meter. The signal includes contributions from scalp and extracranial blood vessels, not only cortical tissue. **pirHEG** (passive infrared, developed by Jeffrey Carmen) measures infrared thermal radiation from the forehead. It is a thermal proxy that reflects a mix of cortical metabolic heat and scalp blood flow; the relative contributions are not cleanly separable. Both methods have extracranial confounds: scalp blood flow, skin temperature, and forehead muscle activity can influence the signal. Neither directly measures cerebral blood flow in the way an MRI perfusion scan or Doppler ultrasound does.

Both have clinical track records. Carmen's original uncontrolled case series (100 migraine patients seen over four years) reported that roughly 90 percent of those who completed at least six sessions showed significant self-reported improvement, in a completer analysis with no control group and no sham comparison. The migraine evidence is the strongest single-condition case for HEG; evidence for other applications remains preliminary and largely observational.

We use continuous pirHEG in our clinical practice. Sessions are short, typically ten minutes of continuous activation run immediately before EEG neurofeedback, up to five times per week. Carmen's original protocol uses thresholded pirHEG at longer durations (up to thirty minutes), but continuous delivery at shorter duration achieves the activation we target without overtaxing the system.

16.1.1 Consumer HEG: Mendi

Consumer devices like **Mendi** are essentially nirHEG for home use, measuring prefrontal oxygenation with a headband and providing gamified feedback through a mobile app. The underlying principle is the same; the precision and the evidence base are not. Mendi is a reasonable entry point for prefrontal activation training, particularly if clinical HEG isn't accessible, but the published research on consumer HEG outcomes remains thin.

16.2 HRV Biofeedback: Training Your Autonomic Nervous System

If HEG trains the brain's blood supply, **HRV (heart rate variability) biofeedback** trains the body's autonomic regulation: the balance between your sympathetic ("gas pedal") and parasympathetic ("brake") nervous systems.

16.2.1 The Vagus Nerve: Why This Works

The parasympathetic brake runs through the vagus nerve, the longest cranial nerve in your body, winding from the brainstem through the neck, around the heart and lungs, and into the gut. What surprises most people: roughly 80 to 90 percent of vagal traffic is afferent, meaning it carries information *up* from the body to the brain, not down. Your gut, your heart, your lungs are constantly reporting to the brainstem about what's happening in the periphery. The brain listens and adjusts.

Vagal tone is a concept used to describe parasympathetic cardiac influence. High vagal tone means the parasympathetic brake is strong, flexible, and responsive. The heart speeds up on the inhale and slows on the exhale with a wide swing. Low vagal tone means the brake is weak: the heart rate is flatter, and the capacity to recover from stress is compromised.

Heart rate variability is the most accessible index of cardiac vagal influence, but it is not a pure vagal-tone meter. HRV, and specifically respiratory sinus arrhythmia (RSA), is best described as a cardiac vagal-related index that is valid primarily under controlled resting conditions. It depends on respiration rate and depth, age (HRV declines substantially with age), aerobic fitness, heart rhythm regularity, medications (beta-blockers, anticholinergics, and others directly alter HRV), and acute or chronic illness. All of these must be accounted for before interpreting HRV as a straightforward readout of autonomic health. With those caveats in place: higher resting HRV is broadly associated with better autonomic flexibility, and HRV biofeedback targets the vagal brake by training the body to produce larger, more coherent oscillations in heart rhythm at the individual's resonance frequency.

For the full neuroanatomy and the clinical implications of vagal tone for emotional regulation, *Half a Second More* Chapter 14 develops this at length.

16.2.2 How HRV Biofeedback Works: Resonance Frequency

A sensor on your fingertip or earlobe measures your heart rhythm in real time. A screen shows your HRV pattern. You learn to breathe at your **resonance frequency**, the specific breathing rate that maximizes the amplitude of your heart rate oscillations and entrains the baroreflex (the feedback loop between heart rate and blood pressure).

Most popular descriptions get this wrong: your resonance frequency is not simply "six breaths per minute." It is an individualized rate, typically falling between 4.5 and 6.5 breaths per minute, that varies from person to person. Some people resonate at five breaths per minute. Others at six and a half. The difference matters. Breathing at your specific resonance frequency produces HRV amplitudes two to four times larger than breathing at a generic pace. A skilled HRV practitioner finds your resonance frequency in the first or second session by testing several rates and watching which one produces the largest, cleanest oscillations.

The breath itself is the biofeedback mechanism. You are not waiting for a machine to train your nervous system as neurofeedback trains your cortex. You are learning a skill: how to recruit the vagal brake voluntarily through paced breathing. The device confirms whether the skill is working. Once learned, the skill transfers. You can use it in traffic, before a meeting, during an argument. The device becomes a training tool you eventually outgrow, not a permanent dependency.

This is the voluntary / involuntary distinction Chapter 3 introduced, and it shapes everything about how HRV is learned and why its results vary. *Half a Second More* develops it in clinical depth, including how to find your resonance frequency and build a daily practice.

16.2.3 When HRV Biofeedback Varies in Response

Because HRV biofeedback is a voluntary skill, variability in response tracks skill acquisition, not fixed brain properties. This is fundamentally different from how neurofeedback non-response works (Chapter 18), and conflating the two leads to confusion.

Did the skill acquire in-session? Within the first two to four sessions, RSA amplitude should increase during paced resonance breathing. If it doesn't, the resonance frequency probably needs adjusting, or the breathing technique needs coaching. This is a technique problem, not a person problem.

Did the skill transfer out of session? The harder question. Does the client recruit the breath when they need it: in traffic, before a presentation, after an argument? Practice adherence and interoceptive awareness are the dominant variables here. Some people internalize the rhythm quickly. Others need structured practice routines to bridge the gap between session and life. This is where the device-to-life translation lives, and it is the primary determinant of long-term benefit.

Low resting HRV and physiological constraints. Some clients have low resting HRV in the context of age, chronic illness, physical deconditioning, cardiac conditions, medication, or long trauma history. They can still acquire the breathing skill. Per-session effects may be smaller, and the longer arc matters more. Adjunctive practices that may modestly influence vagal activity (slow exhale extension, humming, or gargling, though the evidence for the latter two is limited) are sometimes suggested for this group. A note on cold exposure: acute cold (cold showers, ice baths) is commonly described in wellness culture as "activating the vagus" or "building parasympathetic tone." The acute physiological reality is closer to the opposite: the cold pressor response is primarily a sympathetic activation (vasoconstriction, heart rate increase, blood pressure spike, catecholamine release). Longer-term cold habituation may involve parasympathetic adaptations, but the acute response is sympathetic, and framing cold exposure as a straightforward parasympathetic practice is inaccurate.

The framing throughout is continuous, not binary. Most people can acquire the HRV biofeedback skill to some degree, though starting vagal tone, practice adherence, age, fitness, medications, and life context all influence how much the skill moves the needle in daily life. The term "nonresponder" is less useful here than in the neurofeedback literature, because the variable is primarily skill acquisition and transfer rather than a fixed brain property, but individual variation in response is real.

16.2.4 Why It Pairs with Neurofeedback

EEG neurofeedback works top-down: training cortical regulation. HRV biofeedback works bottom-up: training autonomic regulation. Together, you're training regulation from both directions. The brain learns to modulate its electrical patterns while the body learns to modulate its autonomic balance. For anxiety, trauma, and stress-related conditions, this combination is more powerful than either alone.

The evidence: A meta-analysis found large reductions in self-reported stress and anxiety with HRV biofeedback (Goessl et al., 2017). A mechanistic review (Lehrer & Gevirtz, 2014) traces how resonance-frequency breathing produces its effects and notes clinical applications across conditions including asthma and depression. The broader clinical literature extends to PTSD and blood pressure regulation, though the meta-analytic evidence is strongest for stress and anxiety. It is simpler than neurofeedback (no QEEG needed, fewer sessions, lower cost) and often serves as either a complement to or entry point for brain training.

Practical note: Many neurofeedback clinics offer HRV training as part of a broader protocol. Some clients start with HRV to build basic autonomic regulation before adding EEG neurofeedback. Others do both concurrently: HRV at home between clinic NF sessions. Consumer HRV devices (chest straps paired with apps like Elite HRV or HRV4Training) are adequate for home practice because HRV biofeedback is a voluntary skill with clear real-time feedback. The device quality threshold is lower than for EEG, where signal fidelity determines everything.

16.3 Temperature Biofeedback: The Body's Relaxation Signal

Temperature biofeedback is the simplest modality in this chapter, and one of the oldest. A sensor on your fingertip measures peripheral temperature. Cold hands = sympathetic activation (blood flow diverted from extremities). Warm hands = parasympathetic activation (blood flow returning to the periphery).

You learn to warm your hands through relaxation, and in doing so, you're conditioning a parasympathetic response. This was a core component of Peniston's alpha-theta protocol (Chapter 12): temperature biofeedback established the body's capacity for deep relaxation before the brain-level alpha-theta work began.

Temperature biofeedback is rarely used as a standalone intervention today, but it remains valuable as a stabilizing pre-training step, particularly for trauma and addiction work.

16.4 How These Tools Fit Together

Modality	What It Trains	Direction	Typical Use	Typical Course
EEG Neurofeedback	Brain electrical dynamics	Top-down (cortical)	Attention, anxiety, sleep, trauma, performance	25–50+ sessions
HEG Neurofeedback	Prefrontal metabolic activity (optical/thermal proxy)	Top-down (vascular)	Migraine (best evidence); other applications preliminary	Variable
HRV Biofeedback	Autonomic balance (vagal tone)	Bottom-up (autonomic)	Stress, anxiety, PTSD, blood pressure	6–12 sessions
Temperature Biofeedback	Parasympathetic conditioning	Bottom-up (peripheral)	Relaxation, pre-training for alpha-theta	As needed

The relationship between these modalities is complementary, not competitive:

EEG neurofeedback trains the brain's electrical dynamics, the patterns of oscillation, connectivity, and regulation that drive cognition, emotion, attention, and sleep.

HEG neurofeedback trains prefrontal metabolic activity through optical or thermal proxy signals. It targets the vascular and metabolic infrastructure that supports cortical electrical dynamics, though the measurement has extracranial confounds (see above).

HRV biofeedback trains the body's autonomic balance, the sympathetic/parasympathetic regulation that underlies arousal, stress response, and recovery capacity.

Temperature biofeedback trains basic parasympathetic conditioning, the body's ability to shift into a recovery state.

A comprehensive training plan might use all of these at different points: HRV for autonomic foundation, temperature biofeedback for relaxation conditioning, EEG neurofeedback for cortical regulation, and HEG for prefrontal vascular endurance. The specific combination depends on what your brain map shows and what your goals are.

Not every client needs every tool. But understanding that the toolkit extends beyond brainwaves helps you evaluate whether your provider is thinking about the full picture or just one slice of it.

16.4.1 Going Deeper

- For HRV biofeedback, the vagus nerve, and breath-based training in full clinical depth, see *Half a Second More* Chapter 14.
- For ERP methodology (including P300 and ERP-adjacent work), see *QEEG Field Guide* Appendix F (ERP Normative Reference).

Your Move:

1. **Reflect:** Has anyone ever measured your heart rate variability? If you wear a fitness tracker, check whether it reports HRV. Low HRV is a signal that your autonomic regulation could use attention, and it's trainable.

2. **Act:** Try this: breathe at roughly six breaths per minute for five minutes (five seconds in, five seconds out). Notice what happens to your body. Six is a common starting point, not your exact resonance frequency (which a practitioner finds by testing several rates), but it's close enough to feel the effect. If it feels calming, HRV biofeedback might be a useful complement to whatever else you're doing.

3. **Start a conversation:** Ask your neurofeedback provider: "Do you use HRV biofeedback or HEG alongside EEG training? How do you decide when to add those?" A provider who thinks about the full toolkit will have a clear answer.

Ch 17: How to Choose Well

The neurofeedback marketplace ranges from world-class to exploitative. This chapter is your buyer's guide.

A map can point you toward sleep, exercise, stress load, a medication conversation, or training. This chapter is about the last of those. If training is where you land, everything you've learned in this book, the mechanism, the evidence, the phenotypes, the honest limitations, comes down to one practical question: **can you find someone who does it well?** Good neurofeedback and bad neurofeedback aren't just different in degree. One is an individualized, data-driven training program. The other is an expensive placebo wrapped in brain-science language. The Neurofeedback.space directory (neurofeedback.space) is a good starting point, a searchable global directory of verified providers, alongside the BCIA and ISNR directories referenced in Appendix B and Appendix I. (Disclosure: the authors operate Peak Brain Institute, which appears in these directories. The directory is open to any qualified provider.)

17.1 What Good Neurofeedback Looks Like

Competent neurofeedback follows a clear arc: thorough intake, QEEG brain map, individualized training plan, regular sessions with monitoring and adjustment, periodic reassessment (re-mapping every twenty to twenty-five sessions), clear communication about what is being trained and why, and built-in off-ramps if you are not responding. Missing any of these elements removes the mechanism by which you would even know the training is working. If a provider skips the intake or the brain map, or if they cannot explain what protocol they chose and why, that tells you something before the first session starts.

17.2 Red Flags

Guaranteed cures. "Neurofeedback will eliminate your ADHD/anxiety/depression." No responsible clinician guarantees outcomes for any intervention. Neurofeedback is training, not magic.

No baseline assessment. If they start training without a QEEG or at minimum a thorough clinical intake, they have no way to know what to train or to tell whether it is working. You deserve a baseline.

One protocol for everyone. "We do theta-beta for all ADHD clients." This ignores everything we know about phenotype diversity. Your brain is not everyone's brain.

Large prepaid packages with no reassessment. "Sign up for 60 sessions at $150 each, $9,000 upfront." Without built-in checkpoints at sessions 15-20 and 25-30, this is a business model, not clinical care.

No outcome measurement. If they're not tracking your progress with standardized measures, QEEG re-assessment, validated symptom scales, functional outcomes, they have no way to know if the training is working. Neither do you.

"FDA approved" claims. Neurofeedback devices are Class II biofeedback devices, typically 510(k)-exempt for "relaxation training." They are NOT FDA approved for specific psychiatric conditions. One PTSD-targeted device has received 510(k) clearance. If someone tells you their system is "FDA approved for ADHD," that's inaccurate, and it tells you something about their understanding of their own field.

Pressure tactics. High-pressure sales, urgency messaging ("your brain is deteriorating without treatment"), or emotional manipulation of parents. Walk away.

17.3 What Happens When the Protocol Needs Adjustment

Protocols sometimes miss. A responsive clinician catches this by session fifteen to twenty and adjusts; Chapter 18 covers the full troubleshooting framework when training stalls or needs a change in direction.

17.4 Green Flags

They ask questions before selling anything. Good clinicians want to understand your situation before recommending a course of action.

They use QEEG data to guide protocols. Not symptom checklists alone. Not a proprietary "brain type" quiz. Actual brain data, properly recorded and interpreted.

They track outcomes. They can show you what metrics they'll measure and when they'll reassess. They have a plan for what happens if you're not responding.

They explain what they're doing and why. You should understand your protocol, your targets, and the rationale. If you ask "why are you training this frequency at this site?" and get a clear answer, that's a good sign.

They acknowledge limitations. "This protocol has good evidence for your pattern, but not everyone responds the same way, we'll check in at session 15 and adjust if needed." Honesty is a green flag.

They coordinate with your other providers. Good neurofeedback clinicians communicate with your therapist, psychiatrist, or primary care doctor. They're part of a team, not a silo.

17.5 Credentials: What They Mean (and Don't Mean)

BCIA-BCN (Board Certified in Neurofeedback): The most recognized certification. Requires 36 hours of didactic training, 25 hours of mentorship, 10 personal sessions, 100 client sessions, and a written exam. Recertification every 4 years with 48 hours of continuing education.

QEEG-D (QEEG Diplomate): Advanced credential in QEEG interpretation. Requires professional degree plus specialized coursework in EEG acquisition, artifacting, normative databases, and clinical interpretation.

The honest fact: **no research links specific neurofeedback credentials to better patient outcomes.** BCIA certification means someone has met a baseline of training. It doesn't guarantee clinical mastery. And some of the most skilled neurofeedback practitioners we know, people with decades of experience and thousands of clients, are retired nurses, teachers, and scientists who developed deep clinical intuition through years of practice, not through a specific certification pathway.

That said, clinical scope matters. The field includes three distinct roles, and the distinctions are not optional:

- **Independently licensed clinician** (psychologist, LMFT, LCSW, MD, DO, or equivalent): can assess, diagnose, and treat diagnosed mental health conditions using neurofeedback as part of a clinical practice. Full clinical scope.
- **Technician or associate** (no independent clinical license): can operate neurofeedback equipment and run sessions, but only under documented supervision by a licensed clinician when working with diagnosed conditions. BCIA certification itself requires either a health-care license or a formal supervision arrangement for clinical work.
- **Performance/wellness coach** (no clinical license, no supervision arrangement): can provide neurofeedback for non-clinical goals (focus, relaxation, peak performance) but should not assess, diagnose, or treat diagnosed mental health conditions.

An appropriate professional license, or documented legal supervision by a licensed clinician, is a non-negotiable requirement before any provider takes on clinical neurofeedback for diagnosed conditions. Skilled practitioners without independent licenses do excellent work, but they need to be operating within a supervised structure when the work involves clinical assessment and treatment. Ask about this directly. If the answer is unclear, keep looking.

Credentials are a positive signal. They're not a guarantee. The questions that matter more:

- Does this clinician adjust protocols based on what they see in your data?
- Do they notice subtle changes and communicate them to you?
- Do they monitor outcomes with objective measures?
- Do they know when something isn't working and change course?

These are clinical skills. They come from experience, mentorship, and attention.

17.6 The Provider Scorecard

Use this when evaluating any neurofeedback provider. Score each item 0 (no/absent), 1 (partial), or 2 (yes/strong). A score below 11 out of 22 should give you pause.

Question	Score (0–2)
Do they conduct a thorough intake before any assessment or training?	______
Do they use a full 19-channel QEEG with normative database comparison?	______
Is the protocol individualized based on your brain data, not just your diagnosis?	______
Do they track outcomes with standardized measures (not just "how do you feel")?	______
Do they have a reassessment schedule (re-map every 20–25 sessions)?	______
Can they clearly explain what they're training and why?	______
Do they acknowledge limitations and non-response possibilities?	______
Do they hold an independent clinical license, or work under documented supervision by a licensed clinician? (Required for clinical work with diagnosed conditions.)	______
Are they willing to coordinate with your other providers?	______

Question	Score (0–2)
Is pricing transparent with no high-pressure prepaid packages?	_____
Do they individualize frequency targets to your IAF, or use generic band definitions?	_____

Photograph this page or photocopy it and bring it to your consultation. A provider who scores well will appreciate the questions. A provider who doesn't will tell you everything you need to know.

17.7 Conversation Scripts

When calling to inquire: "I'm considering neurofeedback for [your concern]. Can you tell me: do you do a QEEG brain map before starting training? What normative database do you use? How do you decide which protocol to use for each client?"

At your first consultation: "How will we know if this is working? What metrics will you track? When will we reassess? What happens if I'm not responding after fifteen sessions?"

If you're already in training and unsure: "I've been doing [X] sessions. Can we look at the data and see whether things are changing? What would you expect to see by now, and are we on track?"

These questions aren't confrontational. They're the questions any competent clinician expects, and welcomes.

17.8 Consumer Devices vs. Clinical Neurofeedback

Consumer EEG headbands, Muse, FocusCalm, Narbis, BrainBit, Sens.ai, exist and are increasingly popular. The honest assessment:

	Consumer Devices	Clinical Neurofeedback
Electrodes	1–4 dry sensors	19-channel cap, conductive gel
Signal quality	Adequate for gross states	Research/clinical grade (see Chapter 1)
Database comparison	None or proprietary	Validated normative databases
Protocol individualization	One-size-fits-all	QEEG-guided, adjusted per session
Artifact handling	Minimal; home environment	Clinician-monitored; controlled setting
Evidence base	Minimal for clinical outcomes	Extensive (see Chapter 5)
Best use	Meditation support, curiosity	Clinical assessment and targeted training
Typical cost	$200–500 one-time	$4,000–10,000 for full course

The regulatory reality: Most consumer devices are marketed as wellness tools, not medical devices. They typically don't have FDA clearance for therapeutic claims. "FDA registered" means the company notified the FDA of their product, it doesn't mean the FDA evaluated it for efficacy.

Our recommendation: Consumer devices are entry points. If a headband gets you interested in your brain and leads you to seek proper assessment, great. If it becomes a substitute for clinical care when clinical care is what you need, that's a problem. The evidence for consumer-grade neurofeedback producing clinical-level outcomes is minimal.

17.9 What It Costs

Neurofeedback is predominantly an out-of-pocket service. Insurance coverage is patchy, some commercial insurers reimburse under biofeedback CPT codes, but many classify neurofeedback as "investigational" or "not medically necessary." Medicare changed its classification in 2023 (effective early 2024) from "experimental/investigational" to "not medically necessary," still denied but under a different rationale (ISNR CPT Update, 2025).

Typical cost ranges (U.S., as of 2026):

Service	Typical Market Range
Individual neurofeedback session	$100–250 per session
QEEG brain map (acquisition + interpretation)	$500–1,500
Full course (20–40 sessions)	$4,000–10,000

These prices vary by city, provider experience, and how much is included (some clinics bundle the initial QEEG into a package; others charge separately). Some practices, including ours at Peak Brain Institute, work to make brain mapping more accessible than the ranges above. Ask about pricing when you call.

This is real money. It deserves real results. The Provider Scorecard and conversation scripts above exist to help you spend it wisely.

17.10 What to Do With What You Know

The scorecard above tells you how to evaluate a clinician. But before that question comes a more personal one: now that you have a map of your brain, what do you do with it?

The map is not a gate. It does not decide whether you should be treated. You arrived already knowing your goals and where you are struggling. What a brain map adds is perspective on your own resources and constraints: which systems are running hot, which are running quiet, where the bottlenecks sit. That perspective helps you choose and shape what you try next.

Not every pattern on a brain map requires action. But everyone's brain is unusual in some way. When the pattern that shows up lines up with what you are actually struggling with, you have a rough working model of how things work for you. That is what the map is for.

Neurofeedback is one of several things that model can point toward. Sleep hygiene, exercise, diet, meditation, and stress load are all legitimate targets, and an EEG pattern can sometimes inform a medication conversation with a prescriber. A map that leads you to fix your sleep instead of starting training has still done its job. Because phenotypes are not diagnostic, they neither rule neurofeedback in nor rule it out. They give you information. You decide what to do with it.

Hold the model loosely. Phenotypes are not perfect. But they are yours, and they are stable, which is what makes them useful. Try something, notice how you feel, and come back to the assessment data later. That cycle of acting and reassessing is how the map stays useful over time.

Reasons to wait before acting:

- Patterns are mild and you are functioning adequately. A deviation that does not cause real-world disruption may not need real-world intervention.
- You are in a temporary stressor (a move, a loss, a work crisis) that may be driving the map. Re-test when life stabilizes.
- Medications you are currently taking may be shaping the recording. A repeat map after adjustments will be more informative than training against a pharmacological state.
- You are in a developmental period where patterns naturally shift (adolescence, perimenopause). Wait and watch.
- The cost or time commitment is a genuine barrier right now. A half-committed training course is less useful than waiting until you can do it properly.

When you wait, wait deliberately: track sleep, stress, attention, mood, and functional output over three to six months. If patterns worsen or function declines, reassess. If things stabilize on their own, you have useful information too.

Seek a second opinion when:

- The map interpretation does not match your lived experience. The clinician says "everything looks fine" but you are clearly struggling, or the reverse.
- Treatment has not produced meaningful change after a reasonable trial (twenty to thirty sessions of neurofeedback, six to eight weeks of a medication trial) without an explanation for why and a specific adjustment.
- The proposed course feels disproportionate to your symptoms: an expensive, extended program for a presentation that does not clearly warrant it.
- The clinician could not explain their reasoning clearly, or could not answer basic questions about what they are training and why.
- You want a second database comparison, since different normative systems can produce different readings from the same raw EEG.

A good second opinion reviews the raw data, not just the report, and reaches its own conclusions before seeing the first clinician's interpretation. Areas of agreement across clinicians carry higher confidence; areas of disagreement deserve further investigation before committing to a course of action.

17.11 The Remote Option

If you don't have a qualified local provider, and many people don't, remote neurofeedback exists. Cloud-based platforms allow clinicians to prescribe protocols, review data, and adjust training remotely while you do sessions at home with a portable EEG system.

The evidence for remote neurofeedback is limited but growing. It appears safe and feasible. Whether it produces the same results as in-clinic training is an open question, the data quality is typically lower, and the clinician can't observe you in real time.

If you're considering remote training, apply the same standards you'd apply to an in-person provider, plus a few remote-specific checks:

- **Verify the provider's identity and license**, including whether they are licensed in your state or jurisdiction. Telehealth licensing rules vary across state lines; confirm that the provider is authorized to deliver services where you live.
- **Confirm that data transmission is secure and encrypted.** Your brain data and clinical records should travel over encrypted connections, not emailed as open files.
- **Establish an emergency contact plan.** Know who to call if you experience an adverse reaction during or after a remote session. This is especially important if you have a seizure history, active trauma, or are managing a psychiatric condition alongside training.
- **For minors, a caregiver should be present** during remote sessions to monitor the child's response and handle any equipment issues.
- **Some presentations are better handled in person.** Active seizure disorders, acute psychiatric crises, complex trauma with dissociative features, and very young children are situations where in-person clinical observation matters more than convenience.

QEEG assessment (which may require an in-person visit or a supervised recording kit), individualized protocols, outcome tracking, and regular clinical review all still apply. Remote doesn't mean unsupervised.

Decision Point: You now know more about how to evaluate neurofeedback providers than 99% of consumers. Use it. Ask the questions. Demand the baselines. And if a provider can't answer these questions clearly, find one who can.

Your Move:

1. **Reflect:** If you've already done neurofeedback, score your provider on the scorecard. If you haven't, use it to evaluate your options before committing.

2. **Act:** Call two or three providers in your area. Use the conversation scripts. Compare their answers. The differences will be illuminating.

3. **Share:** Photograph or photocopy the Provider Scorecard and give it to someone considering neurofeedback. It's designed to be passed around.

Ch 18: When It Doesn't Work

You've read Chapter 5. You know that a meaningful minority of participants in neurofeedback studies don't show clear improvement at the group level. That finding is real, and it's honest, and if you've been training for weeks without seeing change, it probably feels personal.

Before you stop, understand this: apparent non-response is often not a fixed property of your brain. In our clinical experience, the most common explanation is a mismatch between your brain and the protocol it's being given. The wrong exercise does not produce the right change, and it doesn't matter how many sessions you do. However, this framing has not been tested in a decisive trial (see below), so we present it as a working clinical model, not an established fact.

This chapter explains why, walks you through the most common reasons training stalls, and gives you a concrete decision tree for what to do next.

18.1 The Myth of the Non-Responder

The label "non-responder" implies something fixed about the person. As if some brains can learn from neurofeedback and others simply cannot. The research literature uses this framing because it's convenient for statistics: divide participants into responders and non-responders, count the proportions, report the split.

But that framing hides an important distinction. In most studies reporting non-response rates, every participant received the same protocol. The same frequency targets, the same electrode sites, the same reward and inhibit parameters, applied to brains that were physiologically different from each other. Some of those brains had excess frontal theta. Others had high beta driving their symptoms. Others had connectivity problems that amplitude training doesn't address. Others had undiagnosed sleep disorders generating the very EEG patterns the protocol was trying to change.

Calling someone a "non-responder" after giving them a protocol that didn't match their brain conflates the person with the protocol. The problem isn't the person. The problem is the match.

Across thousands of clients, this is the clinical pattern we see: when someone isn't responding, the first question isn't whether their brain can learn. The first question is whether the training is targeting the right thing.

18.2 Why This Is Different from Missing a Skill

Chapter 3 drew a distinction that becomes essential here. HRV biofeedback is voluntary: you learn a skill, you feel the shift, and the gains depend on whether you practice it and can reach it under stress. When HRV "doesn't work," the question is usually about skill acquisition and transfer.

Neurofeedback is different. The brain learns from contingent reinforcement of its own electrical activity without you consciously trying to do anything, the same way Sterman's cats didn't decide to produce more SMR; their brains learned because the contingency was set up correctly. So when neurofeedback stalls, the question is almost never "did you get it?" It's "did we set up the contingency correctly for your brain?" The targets, the sites, the frequencies, the inhibits, the thresholds, the pacing. If any of those are wrong for your specific pattern, the brain receives a reward signal that doesn't align with anything useful. It's not that your brain can't learn. The training is asking it to learn the wrong thing, or the right thing at the wrong frequency or site.

This is why non-response in neurofeedback is a target problem. Not a skill problem, not a motivation problem, not a "your brain is broken" problem. A target problem.

18.3 What Individuation Actually Means

"Individualized neurofeedback" has become a marketing phrase. Clinics use it the way restaurants use "farm-to-table": it sounds good, but the range of what it actually means is enormous. For you, genuine individuation comes down to a few questions worth asking.

Is the protocol matched to the patterns your brain actually shows, not just to your diagnosis? Most brains present with two or three stacked patterns (Chapter 1), and the primary target should be the one driving the most dysfunction. Is it tuned to your own rhythms rather than textbook averages? Your individual alpha frequency, for instance, may not sit at the 10 Hz a generic protocol assumes, and a mismatch there is one of the most common and most fixable reasons training stalls. The same applies to SMR and beta reward bands on the motor strip. SMR is usually described as 12 to 15 Hz, but the range that works for a given person can be wider or narrower. If the reward band overshoots their natural range, training at C4 15 to 18 Hz for instance, focus may show up but so do sleep onset problems and physical activation, clients feel itchy, twitchy, or wired during training. The band is too fast. If it undershoots, say rewarding 14 to 17 when they actually need 14.5 to 17.5, you get a different kind of mistuning: low energy, weepiness, feeling more emotional than usual, and paradoxically, sleep onset difficulty as well, often with sleep maintenance issues too, more awakenings through the night. These are signs that the reward band needs tuning.

Why frequency direction matters at all comes from the arousal model, one of the foundational frameworks in neurofeedback. Sterman's SMR work established that reinforcing a specific rhythm could alter cortical excitability. Lubar extended the framework to ADHD, framing inattentive presentations as cortical underarousal, treatable by uptraining beta or SMR. The Othmers developed an explicitly arousal-indexed approach to protocol selection, progressively adjusting training frequencies based on where the client's nervous system sat on the activation spectrum. Johnstone, Gunkelman, and Lunt formalized EEG phenotypes as intermediate biomarkers carrying arousal-regulation signatures, moving protocol selection toward pattern-based assignment rather than diagnosis-based recipes.

The core idea is straightforward: cortical arousal sits on a spectrum, and the frequency you reward pushes it in a direction. SMR calms and stabilizes. Higher beta activates and sharpens. Train too fast for the person and you push arousal past their optimum. Train too slow and you pull it below where they function well. The arousal model is a simplification. The brain is a network, not a thermostat, and modern frameworks (connectivity-based neurofeedback, source-level analysis, the vigilance model) add dimensions that a single arousal axis does not capture. But as a first-order clinical heuristic for understanding why a half-hertz shift in the reward band changes what the client feels, it holds.

In our clinical practice, we work from the arousal model alongside a laterality model (left versus right hemisphere contributions to the pattern) and the triple-network model (default mode, salience, and central executive networks). These perspectives come from different parts of the training: neurodevelopmental work with children and adolescents at Laurence Hirshberg's NeuroDevelopment Center in Providence teaches you that activation level drives everything downstream. Substance use treatment and crisis psychiatric inpatient work teaches you that dysregulated brains look nothing like the textbook cases. Hemispheric specialization research in Eran Zaidel's lab at UCLA teaches you that the two hemispheres contribute differently to cognition and emotion in ways that matter for where you place electrodes. And a systems neuroscience perspective ties it together, because the brain's large-scale networks (default mode, salience, central executive) organize the regulatory stability that training is ultimately trying to build. No single framework captures the whole picture, but together they give the clinician three angles on the same brain.

The tuning signal is what happens after a session. Changes in sleep, stress, and attention from immediately post-session out to about twenty-four hours tell the clinician how a protocol is starting to shift the brain's regulatory resources. Sleep onset problems point one direction. Maintenance issues point another. A shift in stress reactivity or attentional stamina tells you whether the protocol is building the capacity it should be building. This is why telling your provider what changed matters so much, and why the daily tracking log in Chapter 4 exists. Those four ratings are the clinical feedback loop. Even changes that seem unrelated to your protocol's specific goal are informative. You came in for focus, but your sleep onset shifted. You came in for anxiety, but your attention span changed. These responses tell a skilled clinician how the brain is reorganizing its regulatory resources, and that information drives the next adjustment: a half-hertz shift in the reward band, a site change, an inhibit modification. Without your report, the clinician is flying partially blind.

This is also why understanding physiology and the QEEG matters more than following recipe books of clinical lore. People are strange. Their brains do not always behave the way the textbook says they should. A clinician who knows brains well, who reads the map in the context of the person sitting in the chair, has a much better chance of adapting protocols to what that person actually needs than one who runs the same preset for every client who walks in with the same diagnosis. And is your provider re-checking the map and adjusting as your brain changes, rather than running the same file from day one to session forty?

Generic delivery, the same protocol for everyone, misses most of this. That is a large part of why standardized-protocol studies report substantial non-response: in our view, much of that "non-response" reflects protocol mismatch rather than brain incapability, though this has not been confirmed in a head-to-head trial of individualized versus standardized protocols. The full practitioner checklist (individual frequencies, inhibit bands, threshold strategy, session-level tracking) is developed in *Peak Brain Coaching*. On your side, the questions above are enough to tell a tuned program from a generic one.

18.4 What Looks Like Non-Response in Clinical Practice

In rough order of how often we see each one:

1. Wrong target for the actual phenotype. In our clinical experience, this is the most common cause we identify. The protocol is targeting a pattern the brain doesn't primarily have. This happens when training is selected based on diagnosis rather than brain data, or when the brain map was read incorrectly, or when the provider defaulted to a familiar protocol rather than matching the specific presentation.

What this looks like: no change in any direction. Not worse, not better. The training is moving the brain, but the movement doesn't connect to the client's actual symptoms because the symptoms are driven by a different pattern.

2. Right target but wrong frequency, site, or inhibit configuration. The provider identified the correct phenotype but the execution is off. Training alpha but at a frequency that doesn't match the client's IAF. Targeting theta reduction frontally when the excess is actually midline. Rewarding SMR but forgetting to inhibit the high beta that's masking the SMR gains. Or the reward band on the motor strip is a half-hertz too wide or too narrow for the client's brain, producing the paradoxical sleep and activation signs described above.

What this looks like: partial improvement that plateaus, or improvement in one domain but not others. Focus sharpens but sleep deteriorates and the client feels wired. Or energy drops, mood gets fragile, and sleep maintenance deteriorates. The brain is learning, but the fine-tuning isn't optimized.

3. Un-addressed primary problem. The neurofeedback targets are correct, but another factor is interfering with what the training can accomplish. Untreated sleep apnea generates theta every night that the daytime training spends sessions correcting. An active thyroid condition destabilizes arousal regulation faster than training can stabilize it. Unresolved acute trauma keeps the nervous system in a state that overrides training gains between sessions.

What this looks like: initial improvement that doesn't hold between sessions. The client feels better on training days and worse by the weekend. Progress resets repeatedly.

4. Lifestyle confounders masking the signal. Active substance use (alcohol, cannabis, stimulant misuse) changes the EEG between sessions in ways that obscure training effects. Chronic sleep deprivation generates the very patterns training is trying to correct. A recent medication change shifted the EEG baseline without anyone accounting for it.

What this looks like: variable session quality, inconsistent self-reports, a sense that "it works sometimes but I can't tell." The signal is there, but the noise is louder.

5. Provider quality is low. The provider doesn't re-map. Doesn't adapt the protocol when the EEG changes. Uses generic thresholds. Doesn't check whether the frequency targets match the client's actual IAF. Doesn't track session-level learning metrics. Just runs the same file, session after session, and hopes.

What this looks like from the client's side: you show up, sit in the chair, watch the screen, go home, and nothing changes. You're told to "be patient." After thirty sessions of patience, you're told "some people just don't respond."

6. The genuine residual. A small fraction of clients, after honest individuation, intact lifestyle, competent provider, and primary problems addressed, still don't show the expected training effects. In the alpha-training literature, baseline alpha amplitude correlates modestly with learning rate (Wan et al., 2014): some brains arrive with more raw material for alpha-class training to work with. In our clinical experience, this category appears smaller than group-level data suggest, because many cases that are labeled "non-response" in standardized trials may belong in categories one through five. But we have not measured this in a controlled way, and the true size of the genuine residual remains unknown.

The order matters. The categories above are listed in the order we most often identify them clinically. Checking the earlier categories first is practical, not because the later ones are unimportant. If your training isn't producing change, it is worth checking whether the protocol matches your map before concluding that your brain can't learn.

But it is equally important to know that stopping, pausing, or seeking a referral are always legitimate options at any point, not just after exhausting every protocol variation. A decision to stop training is not a failure; it is a clinical judgment that the current approach is not serving you.

What would disprove the "non-response is a target problem" framework. The honest version of this argument is testable. If a well-designed, adequately powered RCT of expert-individuated, QEEG-guided neurofeedback (with rigorous protocol-phenotype matching verified by independent review, lifestyle factors controlled, and at least forty sessions at correct dose) still produced non-response rates comparable to standardized protocol trials, the framework would lose much of its clinical support. That trial has not been run. The residual non-response in the face of genuine individualization might be smaller than group-level data suggest, or it might not be. We do not know. The framework in this chapter is a working clinical model based on pattern recognition across thousands of cases. It is a useful guide for troubleshooting. It is not a guarantee, and it should not be presented as one to patients who have tried well-individuated training without response.

18.5 The Diagnostic Order When Training Stalls

If you're not seeing change after fifteen to twenty sessions, the following sequence gets to the answer most efficiently.

Step 1: Re-map. Get a new QEEG. Compare it to your baseline. If the EEG has shifted, the training is working. The brain has moved, which means the original protocol may no longer be targeting the right pattern. The protocol needs to follow where the brain went. A re-map after fifteen to twenty sessions is standard clinical practice, and a provider who doesn't offer one is missing the most important diagnostic information available.

Step 2: Check the protocol-phenotype match. Does the current protocol target the patterns your brain actually shows right now? The patterns the current map reveals, which may differ from intake or from what the diagnosis would predict. If there's a mismatch, change the protocol.

Step 3: Check the lifestyle and medication context. Sleep quality. Substance use. Medication changes. Caffeine timing. Exercise. Stress load. Any of these can mask or undermine training gains. A conversation about what's happening between sessions is as important as the sessions themselves.

Step 4: Consider the residual. Only after steps one through three have been honestly addressed. If the protocol matches the current map, the lifestyle context is clean, the provider is adapting the training, and the brain still isn't moving, then you may be in the group where current methods aren't sufficient. This is a limitation of the current tools. Some combinations of physiology and circumstance fall outside their reach. The alternatives in this case include trying a different protocol family (switching from amplitude training to coherence training, or from frequency training to infra-low frequency), adding peripheral biofeedback (HRV training at resonance frequency; see Chapter 16), or pausing training and addressing other priorities first.

18.6 Medication, Lifestyle, and Substance Interference

Certain substances and conditions change the EEG in predictable ways that interact with training, which is why your provider needs an honest, complete picture of what you take and when.

Medications. Several common ones leave a fingerprint on the EEG. Benzodiazepines and high-dose stimulants can work against certain protocols in real time; opioids slow the dominant rhythms; SSRIs and beta-blockers have milder effects. None of these is necessarily a reason to stop a medication or to avoid training. They are reasons your provider needs the full list, including doses and timing, so the protocol design and the expected rate of change can account for them. Never change a prescription to "help" your training without talking to the prescriber.

Sleep deprivation is the single most common training confound. It elevates theta, suppresses alpha, and degrades executive function in ways that look identical to the patterns neurofeedback is trying to change. Training a sleep-deprived brain can still produce change, and it's working against a headwind that resets every night. If your sleep is poor and your training is stalling, fix the sleep first. Chapter 13 covers this in detail.

Alcohol and cannabis both alter the EEG in ways that can interfere with training. Neither is an absolute contraindication, but both should be disclosed to your provider, and both reduce the efficiency of training.

Caffeine timing matters more than most people realize. A session after a double espresso produces a different EEG than the same session after a glass of water. Consistency matters: if you always train caffeinated, the brain learns in that state. If you alternate, the signal is noisier.

18.7 A Note on Stance

Even though neurofeedback is largely involuntary, there is a behavioral component that occasionally matters.

For protocols that target alpha or involve alpha-theta work, active cognitive effort can interfere. "Trying harder" to make the feedback respond desynchronizes the very rhythms the training is trying to strengthen. The clients who struggle with this tend to be high-achievers who approach the session like a test to ace. Their cortex engages effortful processing, and the alpha drops.

The coaching here is simple: be present, don't perform. Keep your eyes where the provider asks them (open or closed, depending on the protocol). Don't try to figure out what your brain is doing. Let it work.

For most neurofeedback protocols, stance is a minor factor at best. SMR training, beta training, coherence training, Z-score protocols: none of these depend on your psychological stance in any meaningful way. The brain learns from the contingency regardless of your attitude. The stance issue is real but narrow, and it applies primarily to alpha-class and alpha-theta protocols.

If you've been told that your "mindset" is the reason neurofeedback isn't working, be cautious. For HRV biofeedback, where the training is voluntary and skill-based, stance matters (Chapter 16 and *Half a Second More* cover this in depth). For neurofeedback, where the training is involuntary, stance is rarely the explanation. The targets, the sites, the frequencies: those are where the answer usually lives.

18.8 The Decision Tree

If your neurofeedback training isn't producing change, start here.

First, take stock. Before spending anything further, review four things: function (is daily life better, worse, or the same?), burden (what is this costing you in money, time, and energy?), adverse effects (have any new symptoms appeared or existing ones worsened?), and alternatives (what else could you be doing with these resources?). Stopping or pausing is a legitimate clinical decision at any point. No minimum session count, no re-map, no protocol switch should be required before you may rationally decide to stop. If the answer after this review is "I want to continue and troubleshoot," the steps below can help.

Have you had a re-map since starting training? If no: get one. Compare it to your baseline. This is the single most informative diagnostic step available.

Does the protocol match what the current map shows? If the map has shifted, the protocol should shift with it. If your provider isn't adjusting based on re-map data, ask why. If the answer isn't clear, consider a second opinion.

Is another factor interfering? Sleep problems, active substance use, recent medication change, untreated medical condition. If any of these are present, address them before concluding that neurofeedback isn't working.

Are you very early in the process? If you are fewer than fifteen sessions in, you may not be stalled. Some changes take time to emerge, particularly for complex presentations. That said, early is not the same as "too early to evaluate." If nothing at all is shifting, including sleep, energy, and daily function, a protocol review is reasonable at any point.

Is the provider adapting? Are they tracking learning metrics? Adjusting thresholds? Reviewing session data? Or running the same protocol on autopilot? You can tell the difference by whether the conversation changes over time or repeats the same script.

Have you considered a different provider or a different protocol family? Not all providers are equally skilled. Not all protocol families address the same things. If you've had a thorough re-map, the lifestyle context is clean, and you're still not seeing change, a second opinion from a different provider with a different approach is a reasonable next step. Chapter 17 gives you the evaluation criteria.

For clinicians wanting the detailed troubleshooting protocol, the *QEEG Field Guide* Chapter 7.7 covers re-mapping methodology, threshold recalibration, and protocol switching in clinical depth. For the peripheral biofeedback and mindfulness side of the stack, *Half a Second More* Chapter 14 covers HRV skill transfer and the voluntary-training dimension that this chapter intentionally keeps brief.

18.9 The Honest Residual

After all of the above, a small number of clients don't respond as expected. Their protocol matches their map. Their lifestyle is intact. Their provider is competent and adaptive. And the brain still doesn't move the way most brains do under the same conditions.

The research literature on this residual is thin, but it converges on a few findings. Baseline alpha amplitude correlates modestly with alpha-class learning rate (Wan et al., 2014). Putamen volume predicts neurofeedback learning success across paradigms (Zhao et al., 2021). These are real physiological constraints, but they are small-effect, population-level correlations. They are not diagnostic tools. No provider has a reliable way to tell you before training starts whether your brain will be in this group.

If you are in this group, you have not failed. The tools currently available are good but not perfect, and they will get better. The alternatives include exploring different protocol families, adding HRV biofeedback and breath-based training to the stack, working with a skilled therapist on the functional impact of the patterns that training hasn't fully shifted, and keeping sleep, exercise, and metabolic health optimized. The regulatory capacity you build through those channels is real and cumulative, even if the neurofeedback component delivered less than expected.

One more option belongs on the list alongside protocol-switching and HRV biofeedback: **acceptance and accommodation**. Some constitutional patterns are better worked with than changed. A brain that processes slowly, generates less amplitude, or sustains a particular arousal floor is not necessarily a brain in need of further intervention; it may be a brain that benefits most from matching its environment and demands to its actual wiring rather than continuing to push for a metric shift. That is a different and sometimes wiser form of optimization, not defeat.

If you tried a generic protocol and it did not work, that tells you about the protocol, not about your brain. And if you decide to stop, that is a legitimate clinical decision, not a failure of nerve or effort. The field is getting better at matching brains to protocols. The match for your brain may not have existed yet in the provider's toolbox. That's a limitation of the field, not of you.

Decision Point: If you've read this chapter and recognized your situation, the next step is concrete: ask your provider about a re-map if you haven't had one. If you have had one and the protocol hasn't changed, ask why. If the conversation doesn't satisfy you, Chapter 17 gives you the criteria for finding a second opinion. And if you're a parent whose child isn't responding, everything in this chapter applies with one addition: children's brains change faster than adults' in most cases, so the re-map cadence should be tighter.

18.9.1 Going Deeper

- For re-mapping methodology, threshold recalibration, and protocol switching, see *QEEG Field Guide* Chapter 7.7.
- For HRV skill transfer and the voluntary-training dimension, see *Half a Second More* Chapter 14.
- For provider evaluation criteria, see Chapter 17 in this book.

Your Move:

1. **Reflect:** If you've trained without clear results, which of the six categories in this chapter sounds most like your situation? The answer shapes your next conversation with your provider.
2. **Act:** If you're currently in training and haven't had a re-map in the last twenty sessions, schedule one. If your provider doesn't offer re-mapping, that tells you what you need to know.
3. **Start a conversation:** Ask your provider: "What has changed in my brain data since we started? How has the protocol adapted based on those changes?" The answer, or the lack of one, is diagnostic.

Ch 19: The Brain Optimization Stack: And Your Next Step

Neurofeedback doesn't exist in a vacuum. We see it constantly, in biohackers and in clients who've done years of clinical work: people train hard, get real results, then plateau because they're treating the brain as if it operates independently of everything else. It doesn't.

Your brain is an organ. It depends on the environment it operates in. Sleep quality, fuel, movement, stress load, and whatever other therapeutic work you're doing all determine how much neurofeedback can accomplish. Training a brain running on five hours of sleep and a caffeine drip is like doing physical therapy while still sitting in the position that caused the injury.

This chapter is about the stack: the full set of interventions that work together, in the right order, to produce the best outcomes.

19.1 The Order of Operations

Not everything has equal priority. The sequence that works, based on what we see across thousands of clients:

Sleep comes first. Sleep deprivation mimics ADHD, amplifies anxiety, deepens depression, and impairs every regulatory function your brain performs. Neurofeedback often improves sleep directly through SMR training, so you do not need perfect sleep before starting. You do need to eliminate the obvious saboteurs: caffeine after noon, screens before bed, inconsistent timing.

Exercise is next. Thirty minutes of moderate aerobic activity, three to five times per week, increases BDNF, improves cerebral blood flow, enhances sleep, reduces inflammation, and produces measurable cognitive benefits. If you are not exercising, this is the lowest-hanging fruit in the stack.

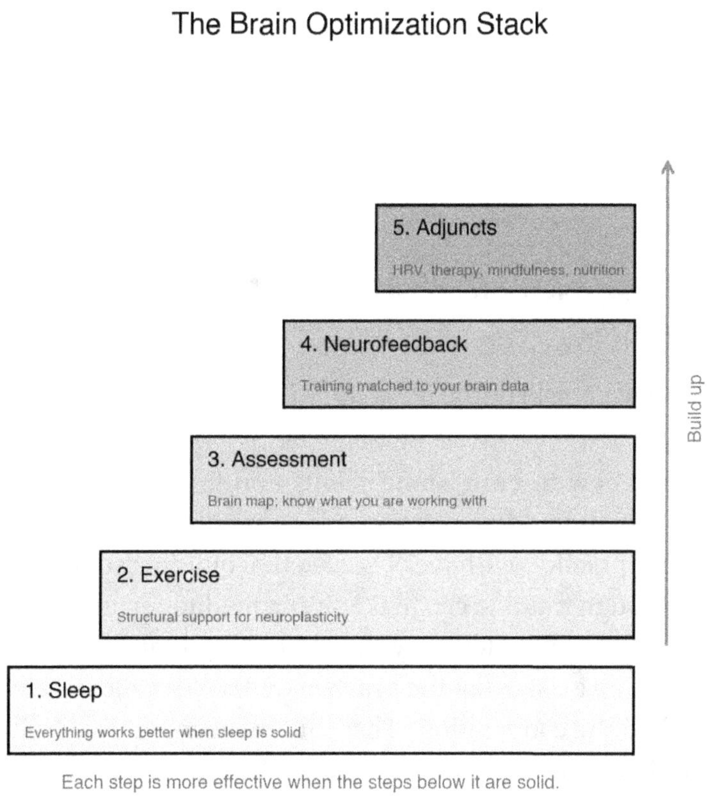

Figure 19.1: The Brain Optimization Stack

Assessment before training. Get a brain map. A QEEG shows you what your brain is doing, which regulatory dimensions need attention, and what a realistic training plan looks like for your specific pattern.

Neurofeedback training with protocols matched to your map, specific targets, and measurable progress.

Adjuncts layered as appropriate. HRV biofeedback pairs naturally with neurofeedback, training autonomic regulation from the bottom up while neurofeedback works top-down. Therapy and neurofeedback combine well; the sequencing and coordination decisions are best made between you and your clinical team. Chapter 16 covers HRV biofeedback and HEG in detail.

19.2 Pairing Neurofeedback with Meditation and Other Practices

Neurofeedback thickens the regulatory floor. Meditation sharpens the steering. The two are complementary, not redundant.

If you are new to both, some clients find it helpful to start neurofeedback first and add meditation once a regulatory foundation is in place. In our practice, we have observed that building some regulatory capacity through training can make sitting meditation more accessible. Many clients who insisted they "could not meditate" discover, once that foundation exists, that the practice was never a moral failure; the cortex lacked the cooperation. That said, no comparative trial has established that sequencing neurofeedback before meditation produces better results than the reverse order, or than starting both simultaneously. This is our practice model, not an evidence-based prescription. If you want to meditate now, there is no reason to wait.

If you already meditate, running neurofeedback alongside your sitting practice is natural. A brief daily practice between sessions functions like consolidation homework: you rehearse the qualities the training rewards.

Therapy and neurofeedback combine well. The sequencing and coordination decisions belong with you and your clinical team, not in a general consumer book. What we can say: neurofeedback is not a replacement for therapy, and therapy is not a replacement for neurofeedback. Each addresses a different layer.

Half a Second More develops the neurofeedback + meditation pairing in full clinical depth for readers who want to go further.

Nutrition and metabolic health. Your brain uses 20% of your metabolic energy. Feed it poorly and it performs poorly. The specifics matter less than the basics: stable blood sugar, adequate protein, sufficient omega-3 fatty acids, hydration, and micronutrient coverage. No supplement replaces a solid dietary foundation. Plasticity requires metabolic support. Training a brain running on caffeine and processed food still works, but the ceiling is lower.

19.3 What About Nootropics?

People ask. The honest answer: most nootropics have minimal evidence for cognitive enhancement in healthy adults. Caffeine works. Creatine has some support for cognitive function under stress and sleep deprivation. After that, the evidence thins rapidly.

If you're interested in cognitive enhancement, the interventions in this chapter, sleep, exercise, brain training, stress management, have far stronger evidence than any supplement stack. Build the foundation before spending money on pills.

19.4 Gamma: The Integration Rhythm and the Meditator's Trait

When distant patches of cortex need to agree on a single object, a flash of insight, or a stable focus, they often coordinate through fast oscillations in the gamma band, roughly 30 to 100 Hz and sometimes higher depending on how a given lab draws the borders. Gamma is easy to misread as a mood or a mystical buzzword; in systems neuroscience it is more like temporal glue. It helps binding, the process by which color, motion, and meaning snap together into one percept, or by which separate working-memory streams line up into a coherent thought. The full story includes arguments about inhibition, prediction, and cross-frequency coupling that we will not litigate here. The useful takeaway for a stack chapter is narrower: when distributed regions must integrate signals on short time scales, gamma is one of the rhythms that shows up in the conversation.

Meditation research keeps colliding with unusually strong gamma in people who have logged extraordinary practice hours. The paper everyone still cites is Lutz et al. (2004), who recorded Tibetan monks with more than ten thousand cumulative hours of meditation. During practice, and as a kind of baseline trait compared with novice controls, these practitioners showed dramatic elevations in gamma power, especially over frontoparietal territory tied to attention and executive control. The sample was small. That matters. So does how large the effect looked, which is why the finding survived twenty years of argument instead of fading into a footnote.

Trait-like persistence showed up in a different design nearly a decade later. Ferrarelli et al. (2013) reported that long-term meditators carried elevated gamma into NREM sleep, a stage not famous for the kind of voluntary control you rehearse on a cushion. If gamma shifts were only a brief state you manufacture while "trying," you might not expect them when the cortex is supposedly offline for consolidation. The sleep result nudges the interpretation toward durable changes in how cortex generates and couples fast oscillations, not only toward what happens during formal practice.

Braboszcz et al. (2017) stretched the question across traditions. Vipassana, Himalayan Yoga, and Isha Shoonya practitioners with long histories showed a similar gamma-linked phenotype compared with controls, which undercuts the idea that one exotic lineage produced a one-off quirk.

Now the caveats, and they deserve real weight. These studies are almost all small. They are cross-sectional: you cannot prove meditation caused the gamma from designs that compare people who already arranged their lives around practice with people who did not.

Self-selection is real. Committed meditators differ on sleep, diet, personality, social support, and expectancy in ways statistics only partly absorb. Scalp-recorded gamma is also notoriously artifact-prone. Eye movement, micro-saccades, and temporalis tension can inject broadband power that masquerades as neural gamma until you test aggressively. Treat the whole storyline as suggestive, not definitive.

What does that imply for neurofeedback? Most clinical protocols that earn their keep in routine practice focus on slower bands you can train with cleaner sensors and clearer reinforcement rules: sensorimotor rhythm, alpha reactivity, theta-to-beta balance, and similar targets tied to sleep, attention, and arousal regulation. Training high gamma directly is uncommon, both because of contamination risk and because large, standardized validation for "raise your gamma to fix X" mostly does not exist yet. That leaves a real gap on the map. Meditation may be one of the few repeatable behaviors that reliably pushes cortical dynamics toward the fast integration regime gamma points to, at least for some dedicated practitioners.

So the stack-level conclusion is complementary. Neurofeedback builds foundational regulatory machinery: steadier alpha when you need restful awareness, cleaner SMR when you need calm focus, less runaway default-mode chatter when rumination drives suffering. Long-form contemplative practice may sculpt the higher-order binding and metacognitive precision that gamma-heavy signatures hint at. You are not joining a cult of one technique. You are sequencing tools that touch neighboring layers of the same hierarchy.

For a fuller treatment of the meditation and gamma evidence, including how studies succeed or fail and what we think it means for practice, see Chapter 13 in *Half a Second More*.

19.5 The "Periodization" Concept

Athletes don't train the same way year-round. They periodize: build phases, peak phases, recovery phases. We find a similar phased approach useful for brain training, though no comparative trial has tested this periodization model against other scheduling approaches for healthy optimization. What follows is our practice model, offered as one reasonable framework rather than an established protocol.

Build phase (months 1-3): Establish the foundation. Sleep optimization, exercise habit, brain map, begin neurofeedback. This is where the regulatory capacity is being constructed.

Peak phase (months 3-6): Active training at full intensity. Two to three neurofeedback sessions per week, adjuncts layered in, progress tracked. This is where the biggest changes tend to happen in our experience.

Consolidation phase (months 6-12): Reduce session frequency. The gains from the peak phase are consolidating, the brain is integrating the new patterns into daily operation. Some people transition to maintenance sessions (monthly or quarterly). Others are done.

Maintenance (ongoing): Sleep, exercise, mindfulness, and periodic brain assessment. The regulatory capacity you've built needs the same maintenance as physical fitness, use it or lose it, but the foundation makes recovery faster if you slip.

19.6 Building Your Personal Protocol

Step 1: Rate your current stack honestly. Sleep (1-10), exercise (1-10), nutrition (1-10), stress management (1-10), therapeutic support (1-10). Where's the weakest link?

Step 2: Fix the weakest link first. If sleep is poor, start there: two weeks of basic sleep hygiene (consistent timing, no screens before bed, caffeine cutoff) before adding anything else. That said, neurofeedback often improves sleep directly (see Step 1 above), so "fix sleep first" means address the obvious saboteurs, not achieve perfect sleep before starting.

Step 3: Get assessed. Brain map, clinical intake, individualized plan.

Step 4: Train with clear targets and checkpoints. Protocol matched to your map. Progress reviewed every 20-25 sessions.

Step 5: Layer adjuncts based on your specific needs. Therapy if you need processing work. HRV if autonomic regulation is weak. Mindfulness if attention flexibility is the goal.

Step 6: Transition to maintenance. Reduce intensity, maintain the foundation, reassess periodically.

Then ask your neurofeedback provider: "What else should I be doing alongside training to get the best results?" A provider who thinks about the full stack will have a clear answer.

19.7 Where the Field Is Actually Going

Neurofeedback in 2026 looks nothing like neurofeedback in 1996. The next decade will change it again. We'll say what we think is coming as soberly as we can, which means naming the conditions that have to hold.

The central bet the field is making is on personalization. The work on individual alpha frequency as a treatment-matching predictor (Voetterl et al., 2023) is the leading edge of a broader shift: from standardized protocols assigned to diagnoses, toward protocols matched to quantitative brain signatures. IAF, coherence phenotyping, source-level connectivity patterns, possibly genetic and metabolic markers alongside EEG. The infrastructure for this approach already exists; the validation trials are what's missing. The next generation of RCTs, several in design or early enrollment now, will test QEEG-guided protocol selection against standardized protocols and sham. If individualization produces the effect sizes that clinical practice consistently suggests, those trials will generate the evidence that's currently absent. If they don't, the field will have to reckon with that honestly. Either way, the answer is coming, probably inside this decade.

What happens in parallel: machine learning transforms QEEG interpretation from a skill that lives in a handful of expert clinicians to something more reliably distributed. The risk is premature commercialization: black-box algorithms marketed before validation. The opportunity is that reliable, affordable brain phenotyping stops being gatekept by geography. At the same time, cloud-based remote delivery models will extend clinical reach, with the trade-off that quality control at scale is harder than quality control in the room. The best models will combine in-person assessment with remote training and consistent clinical review; the worst will dilute the intervention into a symptom app. Regulatory clarity will move slowly; the devices are Class II biofeedback instruments while the clinical claims increasingly resemble medical ones, and insurance coverage will follow trials, which puts real coverage five to ten years out for most conditions. Cost per session will fall as hardware improves and interpretation becomes more automated. Brain mapping, currently $500-$1,500, will become substantially cheaper on a timeline that's hard to predict but directionally clear.

By the mid-2030s, our expectation is that neurofeedback occupies a position similar to where physical therapy sits today: well-established for some conditions, emerging for others, integrated into multi-modal treatment plans, delivered by trained specialists, and covered by insurance for validated applications. A standard component of brain-informed healthcare, distinguished by its capacity to train the organ directly based on individualized data.

That's a maturation, not a revolution. And the work that will make it happen, or fail to, is being designed in research labs right now.

19.8 Closing

Between us, we've spent over twenty-five years looking at brains, more than 25,000 maps. What stays with us isn't the science, though the science is real. It's the quiet moments in the room.

The woman who hadn't slept in three years, sitting across from her map, seeing for the first time that her sensorimotor strip wasn't producing the stabilizing rhythm it should. The eleven-year-old who couldn't handle the cafeteria, whose parents had been told he lacked empathy, looking at data showing his empathy circuits were running overtime. The therapist who'd processed her own trauma in every way she knew how and still couldn't stop scanning the exits. Each of them, in that first moment of recognition, shifted from asking "what's wrong with me?" to asking "what is my brain doing, and what can I do about it?"

That shift is what this book is for. We wrote it to help you understand your brain, its measurable patterns, its trainable rhythms, and the genuine limitations of the evidence, which we've laid out as carefully as we can.

The field is young. The evidence base is uneven. The best sham-controlled studies don't consistently show what practitioners see in their offices, and we've been direct about why that gap exists and what it means. Some of our explanations will hold up. Some may not. The trials that will resolve the biggest open questions are being designed now, and we'll read those results with the same rigor we've asked you to bring to every claim in this book.

What we can say with confidence: your brain produces measurable electrical patterns. Those patterns shape how you think, feel, sleep, focus, and recover. They can be recorded, compared to what's expected, and trained through operant conditioning. The mechanism is real. The results, when the work is done well, are consistent enough across thousands of clients that we've staked our professional lives on them. And the regulatory capacity that training builds, because it targets circuits you use every day, appears to persist differently from interventions that require ongoing administration, though long-term controlled follow-up data remain limited and the question of whether maintenance sessions are needed is unresolved for most conditions.

We don't claim certainty where certainty doesn't exist. We claim that this is a serious intervention with a real mechanism, a complicated evidence base, and clinical results that warrant informed use and continued investigation.

The best version of this field isn't one where neurofeedback replaces therapy or medication. It's one where a quantitative picture of the brain is a standard part of understanding yourself, the same way a blood panel is part of understanding your body. Where treatment decisions are informed by data, not just diagnoses. Where the conversation between you and your clinician starts with what your brain is actually doing, not just what your symptoms are called.

We're not there yet. But every brain map that gets read, every protocol that gets matched to the individual rather than the label, every clinician who tracks outcomes with real data, moves the field closer.

Your brain has a pattern. But you can understand it, and understanding is the foundation that makes every subsequent decision, about training, about therapy, about how you structure your sleep and your days, informed rather than hopeful.

That's what we set out to give you. Not certainty. Clarity.

19.8.1 Going Deeper

- For the long game of self-regulation, see *Half a Second More* Chapter 18.
- For the meditation-gamma evidence, see *Half a Second More* Chapter 13.
- For character archetypes as an emotional framework for your optimization priorities, see *Gifted and Tortured*.

Your Final Move:

1. **Decide:** Based on everything you've read, is neurofeedback something you want to explore? If yes, what's your first step? Write it down. Put a date on it.

2. **Share:** If this book changed how you think about your brain, share it with someone who needs the same perspective, a friend considering neurofeedback, a parent searching for answers, a therapist looking for better tools.

3. **Stay with it:** This book is a starting point. Your brain changes. The science changes. The best clinicians we know are still learning. Stay curious, stay skeptical, and revisit your brain data as your life evolves.

Before You Go: Your Reader Kit

You read the book. Here is the part you can put to work before your first appointment.

A free **Neurofeedback: Explained Reader Kit** goes with these pages:

- **Full-color QEEG plates** for anxiety, ADHD, trauma, sleep, and the other patterns discussed in this book
- The **Questions to Ask Any Neurofeedback Clinic** printable
- The **Provider Scorecard** for comparing clinics side by side
- A **living bibliography** of the key trials and reviews, kept current

It is free. First name and email, nothing else, and you can unsubscribe at any time. Your email is used only to deliver the kit and occasional book-related updates; it is not sold or shared. If you prefer not to provide an email, the core resources, the Provider Scorecard, the conversation scripts, and the Evidence Lens, are described in the chapters of this book (Chapters 5 and 17).

Scan with your phone's camera

or visit **peakbrainpress.com/nfb-bonus**

Appendix A: Glossary

Alpha gating: The brain's use of alpha oscillations to actively suppress cortical regions not needed for the current task, functioning as a sensory filter that determines what information gets processed and what gets blocked.

Alpha waves (8-12 Hz): Brain oscillations associated with relaxed wakefulness and active inhibition of task-irrelevant processing. Your brain's "idle" rhythm and noise-cancellation system.

Amplitude: The height of a brain wave at a given frequency, measured in microvolts. Higher amplitude means more neurons are producing synchronized postsynaptic potentials at that frequency. Amplitude is not the same as power: power is amplitude squared within a frequency band, the measure most normative databases report. When your clinician says a band is "high," ask whether they mean high amplitude or high power, because the scales differ.

Artifact: Contamination of the EEG signal by non-brain sources: eye blinks, muscle tension, movement, electrical interference. Artifact rejection is critical for accurate brain mapping.

BCIA (Biofeedback Certification International Alliance): The primary credentialing body for neurofeedback practitioners. BCN = Board Certified in Neurofeedback.

Beta waves (13-30 Hz): Brain oscillations associated with active, focused cognitive processing. The brain's "on" signal.

Coherence: A measure of how synchronized two brain regions are at a given frequency. Reflects functional connectivity between areas.

Constitutional phenotype: A QEEG pattern that is largely heritable and stable across the lifespan, such as individual alpha frequency. Constitutional patterns are managed rather than fundamentally changed through training.

Cross-frequency coupling: The interaction between different brain rhythm frequencies, where slow oscillations organize the timing of faster oscillations. Theta-gamma coupling during memory encoding is the best-studied example.

Delta waves (0.5-4 Hz): The slowest brain waves, dominant during deep sleep. Excess waking delta may indicate head injury, medication effects, or severe fatigue.

EEG (Electroencephalography): Recording of the brain's electrical activity from electrodes placed on the scalp. The signal primarily reflects summed postsynaptic potentials from large populations of cortical neurons, not individual action potentials.

Gamma waves (30-100+ Hz): The fastest brain oscillations, associated with information binding, perceptual integration, and higher-order cognitive processing. Elevated baseline gamma has been observed in long-term meditators.

High beta (20-30+ Hz): Fast brain activity often associated with rumination, anxiety, and hyperarousal when elevated at rest.

ILF (Infra-Low Frequency): Neurofeedback training at very slow frequencies below 0.5 Hz. Associated with the Othmer method.

Individual alpha frequency (IAF): The specific frequency at which a person's alpha rhythm peaks, typically between 8 and 12 Hz. Roughly 80 percent heritable. Training protocols should be individualized to IAF rather than using generic band definitions.

LORETA/sLORETA: Mathematical methods for estimating deep brain sources from surface EEG data. Enables "3D" neurofeedback targeting.

Normative database: A statistical model of expected EEG patterns for each age, built from recordings of healthy individuals. The basis for Z-score comparisons.

Operant conditioning: Learning through reinforcement: behavior (or brain activity) that's rewarded becomes more frequent. The core mechanism of neurofeedback.

P300: An event-related potential (ERP) peaking approximately 300 milliseconds after a novel or task-relevant stimulus. Measured during an active oddball paradigm, not during a standard resting QEEG recording. Latency increases with age and serves as a marker of cognitive processing speed.

Phase: The timing relationship between oscillations at two brain sites. Reflects coordination of processing across regions.

Phenotype (QEEG): A recurring, recognizable configuration of brain electrical activity observed across many individuals. Roughly thirty phenotypes are described in clinical practice; most brains present with two or three simultaneously. The phenotype framework used in this book is an author-developed and clinic-derived heuristic, not a validated diagnostic taxonomy. It is a probabilistic description, useful for guiding clinical hypotheses, not a diagnosis.

QEEG (Quantitative EEG): EEG data that has been mathematically processed, including spectral analysis, coherence computation, and other statistical transformations. Comparison against a normative database is the most common clinical application and the basis of the "brain map" discussed in this book, but quantitative EEG more broadly refers to any mathematical analysis of the raw EEG signal.

Regulatory phenotype: A QEEG pattern that is substantially state-dependent and responsive to training, such as frontal theta excess or resting high beta. Regulatory patterns are the primary targets of neurofeedback.

Resonance frequency: The individualized breathing rate (typically 4.5 to 6.5 breaths per minute) that maximizes heart rate variability amplitude and baroreflex sensitivity during HRV biofeedback. Varies from person to person.

SCP (Slow Cortical Potential): Very slow brain voltage shifts that reflect cortical readiness states. Trained in some ADHD and epilepsy protocols.

SMR (Sensorimotor Rhythm, 12-15 Hz): A rhythm over the sensorimotor cortex reflecting stable, inhibited motor readiness. Shares generators with sleep spindles. The foundational neurofeedback protocol.

Sleep spindles (sigma rhythm): Brief 12-15 Hz bursts during N2 sleep that protect sleep continuity and support memory consolidation. The nighttime version of SMR.

Theta waves (4-8 Hz): Brain oscillations associated with drowsiness, daydreaming, and internal processing. Excess frontal theta is associated with underactivation.

Theta-beta ratio (TBR): Theta power divided by beta power. Once considered an ADHD biomarker, now understood as a non-specific arousal index confounded by sleep deprivation.

Vagal tone: A measure of parasympathetic nervous system function, indexed by heart rate variability. Higher vagal tone reflects more flexible autonomic regulation and better stress recovery capacity.

Z-score: A statistical measure of how far a value deviates from the mean of a normative database. A Z-score of 2.0 means two standard deviations from expected.

Appendix B: Provider-Finding Guide + Clinician Tools

The information in this appendix is educational and does not constitute medical advice. Selection and oversight of a neurofeedback program requires professional clinical judgment. Consult a licensed, qualified clinician before pursuing assessment or training.

For Consumers: Finding a Qualified Provider

Step 1: Search for QEEG and neurofeedback providers in your area. Resources:

- Peak Brain Institute: www.PeakBrainInstitute.com (the authors' practice, with locations in Los Angeles and remote services available)
- Neurofeedback.space directory: neurofeedback.space (searchable by location, specialization, and remote availability)
- BCIA practitioner directory: bcia.org
- ISNR member directory: isnr.org
- Ask your therapist, psychiatrist, or primary care doctor for referrals

Step 2: Use the Provider Scorecard from Chapter 17 to evaluate each option. Call at least two providers and use the conversation scripts.

Step 3: Schedule a consultation (not a sales pitch). A good provider will want to understand your situation before recommending anything.

Questions to Ask Before Your First Session:

- Do you do a QEEG brain map before starting training?
- What normative database do you use?

- How do you choose protocols: based on my brain data or based on my diagnosis?
- How many sessions do you typically recommend, and when do you reassess?
- What happens if I'm not responding?
- What are your credentials and training background?
- Do you coordinate with other providers (my therapist, my doctor)?

For Clinicians: Collaboration Framework

When to consider a neurofeedback referral for your client:

- Symptoms persist despite adequate therapy and/or medication
- Client is interested in non-medication or adjunctive approaches
- Sleep, attention, or arousal regulation issues are central to the presentation
- You want objective brain data to inform treatment planning
- Trauma client needs nervous system stabilization before or alongside processing work

How to frame it to your client: "A brain map can show us what's happening at the neurological level, not a diagnosis, but a picture of your brain's patterns that might explain what we're seeing in our work together. It's like getting a blood panel for your brain."

How to collaborate with a neurofeedback provider:

- Share relevant clinical history (with client consent)
- Ask the provider for a summary of the QEEG findings and protocol plan
- Coordinate timing: neurofeedback for stabilization may enhance your therapeutic work
- Request progress updates at regular intervals
- Discuss together when the client may be ready for deeper processing or when training should end

Downloadable resources (companion site):

- "How to Read Your Client's Brain Map Together" one-pager

- "Questions Your Client Should Ask Any Neurofeedback Clinic" printable
- Referral letter template

Online plates: Full-color QEEG brain map examples for anxiety, ADHD, trauma, sleep, and other common patterns are available at neurofeedbackexplained.com/plates.

Appendix C: Research Summary by Condition

Condition	Level	Best Available Evidence	Key Finding
ADHD (children)	Level 1 (neg.)	JAMA Psychiatry 2025 meta-analysis; Arnold 2021 double-blind RCT	NF does not outperform sham at group level; both groups improve. Individualized QEEG-guided protocols may produce different results.
ADHD (adults)	Level 2	Barth et al., 2021 SCP/fNIRS RCT; JAMA 2025	Small, inconsistent effects vs. active controls.
Anxiety (generalized)	Level 2–3	Russo et al., 2022 meta-analysis (26 studies)	Large within-group effects ($g \approx 0.87$) but mostly weak controls. Few sham-controlled trials.
Depression	Level 2–3	Barlas, 2021 meta-analysis; 2024 fMRI NF studies	Large pre-post effects, limited sham-controlled data. fMRI connectivity NF shows specific effects for rumination.
PTSD	Level 2	Voigt et al., 2024; Askovic et al., 2023	Large effects that shrink with better controls. VA/DoD: "insufficient evidence to recommend for or against."
Substance use	Level 2–3	Wan et al., 2026 meta-analysis ($g \approx 0.85$)	Significant symptom reduction across RCTs, stronger for substance than behavioral addictions. Variable controls.

Condition	Level	Best Available Evidence	Key Finding
Insomnia	Level 1 (neg.)	2024 RCT meta-analysis; Schabus 2017	Controls outperformed NF on PSQI. NF is not a proven primary insomnia treatment. Sleep often improves as secondary gain.
Epilepsy	Level 1	Tan et al., 2009 meta-analysis (10 studies); Sterman SMR studies	The strongest evidence base in neurofeedback. Across the pooled studies, 74% of patients reported fewer weekly seizures, all of them medication-refractory cases. SMR training raises seizure thresholds. No modern sham-controlled meta-analysis has revisited this. An adjunct, never a substitute for neurology and antiseizure care.
Autism spectrum	Level 3–4	Rezaee et al., 2025; 2018 Mente RCT	83% of studies report positive cognitive effects. Small samples, variable controls.
TBI / concussion	Level 3–4	Case data, small trials	Supportive but no NF-specific meta-analysis.
Peak performance	Level 3	Treves et al., 2025 (consumer NF + mindfulness meta-analysis)	Small reduction in distress ($k=11$, $g=-0.16$). No significant cognitive effect. Authors conclude consumer device claims are "not currently supported"; effects may reflect "neurosuggestion."
Chronic pain	Level 3	Patel et al., 2020 systematic review	Small-moderate effects, high heterogeneity, limited sham control.

Evidence levels follow standard evidence-based medicine framework: Level 1 = replicated RCTs + high-quality meta-analysis; Level 1 (negative) = Level

1 evidence that goes against neurofeedback for this condition; Level 2 = consistent RCTs but not definitive; Level 3 = emerging/inconsistent; Level 4 = case data only. This is the book's own shorthand. It is not the AAPB/ISNR efficacy scale, which numbers in the opposite direction, where Level 1 means not empirically supported and Level 5 is the highest tier.

Appendix D: Consumer Device Comparison

Device	Type	Ch.	Use	Clin.	Evidence
Clinical EEG systems (BrainMaster, Deymed, Mitsar, etc.)	Medical	19–32+	Full QEEG + NF	Yes	Extensive
Muse / Muse S	Headband	4+PPG	Meditation, attention	No	Small; 2025 meta
FocusCalm	Headband	4	Attention, calm	No	Minimal
Narbis	Glasses	3	Attention	No	Minimal
Sens.ai	Headset	EEG + PBM	NF + PBM	No	Limited
BrainBit	Headband	4	General EEG	No	HW only
Mendi (fNIRS)	Headband	1–3	Prefrontal blood flow	Hemo NF	Small
Dreem (disc. DTC 2021; now Beacon/clinical)	Headband	6+accel	Sleep stim	Not NF	Not NF
Oura Ring (PPG only)	Ring	0 EEG	Sleep tracking	No	PSG-validated

Key distinctions:

- Clinical systems record from 19+ sites with medical-grade amplification and artifact handling. Consumer devices use 2-6 sensors with lower signal quality.

- "FDA registered" (consumer devices) ≠ "FDA cleared for therapy" (clinical devices).
- Consumer devices are wellness tools. Clinical systems are assessment and training instruments.
- No consumer wellness device has been shown in RCTs to produce clinical-level outcomes for ADHD, anxiety, depression, or insomnia. (Note: the Mente Autism device, a clinical / prescription home-use system with a sham-controlled RCT, is not a consumer wellness headband; see Chapter 11 for that evidence.)

This comparison reflects the field as of early 2026. Device availability, pricing, and regulatory status change; see the companion site for updated information.

Appendix E: Recommended Reading

For Consumers

- **A Symphony in the Brain** by Jim Robbins (2000). The origin stories of neurofeedback. Dated but still the best narrative history.
- **The Body Keeps the Score** by Bessel van der Kolk (2014). The book that put neurofeedback on the mainstream radar. Chapter on NF and trauma is essential.
- **Outlive** by Peter Attia (2023). A longevity book. The best available model for thinking about brain health within a broader framework.

For Clinicians

- **Neurofeedback in the Treatment of Developmental Trauma** by Sebern Fisher (2014). The clinical case for neurofeedback in complex trauma.
- **Neurofeedback: The First Fifty Years** by James R. Evans, Mary E. Dellinger & Michael Russell, eds. (2019). The definitive insider history and survey of the field.
- **The QEEG Field Guide** by Andrew Hill & Jonathon Lomeli (2026). The clinical assessment manual for the QEEG methodology this book teaches consumers to understand.

For the Science-Curious

- **Gifted & Tortured** by Andrew Hill (2026). Brain phenotypes in neurodivergence. The companion book that explains the "what" of brain patterns.
- **ADHD Nation** by Alan Schwarz (2016). The pharmaceutical and cultural history of ADHD, essential context for understanding why neurofeedback faces structural headwinds.

Key Research Papers

See Appendix C for condition-specific evidence summaries. The companion site maintains an updated bibliography with links to key meta-analyses and systematic reviews.

Appendix F: Methods (The 25,000-Map Clinical Archive)

Throughout this book, we reference patterns observed across over 25,000 quantitative EEG brain maps. Here's what that number means, and what it doesn't.

The Dataset

These maps come from Peak Brain Institute, the neurofeedback practice founded by Andrew Hill, PhD. They represent clients assessed between approximately 2012 and 2026 (fourteen years of clinical operations at Peak Brain Institute), recorded using 19-channel clinical EEG systems, processed through clinical QEEG analysis software, and compared against established age-matched normative databases validated for clinical use.

The Population

This is a **referral population**, not a random sample. The people who come to Peak Brain are seeking assessment because something isn't working: attention, anxiety, sleep, performance, trauma recovery, cognitive concerns. The most common presentations, in rough order of frequency, are ADHD and attention concerns, anxiety and stress, sleep disruption, trauma and PTSD, performance optimization, and cognitive aging. Less common presentations include autism spectrum and other neurological or medical concerns.

This means the patterns we describe are patterns observed in people who sought help. They may not generalize to the broader population. We are explicit about this limitation throughout the book.

Data Quality Standards

Every map in the dataset meets specific quality criteria:

- **Artifact rejection:** Segments contaminated by eye blinks, muscle tension, movement, or electrical noise are removed before statistical comparison, using visual review by a trained technician. Epochs that do not meet clean-data standards are excluded prior to normative comparison.
- **Recording standards:** All recordings follow a 10-minute eyes-open and 10-minute eyes-closed protocol, with electrode impedance maintained below 5 kΩ per site and a controlled recording environment.
- **Normative comparison:** Data compared against established age-matched normative databases with Z-score computation.
- **Clinical integration:** QEEG findings are always interpreted alongside clinical history, medications, sleep status, and presenting concerns, never in isolation

What We Track

- Absolute and relative power across standard frequency bands
- Coherence and phase relationships between electrode sites
- Frontal alpha asymmetry
- Individual alpha frequency
- Z-score deviations from normative databases
- Pre/post training comparisons at reassessment intervals

What We Don't Track (and Why That Matters)

- We don't have systematic outcome data linked to every map in a publishable research database. Clinical observations are based on patterns seen across cases, not on a formal research protocol with pre-registered hypotheses and independent outcome assessment.
- We don't control for placebo, expectancy, or non-specific treatment factors in our clinical work. This is a practice, not a trial.
- We don't have long-term follow-up data on most clients beyond the training period.

These limitations are real and we don't minimize them. The patterns described in this book are clinical observations from a large, consistent dataset, not controlled research findings. Where we cite published research, we cite it. Where we're sharing clinical observation, we say so explicitly.

Why This Matters

Transparency about method is what separates authority from assertion. We want you to know exactly how the observations in this book were generated, what the strengths of that method are, and where the limitations lie. You deserve to evaluate our credibility the same way we've taught you to evaluate anyone else's.

Appendix G: Consumer Phenotype Atlas

This appendix is a consumer-readable reference for twenty QEEG patterns you will hear about often in neurofeedback practice. It is not a shortcut to self-diagnosis. It is a translation layer between technical reports and lived experience. Each entry tells you what the pattern is in plain language, what it can feel like from the inside, which diagnoses and presentations it commonly keeps company with, what kinds of training plans clinicians typically discuss when the pattern is real and well recorded, and whether we usually treat it as primarily **regulatory** (more responsive to training and state change) or **constitutional** (more stable, more about management and skill than expecting the map to "normalize").

A phenotype is not a diagnosis. Chapter 1 explains why at length: a QEEG phenotype is a measured, reproducible feature of your brain, not a symptom category. It cannot tell you what condition you have. What it can do is show you which resources your brain is running and where the regulatory bottlenecks sit, so that you and your clinician can choose interventions that match your neurology rather than your label. If you catch yourself reading an entry below and thinking "that's my diagnosis," stop and reread this paragraph.

A note on phenotype counts across this portfolio. Chapter 1 references roughly thirty to thirty-five recurring QEEG phenotypes identifiable by a skilled clinician. The *QEEG Field Guide* documents thirty-one individual phenotypes and ten composite signatures at full clinical depth. This appendix covers twenty of those, selected for consumer relevance. The counts are consistent; they describe the same underlying taxonomy at different levels of coverage. The twenty patterns here are the ones a general consumer is most likely to encounter in clinical practice or to recognize from lived experience.

A note on Tortured Character cross-references. Each entry below includes a "Tortured Character" cross-reference pointing to the closest character archetype in *Gifted and Tortured*. The character names in that book and the phenotype names in this appendix were developed on parallel tracks; not every appendix label has a one-to-one character counterpart. Where the match is approximate rather than exact, the cross-reference names the closest functional parallel rather than an identical label. For precise character-to-phenotype mapping, see the full concordance in *QEEG Field Guide* Appendix G.

The regulatory-or-constitutional distinction comes with a humility clause. Brains learn. Trauma resolves. Sleep improves. Medications change. A label that looks fixed at twenty-two may soften at forty-two. The categories are heuristics for expectations and pacing, not moral judgments about how changeable you are.

For clinical-depth treatment of all thirty-one individual phenotypes and ten composite signatures in the Field Guide taxonomy, including normative comparison rules and detection logic as implemented in specialized software, see *QEEG Field Guide* Chapter 6. A full cross-book name-mapping table, linking clinical names, consumer names, taxonomy codes, and *Gifted and Tortured* character archetypes, appears in *QEEG Field Guide* Appendix G. This appendix deliberately avoids specific Z-score cutoffs, narrow Hz band edges, and citation blocks that vary by vendor and age norm, because those details age poorly and invite false precision. When your clinician quotes numbers, ask which database, which montage, and whether the recording was alert and artifact-controlled.

A quick recording checklist (so the map matches your life)

If you are about to be recorded, treat the day like a mild experiment. Sleep is not optional the night before if the question is attention or seizure-adjacent temporal instability. Caffeine is a variable. If you always drink coffee, say so, and keep it consistent across visits if you will compare maps. Medications matter: stimulants, benzodiazepines, anticonvulsants, sedating antihistamines, and cannabis can all repaint power and peak frequency. For the cleanest baseline, stimulants and modafinil are ideally washed out before the recording. In practice that means skipping one day of medication: take your normal dose the day before that, skip the day before the recording, and resume right after. Your prescribing physician needs to agree to this; the decision belongs to them, not your neurofeedback provider. Do not change other prescriptions for EEG day without medical guidance. Bring a list with doses and timing.

During the session, tension is data. If you are white-knuckling the chair, jaw clenched, trying to "do well," say it out loud. Technicians can pause, reset, coach breathing, or mark epochs later as suspect. Eyes-closed segments are "alert rest" (unless the clinical question involves sleep). If you drift, the map may inherit drowsiness that looks like ADHD, depression, or temporal slowing on paper.

Afterward, ask for plain-language anchors: which findings replicated across visits, which were probably state, and which should trigger a medical referral rather than a training plan. The twenty patterns below are common conversational shortcuts in neurofeedback offices. They are not the only patterns that exist, and they are not automatic orders for protocols.

Real humans routinely stack patterns. Anxiety plus ADHD often pairs hyperarousal markers with underactivation markers depending on site and band. Trauma histories may show deficient posterior alpha alongside frontal asymmetry. Post-concussion maps may mix coherence disruption with focal slowing. A good report names the *primary* regulatory bottleneck for the season you are in, not every color on the page at equal volume. If your printout looks like a Christmas tree, ask for a prioritized story: what to treat first, what to monitor, and what might resolve indirectly when sleep or medications change.

Frontal Theta Excess (the underaroused brain)

What it is: At rest, slow "theta" activity over the frontal midline and lateral prefrontal leads is higher than expected for your age. In plain language, the executive cockpit is drifting toward the slow rhythms you would expect when vigilance drops or when frontal networks are underpowered for the job you are asking them to do. The same topography can show up in drowsy recordings, so experienced readers cross-check alertness signs and compare eyes-open and eyes-closed segments before they treat the map as a trait portrait.

What it feels like: You may live behind a thin veil of fog: words arrive late, follow-through frays, and starting tasks feels heavier than it "should." Frustration stacks up because effort does not reliably convert into momentum. Some people describe this as sleepy inattention; others feel irritable rather than sleepy, as if the brain keeps stalling when you try to engage gear. You might compensate with last-minute panic, caffeine, or endless list-making, then crash when the adrenaline drops.

Common conditions:

- ADHD, especially inattentive and combined presentations
- Executive dysfunction after stress, sleep debt, or mood disruption
- Traumatic brain injury and post-concussive syndromes when slowing is frontal-weighted
- Age-related change in frontal regulation (only interpreted with solid age norms and clinical context)

Typical protocols: Clinical practice often targets frontal midline sites with training that discourages slow theta during active states and rewards faster "working" rhythms in the low beta range, sometimes paired with central protocols when motor control or sleep onset is also part of the picture (Arns, de Ridder, Strehl, Breteler, & Coenen, 2009; Arns, Heinrich, & Strehl, 2014). If your recording was sleepy, the plan should address sleep and recording quality before anyone commits you to months of training aimed at a drowsiness artifact. We also watch whether theta drops when you engage a simple cognitive task; if it does, the story may be less about a broken idle state and more about context-dependent regulation that training can target with clearer behavioral hooks.

Regulatory or constitutional: Mixed. Sleep, medications, and alertness move this pattern meaningfully, which is encouraging for training. A persistent baseline can still look stubborn across months, which is why clinicians emphasize behavior, sleep, and sometimes medication collaboration alongside neurofeedback.

Tortured Character: The Fog; The Stabilizer

Frontal Alpha Excess (the alpha ADHD pattern)

What it is: Alpha activity normally dominates the posterior scalp at rest; when it migrates prominently into the frontal regions, the executive cortex is idling rather than holding alert engagement. This pattern, sometimes called the ADHD alpha subtype in research traditions going back to Clarke and Chabot, sits in a distinct neighborhood from frontal theta excess: the mechanism is different, the felt sense is different, and, critically, the training approach is not the same. The frontal lobes need activation, but reaching there by suppressing frontal alpha directly turns out to be the wrong lever for many people with this map.

What it feels like: Inattention that feels passive and drifty rather than effortful and foggy. You may slide away from tasks gently, a soft disconnection rather than a slog through resistance. Affective flatness often rides alongside the attention drift: disengaged rather than depressed. Some people describe it as living behind a pleasant haze that becomes inconvenient when demands require sustained focus.

Common conditions:

- ADHD presentations where stimulant response is inconsistent or muted
- Affective disorders blended with attention complaints
- Overlap with depressive hypoarousal

Typical protocols: The counterintuitive lesson from clinical experience is to avoid directly suppressing frontal alpha, which is repeatedly reported as ineffective or destabilizing for this subtype. The more reliable strategy supports posterior alpha while rewarding frontal engagement in the faster bands, a two-site approach that addresses the gradient rather than attacking one region. If neurofeedback made you feel worse in a previous course of training, bring that history to your current clinician and ask whether the protocol matched your subtype or defaulted to the more common theta recipe. They are not interchangeable. For clinical-depth detail, see *QEEG Field Guide* Chapter 6.

Regulatory or constitutional: Mixed: the frontal alpha distribution has trait-like character in many people, though functional and medication changes can shift the picture.

Tortured Character: The Floater

Global High Beta Excess (the hyperaroused brain)

What it is: Fast "high beta" activity is elevated broadly across the scalp, not just at one tense muscle group under a single electrode. Conceptually, the cortex is running with the gain turned up: more fast-looking activity than is typical for quiet rest. This pattern is one of the easiest to fake with jaw tension, frown muscle bracing, or a cold, uncomfortable room. Frontalis and temporalis EMG peaks in the same 20-30 Hz range as cortical high beta, and on a color map the two are indistinguishable (see the EMG caveat in Chapter 1). Serious clinicians scrutinize the raw EEG waveform and check artifact channels before they narrate your personality from a red topo map. When the elevation is genuine and stable across visits, it often tracks people who describe their nervous system as "always on," even in safe settings.

What it feels like: The mind hums. You may live in pre-worry, body tension, shallow breathing, or the feeling that you never quite downshift after the day is done. Sleep may look like exhaustion without restoration, because the nervous system never fully hands the shift lever to parasympathetic calm. You might notice bruxism, jaw pain, or chronic shoulder armor that mirrors what the electrodes pick up.

Common conditions:

- Generalized anxiety, panic, and hypervigilant PTSD presentations
- Insomnia with a "tired but wired" profile
- Chronic stress and somatic anxiety

- Medication and substance effects that raise fast activity (caffeine, stimulants) before you call the pattern purely trait-like

Typical protocols: Many clinicians prioritize calming central rhythms in the SMR range while placing limits on high-beta runaway, or use posterior alpha support when the map and symptoms suggest the brain forgot how to idle (Arns & Kenemans, 2014). If muscle artifact drives the "global" picture, training plans should not pretend to treat a mythic anxiety brain while ignoring the jaw. Heart rate variability work, paced breathing, and sleep compression protocols sometimes move this phenotype as much as early neurofeedback sessions, especially when hyperarousal is driven by lifestyle rather than a single cortical knob.

Regulatory or constitutional: Mostly regulatory in the sense that state, stress, and skills training move it, but people differ in how low their high beta will go. Some nervous systems have a high floor set by genetics and early experience.

Tortured Character: The Grumpy; The Lifeguard

Frontal High Beta (the worried forehead)

What it is: Fast activity concentrated at the frontal sites, the planning, self-monitoring, and worry circuitry, rather than distributed across the whole scalp. This makes it a distinct presentation from global high beta excess: the engine is revving specifically in the regions responsible for problem-solving, self-criticism, and error-checking. The pattern shows up in clinical practice alongside perfectionism, checking behaviors, and the specific brand of anxiety that lives in the head rather than the body.

What it feels like: The mind races through problems rather than through sensations. Bedtime mind-racing is a signature complaint: the body is tired, the cortex is still running meetings. You may catch yourself rehearsing arguments, planning contingencies, or critiquing your performance from earlier in the day when you would rather be sleeping. OCD-adjacent features are common: not necessarily rituals, but mental repetition, doubt loops, and difficulty letting a thought rest before it is resolved.

Common conditions:

- Anxiety where worry is the dominant feature rather than physical tension or panic
- OCD and OCD-spectrum presentations
- Perfectionism and cognitive overcontrol
- ADHD excess-beta presentations, sometimes mislabeled as straight inattention because the fast-brain component looks like focus from the outside

Typical protocols: Training aimed at calming frontal fast activity, often combined with rewards for a counter-rhythm in the sensorimotor range that provides an alternative to the rumination loop. Late-day or high-dose stimulants can amplify this pattern in people who already carry frontal fast activity as their stress signature; that conversation belongs with your prescriber. Cognitive approaches targeting worry and rumination complement the neurofeedback well. For clinical-depth detail, see *QEEG Field Guide* Chapter 6.

Regulatory or constitutional: Predominantly regulatory: modifiable with appropriate training and lifestyle.

Tortured Character: The Ruminator

Low-Voltage Fast (the brain running on fumes)

What it is: Overall EEG amplitude is low across the head, while the remaining signal leans "fast." Think of a stereo turned down but still bright in the treble. Clinicians who use phenotype language often separate this from "everything is low" patterns that are purely about sedation or poor electrode contact, which is why assessment quality matters so much. Technicians verify impedances, check for bridging between electrodes, and compare the session to known-good hardware before they stamp someone with a constitutional LVF story. Families sometimes hear this pattern described as a reason to be cautious with stimulants in ADHD; that conversation belongs with your prescriber, not a forum thread, because clinical decisions need your full history and safety monitoring.

What it feels like: You might report a thin, brittle focus: mentally revved and depleted at the same time. Some people call it wired-but-tired. Tasks can feel effortful in a slippery way, as if the brain refuses to thicken its signal when you need stable attention. You may notice that stimulants or intense focus hacks help briefly, then leave you more frayed.

Common conditions:

- Chronic anxiety and hyperarousal burnout
- Substance histories that reshape cortical excitability (interpretation belongs with a qualified clinician)
- ADHD presentations where stimulant response is unpredictable or paradoxical in some phenotype-informed frameworks (Arns, Gunkelman, Breteler, & Spronk, 2008)
- Overlap with insomnia and stress-dysregulated autonomic tone

Typical protocols: Because pushing fast rhythms even harder can backfire, many experienced clinicians favor gentle amplitude-building approaches: supporting alpha and SMR-like bands, calming protocols, and very conservative thresholds rather than aggressive "more beta" activation training (Arns, Drinkenburg, & Kenemans, 2012). Expect the conversation to include sleep, recovery, and medical factors, not only electrodes. Some practices layer infra-low-frequency approaches or autonomic-focused methods here; evidence varies by method, so ask what success metrics mean beyond the screen.

Regulatory or constitutional: Predominantly constitutional as a trait-like EEG style in many individuals, with important regulatory overlays from sleep, withdrawal from substances, and medications. Training goals usually emphasize functional stability, not forcing a "normal-looking" amplitude.

Tortured Character: Fog & the Tide

Slowed Alpha Peak Frequency (processing speed deficit)

What it is: The peak of the resting alpha rhythm, usually measured at posterior leads with eyes closed, sits lower than expected for your age. This is about the *clock speed* of the alpha generator, not whether alpha is tall or short. Two people can both show pretty alpha waves while one ticks faster and one ticks slower. Sedation, drowsiness, and some medications also drag peak frequency around, so clinicians ask what you took, when you slept, and whether the tech saw rolling eye movements before they treat a slow peak as your lifelong tempo.

What it feels like: The world can feel like it arrives slightly faster than you can package it. Timed tasks, working memory loads, and rapid context switching cost more than they do for peers. It is the subjective experience people sometimes mislabel as "low IQ" when it is often better framed as a pacing mismatch between brain and environment. You might thrive when deadlines disappear and drown when the room speeds up.

Common conditions:

- Attention complaints with a sluggish processing flavor
- Mood disorders where psychomotor slowing is part of the picture
- Risk and resilience questions in cognitive aging (interpreted only with clinical context)
- Treatment-selection discussions in research contexts that stratify who may respond better to which class of intervention (Arns, Drinkenburg, & Kenemans, 2012)

Typical protocols: Some labs use neurofeedback aimed at gradually shifting alpha frequency or strengthening organized alpha dynamics; others treat this metric primarily as a planning tool for modality choice rather than as a single training target (Arns, Drinkenburg, & Kenemans, 2012). Your clinician should say clearly which strategy they are using and why. If someone promises they will "speed up your alpha peak" in six sessions, hold the claim lightly; the literature on durable peak-frequency shifts from training is thinner than the literature on using peak frequency to choose among broader treatment packages.

Regulatory or constitutional: Predominantly constitutional. IAF heritability is approximately 0.81 in twin studies (Smit et al., 2006), and the metric is famously stable test-retest compared with many EEG features, which makes it valuable for stratification and honest about quick fixes. Some studies report modest training-related shifts, but their size and durability are debated (see Chapter 3 for the three-timescale framework).

Tortured Character: The Timekeeper

Frontal Alpha Asymmetry (withdrawal-motivation bias)

What it is: Left and right frontal resting alpha are not balanced in the way population norms expect. The conventional metric is asymmetry = ln(right alpha power) minus ln(left alpha power). Because alpha reflects cortical idling, lower alpha at a site is read as higher activation. In the classic "withdrawal" formulation, a negative score (relatively lower right-frontal alpha, meaning relatively higher right-frontal activation) tilts affective style toward vigilance, threat sensitivity, and low approach drive. In practice, good clinicians decompose the signal: sometimes the story is "left is underactive," sometimes "right is overactive," and the training logic is not identical. Eye movement and poor frontal artifact control can distort asymmetry metrics, so this is not a party trick to compute at home from a single channel.

Diagnostic value: A 2017 meta-analysis (van der Vinne, Vollebregt, van Putten, & Arns, 2017) found that frontal alpha asymmetry has negligible diagnostic effect size for depression. The pattern is not a diagnostic marker for depression, anxiety, or any other psychiatric condition. It may inform clinical thinking as an individual difference (see Chapter 1's INFORMS-not-diagnoses framework), but it should not be presented or interpreted as a diagnostic test.

What it feels like: Motivation may feel muted while worry stays online. Pleasure and "forward motion" can feel out of reach even when you know what you value. Social initiation takes more fuel. Some people describe an internal climate that is gray and braced at the same time. You might notice that your body believes relaxation is unsafe even when your mind knows better.

Common conditions:

- Depression and dysthymia, especially anhedonic presentations
- Anxiety-depression blends
- Post-trauma mood states with chronic hypervigilance
- Bipolar-spectrum presentations require careful state-aware interpretation; asymmetry is not a lab test for diagnosis

Typical protocols: Approaches often aim to support healthier left-frontal engagement and calm right-frontal overdrive, using frequency targets chosen after reviewing your exact asymmetry and artifacts (van der Vinne, Vollebregt, van Putten, & Arns, 2017). Evidence for any single protocol here is more modest than for classic attention-training recipes, so we usually frame this as adjunctive work aligned with therapy and, when appropriate, medication. Behavioral activation, light exposure, and movement also nudge frontal systems; neurofeedback rarely replaces those foundations when mood is the primary complaint.

Regulatory or constitutional: Mixed. Mood state moves the measure; trait-like stability is partial, not perfect.

Tortured Character: The CEO

Excess Alpha (cortical idling / hypoarousal variant)

What it is: This label covers patterns where alpha is doing the wrong job at the wrong address. A common clinical story is frontal alpha that is high relative to what should be a posterior-dominant alpha landscape: executive cortex idling like occipital cortex on a quiet afternoon. A separate but related story is globally high posterior alpha with poor reactivity when you open your eyes or engage tasks, tying into under-aroused inattention. Readers compare eyes-open suppression to eyes-closed baselines because healthy alpha should drop when you look at the world; if it does not, the "spacey" story strengthens.

What it feels like: Daydreamy drift, "spacing out," slow reorientation when someone calls your name, or reading the same paragraph twice without traction. It can feel gentle from the inside, even when it wrecks deadlines. Some people experience shame because the struggle does not look like effort from the outside. Teachers or bosses may have called you lazy while you felt underwater.

Common conditions:

- ADHD inattention presentations that do not match the classic "theta excess" cartoon
- Sluggish cognitive tempo and cognitive disengagement constructs discussed in the literature
- Hypoarousal features in mood disorders
- Situations where drowsiness or medications inflate alpha; those must be ruled in or out

Typical protocols: A reflex to hammer frontal alpha downward can misfire. Many supervisors teach posterior alpha support paired with frontal activation via appropriate fast-band rewards, aiming to restore a normal gradient rather than attacking one site in isolation (Ros, Theberge, Frewen, et al., 2013). The difference between subtypes here is a real clinician skill. If you have been told you "failed" prior neurofeedback because alpha training destabilized you, bring that history forward; it may be a phenotype mismatch rather than a personal failure of attention.

Regulatory or constitutional: Mixed. Some people show this pattern across years; others mainly when sleep, mood, or burnout slide.

Tortured Character: The Spacer

Posterior Cingulate Hyperactivation (the default mode that won't stand down)

What it is: The posterior cingulate cortex is the posterior hub of the default mode network, the brain's internally focused, self-referential system that activates during mind-wandering and quiet rest. In typical function, the default mode quiets when you shift attention outward. When it does not, the resting map shows elevated slow-to-medium activity at the posterior midline site, and the subjective experience is a default mode that will not disengage: self-referential processing that runs even when you would rather it stop. Research linking default mode overactivity to rumination and intrusive recollection converges across depression and PTSD literatures, though the specific EEG signature at the posterior midline is a softer signal than the frontal and arousal patterns with more established research records (Hamilton et al., 2015; Knyazev, 2013).

What it feels like: Your mind returns to itself even when you direct it elsewhere. Rumination (replaying conversations, imagining scenarios, rehearsing what you should have said) is the signature texture. Mind-wandering arrives uninvited and is hard to interrupt deliberately. In trauma contexts, this can manifest as intrusive recollection: the default mode replays material from the past rather than generating imaginary futures. Some people find that stillness amplifies the problem; externally focused activity is the only reliable pause.

Common conditions:

- Depression with prominent rumination
- PTSD with intrusive recollection
- Anxiety organized around self-referential loops
- Presentations where conventional meditation practices initially make things worse before improving

Typical protocols: Posterior-site alpha and alpha-theta approaches, mindfulness training, and cognitive strategies targeting rumination directly (rumination-focused cognitive therapy) can work along parallel tracks. SSRIs have documented effects on default mode overactivation in some people. External engagement, absorbing tasks and aerobic exercise, provides reliable interruption even when training is ongoing. For clinical-depth detail, see *QEEG Field Guide* Chapter 6.

Regulatory or constitutional: Regulatory: responds to intervention, though in strongly rumination-prone individuals the pattern has trait-like persistence across years.

Tortured Character: The Storyteller

Theta-Beta Ratio Elevation (classic ADHD marker, with caveats)

What it is: A ratio comparing theta-band power to beta-band power at central or midline leads is higher than expected. It was once packaged as a star biomarker for ADHD. Contemporary reviews are humbling: group differences exist, but individual classification is messy, and the ratio can climb for reasons unrelated to attention diagnosis. The ratio is a compression algorithm. It hides whether theta is truly high, beta is truly low, or a recording was sliding toward sleep.

What it feels like: Subjectively, it often tracks "underregulated attention and arousal": mind wandering, impulsive errors, inconsistent effort, feeling fine one hour and useless the next. None of that proves the ratio caused the feeling; it is a correlate to interpret. Parents may see it as "lazy," coaches as "inconsistent," partners as "checked out," when the story is often regulation, not effort.

Common conditions:

- ADHD symptom clusters
- Sleep deprivation and sleep disorders
- Drowsiness during recording
- Mood disorders with attention complaints
- Technical issues when slow alpha bleeds into fixed theta bands in people with slow alpha peak frequency

Typical protocols: The training tradition that made this famous usually suppresses slow activity and rewards beta during active training, often at midline sites (Arns, Conners, & Kraemer, 2013). Modern clinical teaching stresses *decomposing the ratio* first. If beta is genuinely low, you may need beta support. If theta is inflated only because the recording was sleepy, training should not pretend it found ADHD. In pediatric work, we sometimes screen sleep-disordered breathing when the ratio looks dramatic but the child snores or mouth-breathes; fixing oxygen can change the map faster than thirty sessions of misdirected training.

Regulatory or constitutional: Predominantly regulatory. The ratio swings with state, which is both an opportunity and a reason to distrust one snapshot.

Tortured Character: The Supervisor

Low SMR (sensorimotor readiness deficit)

What it is: The sensorimotor rhythm is generated over the motor strip, the band of cortex that runs ear-to-ear across the top of the head, and reflects a calm, physically ready state at roughly twelve to fifteen cycles per second. Barry Sterman's foundational work is the bedrock here: training cats to produce more of this rhythm also protected them from seizure induction, and subsequent human work extended the findings to sleep onset. When SMR is low at the central sites, the thalamocortical gate that creates smooth physical stillness is not functioning at full efficiency. The body does not settle even when the situation calls for it.

What it feels like: The body wants to move even when the mind does not need it to. Sitting through long meetings, dinners, or car rides is uncomfortable in a physical way: restless legs, fidgeting, the urge to shift position or pace. Sleep onset is often the most noticeable problem: despite real tiredness, the body cannot find the transition between awake and asleep. Some people describe this as having an engine that idles too rough, not racing, not flooded, just unable to settle into smooth neutral.

Common conditions:

- Sleep-onset insomnia, especially with physical restlessness at bedtime

- Hyperactive and combined ADHD presentations where motor restlessness is prominent
- Restless-leg-adjacent presentations
- Difficulty sustaining stillness in meditation, long travel, or formal settings

Typical protocols: SMR uptraining at the central sites is among the most evidence-supported neurofeedback applications, with a research lineage going back to Sterman's original work and replicated specifically for sleep-onset latency. Effects on sleep often appear earlier in a training course than attention effects, sometimes within five to ten sessions. Sleep hygiene and circadian regulation support and consolidate the training gains. For clinical-depth detail, see *QEEG Field Guide* Chapter 6.

Regulatory or constitutional: Predominantly regulatory and trainable. SMR training shows medium-to-large effects on sleep onset latency in controlled studies.

Tortured Character: The Pacer

Posterior Dominant Rhythm Suppression (anxiety-related alpha deficiency)

What it is: At rest, especially with eyes closed, posterior alpha power is lower than expected: the visual association cortex and nearby hubs are not producing a strong, well-shaped idle rhythm. Clinicians link this to a brain that does not gate sensory traffic cleanly when it could be resting. Sometimes the low alpha is relative: fast beta runs hot and alpha looks absent in the mix, which is why readers look at more than one metric before they tell you your visual cortex "forgot" how to rest.

What it feels like: You scan even when you are safe. Sounds feel closer than they are, lights dig in, relaxation techniques backfire because stillness invites intrusion. Some people describe lying in bed awake with a body that is exhausted and a brain that will not switch modes. You might crave distraction because silence feels loud.

Common conditions:

- Anxiety disorders and hypervigilant stress physiology
- PTSD with tonic arousal
- Chronic pain and central sensitization presentations (as a correlate, not a standalone explainer)
- Medication and caffeine states that suppress alpha

Typical protocols: Alpha uptraining at posterior sites, calming SMR-centered work, and careful pairing with high-beta limits when the map shows coactivated fast activity are common starting points (Ros et al., 2013). Trauma-informed pacing matters: flooding the nervous system while chasing metrics helps nobody. Gentle titration, shorter sessions early on, and explicit stop signals in the therapy relationship often predict whether alpha work lands as relief or as threat.

Regulatory or constitutional: Mixed with a regulatory lean. Many people can rebuild alpha generation with skilled training, sleep stabilization, and appropriate therapy. Chronic developmental trauma and long illness histories may lengthen the arc.

Tortured Character: Princess & the Pea

Temporal Dysrhythmia (intermittent slowing or sharp activity)

What it is: Temporal lobes show unstable rhythm organization: focal or lateralized slow activity in theta and delta, bursts of temporal fast activity, or sharp-looking transients that demand careful clinical EEG judgment. In phenotype systems influenced by Gunkelman's teaching, "temporal dysrhythmia" names a family of temporal instability patterns rather than one tidy line on a spreadsheet (Arns, Gunkelman, Breteler, & Spronk, 2008). Laterality matters for interpretation: language-dominant temporal change and nondominant temporal change carry different clinical guesses, always secondary to history and exam.

What it feels like: Emotions may spike and vanish with confusing timing. Memory feels unreliable in specific ways: names, context, sequences. Some people report brief strangeness: déjà vu, dissociative shimmer, auditory hypersensitivity, or "out of nowhere" drops in mood that do not fit neat storylines. You might distrust your own reactions because they seem out of proportion even when the trigger looked small.

Common conditions:

- Trauma-related dysregulation with limbic flavor
- Mood lability when temporal generators are involved
- Head injury histories that whiplash temporal networks
- Seizure disorders or seizure-adjacent phenomena belong in neurology, not in a self-help appendix

Typical protocols: If a neurologist clears training, clinicians may sequence temporal calming work: slow-activity inhibits paired with organized rewards, sometimes alongside frontal regulation plans. Aggressive temporal training without medical clarity is unsafe theater. If you carry a history of staring spells, déjà vu clusters, or sudden fear waves with blanking, advocate for standard EEG and medical input even when a QEEG report looks "mild."

Regulatory or constitutional: Mixed and etiology-dependent. Functional stress patterns can soften with treatment; structural temporal injury may leave a long-lasting signature.

Tortured Character: The Storm Glass

Temporal Beta (the emotional amplifier)

What it is: Beta and high-beta activity elevated at the temporal lobes, the regions that handle emotional processing, auditory interpretation, and memory, rather than globally. The temporal cortex is, broadly, where sound acquires emotional meaning and where experience gets contextually tagged. When fast activity runs high there, the system is specifically amplifying emotional and auditory signals. An important clinical note: temporal fast activity warrants careful evaluation before any training plan is built, because fast transients that look sharp or spike-adjacent require neurological clearance first. This is one of the few entries in this atlas where "ask your clinician to look at the raw EEG" is the standard of care.

What it feels like: Sounds and emotional signals arrive at full volume with limited filtering. Sudden mood shifts without obvious triggers, a wave of irritability or dysphoria that comes and goes in minutes, are a common presentation. Episodic déjà vu and brief moments of unreality (depersonalization, derealization) are sometimes reported. Misophonia, the intense distress or rage triggered by specific sounds like chewing or tapping, has temporal fast-activity patterns as a candidate EEG correlate. The right temporal region particularly handles social prosody, so elevated right-temporal fast activity can coincide with difficulty reading emotional tone, sarcasm, or subtext in conversation.

Common conditions:

- Emotional reactivity and rapid, unexplained mood shifts
- Misophonia and auditory sensitivity
- PTSD presentations with limbic features
- Head injury histories with temporal involvement

Typical protocols: Temporal beta downtraining under close clinical monitoring, after neurological evaluation for epileptiform activity. A normal routine EEG lowers the concern but does not exclude epilepsy, so the clinical history still governs. If sharp transients are present, the approach shifts substantially and belongs in a separate conversation with your clinician and neurologist. For clinical-depth detail, see *QEEG Field Guide* Chapter 6.

Regulatory or constitutional: Regulatory and modifiable, but caution is the standard of practice. Always rule out epileptiform activity before beginning.

Tortured Character: The Amplifier

Left Temporal Alpha (language-region idling)

What it is: The left temporal lobe is the primary home of language processing in most people, the regions responsible for understanding speech, retrieving words, and encoding the verbal record of experience. When alpha activity is elevated at left temporal sites relative to the rest of the map, those regions are idling rather than engaging efficiently. The pattern is sometimes called the "Quiet Word-Finder" presentation in phenotype-informed clinical practice: language cortex running slow, costing you the word you know is in there. Compared with the other entries in this atlas, the research characterization of this pattern is less extensive; treat timing and response estimates as provisional.

What it feels like: You know what you want to say but cannot access it in the moment. Words arrive late, or you substitute general terms for specific ones: "the thing" instead of its name, "you know" instead of the actual noun. Mid-sentence gaps are a signature. Some people describe feeling less verbally sharp than they know themselves to be: the concept is intact, the retrieval is the bottleneck. The pattern can be more pronounced under fatigue, stress, or mood pressure.

Common conditions:

- Word-finding complaints and verbal fluency difficulties
- Overlap with depressive presentations, where language processing and mood circuitry share temporal real estate
- Attention complaints with a verbal-retrieval flavor distinct from the classic frontal theta story
- Age-related word-finding changes (interpreted against appropriate age norms only)

Typical protocols: Activation-based training at left temporal sites, aimed at reducing the idling and encouraging more engaged rhythm. Speech-language evaluation is appropriate when complaints are significant or progressive. Addressing co-occurring mood patterns often helps the temporal picture as well, since depression and temporal alpha excess interact. For clinical-depth detail, see *QEEG Field Guide* Chapter 6.

Regulatory or constitutional: Not well-characterized. Treat as provisional pending broader empirical study.

Tortured Character: The Interpreter

Coherence Anomalies (hyper-coherence or hypo-coherence between regions)

What it is: Coherence measures the statistical coupling between two scalp sites at a frequency (see the coherence caveat in Chapter 1). **Hyper-coherence** means regions that should decouple for independent work stay tightly coupled. **Hypo-coherence** means regions that should coordinate show weak coupling. Neither map reading is a personality sentence; both show up in concussion, neurodevelopmental differences, psychiatric illness, and medication states. Coherence is not a direct measure of neural communication: volume conduction, shared reference noise, electrode bridging, and common noise sources can all create or inflate apparent coupling, which is part of why connectivity work belongs in experienced hands (Collura, 2014).

What it feels like: Hyper-coherence can feel like mental stickiness: rumination, perseveration, getting trapped in one channel of thought, sensory overwhelm without clean gating. Hypo-coherence can feel like scattered executive function: knowing the plan but struggling to coordinate attention, emotion, and action across the day. You might describe yourself as "all or nothing," either flooded or fragmented.

Common conditions:

- Traumatic brain injury, where connectivity metrics often join power changes in research and clinical reporting (Collura, 2014)
- Autism spectrum presentations in some connectivity-guided training traditions (Collura, 2014)
- Complex trauma and dissociation when disconnection shows up in network metrics (interpreted cautiously)

- Any condition mirrored by medications that globally synchronize or desynchronize cortex

Typical protocols: Connectivity-guided neurofeedback attempts to train coherence down in overheated pairs or up in disconnected pairs, often as phase-two work after power issues are understood (Collura, 2014). Reference montage choices and artifact control dominate quality; this is not beginner terrain. Expect longer courses when the target is network organization rather than a single frequency band at one electrode; progress may show up first as cognitive flexibility or sensory tolerance, not as a dramatic coherence matrix flip.

Regulatory or constitutional: Mixed. Acute injury states can evolve over months. Longstanding developmental or severe injury patterns may change slowly and rarely "normalize" fully.

Tortured Character: The Switchboard

High Beta with Alpha Suppression (the combined hypervigilance pattern)

What it is: This is a composite you will see discussed more than it appears as a single named code in taxonomies: fast activity runs hot while posterior alpha idling is weak. Conceptually, the brain is both revved and unable to mute sensory channels at rest. Your report may list the pieces separately; the clinical story is the intersection. In insomnia research traditions, a similar idea appears as cortical hyperarousal plus poor sleep pressure regulation: the biology does not match the folk theory that tired brains always look slow.

What it feels like: Pure strain. You might report irritability, startle, muscle bracing, poor sleep, and an inner monologue that will not land. People sometimes say they feel "unsafe in their skin" even when life is objectively stable, because the nervous system is reading threat everywhere. Small sensory slights land as big events.

Common conditions:

- Anxiety disorders overlapping insomnia

- PTSD hyperarousal
- Chronic pain states with centralized sensitization features
- Stimulant overmedication or high caffeine intake as confounders

Typical protocols: Sequencing matters. Many clinicians blend posterior alpha support with careful limits on broadband fast activity, using central calming SMR-family approaches as a bridge (Arns & Kenemans, 2014). If medications drive the pattern, neurofeedback alone will mislead everyone. This composite is common in high-performing professionals who downregulate poorly after work: the mind still sprints while the body begs for idle.

Regulatory or constitutional: Mostly regulatory, with individual floors and ceilings.

Tortured Character: The Sentinel

Mu Rhythm Suppression (sensorimotor integration deficit)

What it is: Mu is the central strip's alpha-family rhythm, strongest at sensorimotor cortex. When you move, or imagine movement, mu typically drops. During action observation, many neurotypical brains show mu suppression, which has been linked to sensorimotor and social-motor simulation frameworks (Pineda, 2005; Pineda et al., 2008). This entry uses "Mu Rhythm Suppression" in the clinical sense people intend when they talk about **sensorimotor integration problems**: reduced or absent mu suppression when you watch another person act, or an overly rigid mu landscape at rest that fails to flex with intention. Resting QEEG and task-based EEG tell related but different stories; many offices only measure rest.

What it feels like: You may see clumsy initiation: the body hesitates though intention is clear. Social learning through watching can feel opaque. Some people describe feeling "out of sync" with others in subtle motor-affective ways that are hard to verbalize. Imitation, team sports, and coordinated play may have always cost more than they looked like they should.

Common conditions:

- Autism spectrum presentations in research linking atypical mu dynamics to social-motor cognition (Pineda, 2005; Pineda et al., 2008)
- Sensorimotor coordination complaints that outrun classic ADHD frontal theta stories
- Disorders affecting motor planning; medical diagnosis belongs with appropriate specialists

Typical protocols: Central protocols may target appropriate desynchronization during engagement, SMR-range training, or imagery-supported approaches when clinicians use them (Pineda, 2005; Pineda et al., 2008). Claims should stay modest: this is an evolving area with thinner outcome literature than classic ADHD neurofeedback trials. Occupational therapists and motor coaches sometimes parallel what neurofeedback targets here; the best plans coordinate skills in the real world, not only rewards on a screen.

Regulatory or constitutional: Mixed with a constitutional lean in many developmental presentations, still trainable for some goals over long arcs.

Tortured Character: The Mirror

Diffuse Slowing (the becalmed brain)

What it is: When slow activity is elevated broadly across the scalp rather than concentrated at one frontal bottleneck, the picture is usually systemic rather than focal, meaning the brain is running slow everywhere. Clinicians call this diffuse slowing. In clinical practice, this pattern is among the most important to approach carefully, because the list of conditions that can produce it runs through medications, sleep disorders, metabolic conditions, post-viral syndromes, and past neurological insult before arriving at "this is a stable trait to train against." We include this entry as a conversational frame rather than a training target: if your map shows diffuse slowing, the first questions are medical.

What it feels like: Persistent mental fog that does not resolve predictably with sleep or caffeine. Thinking feels slow and thick. Words are harder to find than usual. Recent memory for names and conversations feels unreliable. Tasks that "should" take minutes take significantly longer. People who had COVID-19 and developed prolonged brain fog often recognize this description. The same pattern shows up in untreated sleep apnea, hypothyroidism, heavy sedating medication burdens, and after head injury.

Common conditions:

- Long COVID and post-viral syndromes
- Untreated obstructive sleep apnea
- Medication side effects, especially with sedating or anticonvulsant medications
- Metabolic conditions: thyroid, vitamin deficiency
- Post-concussive and TBI-related presentations

Typical protocols: Medical workup and medication review come before any training plan. If diffuse slowing is present and you are on multiple medications, the first question is whether any can be adjusted. CPAP for sleep apnea and thyroid correction can shift the map meaningfully, sometimes more than months of neurofeedback aimed at the wrong target. When training is appropriate, conservative approaches come first. Serial mapping after medical treatment provides the clearest evidence of what is modifiable and what remains. For clinical-depth detail, see *QEEG Field Guide* Chapter 6.

Regulatory or constitutional: Mixed: constitutional components (aging, past injury) interact with modifiable medical, sleep, and inflammatory factors. Many people see meaningful improvement when the underlying driver is addressed.

Tortured Character: The Becalmed

Mixed Fast-Slow (the paradoxical map)

What it is: When both slow and fast activity are elevated simultaneously, with the map warm in the lowest frequency ranges and also warm in the high-frequency ranges, while the organized middle range is relatively absent, the pattern raises a different set of questions than any single-direction deviation. A healthy brain should not stably appear underaroused and overaroused at the same time in a way that is regulatory rather than driven by something external. When it does, the first explanation to reach for is pharmacological: sedating medications push slow activity up while the fast components remain or amplify; polypharmacy, antipsychotic regimens, and past toxic or viral encephalopathy are among the most common drivers. This is one of the patterns on this atlas where neurofeedback is typically on hold, because training one band can unmask or worsen the other, and the priority is medical clarity first.

What it feels like: Wired and foggy at the same time. The brain is neither alert nor restful; it is stuck in a state that does not match any clean description. Concentration is poor despite feeling overstimulated or anxious. Sleep does not restore. People sometimes say the experience is exhausting in a way that no amount of rest touches, which is accurate, because the pattern is driven by something the nervous system cannot resolve through ordinary recovery.

Common conditions:

- Complex medication regimens, especially those mixing sedating and activating agents
- Post-COVID encephalopathic presentations
- Long-course chronic fatigue with systemic inflammation
- Past toxic or viral neurological insults

Typical protocols: Your prescriber needs to review the medication picture before any training begins; do not adjust medications on your own. If and when the medical picture stabilizes, conservative training approaches under close clinical monitoring are the starting point. The good news buried in this pattern is that it is often largely medication- or medically-driven, which means it can reverse meaningfully when the underlying cause is addressed. For clinical-depth detail, see *QEEG Field Guide* Chapter 6.

Regulatory or constitutional: Largely medication- and medically-driven. Often reverses when the underlying cause is identified and treated.

Tortured Character: The Paradox

How to use this atlas without overusing it

Patterns echo biology, not destiny. Medications, caffeine, jet lag, menstrual phase, fear of the electrodes, and a bad night's sleep can all repaint a map. Normative databases differ. Montage choices differ. Children are not small adults. Older adults are not broken twentysomethings. Z-scores compare you to a reference group that may not represent your life (Thatcher et al., 1998).

Use this appendix to ask better questions. When someone names a phenotype, ask what state you were in, whether muscle tension could explain temporal or frontal fast activity, whether sleep apnea could explain diffuse slowing, and whether anxiety during the hookup could explain beta. Ask how your clinician separates trait from state, and what success would look like behaviorally in twelve weeks, not only on a printout. Ask for a written tie between each training choice and a reproducible finding, not only a brand name.

If a phenotype sounds like you but your map does not show it, trust the lived experience and keep investigating. If a map flags a pattern you do not feel, slow down and ask what else could explain the deviation. The best clinical encounters sound like informed conversation, like a good coach who watches film with you, not like a machine that prints your future.

Phenotypes are also social objects. A label can relieve shame when it reframes struggle as biology you can work with. The same label can harm when it becomes identity shorthand. Treat the atlas entries as working hypotheses that coordinate sleep, therapy, medicine, and training, not as a fixed cast list you must perform for the rest of your life.

When you want depth, cross-domain links, composites, medication confounds, and the full forty-one-entry list (thirty-one phenotypes plus ten composites) with detection rules, open *QEEG Field Guide* Chapter 6. When you want human-scale framing of how brains like yours learn self-regulation, the main chapters of this book are where to go.

Appendix H: Symptom Observation and Referral Worksheet

This appendix is a self-observation and conversation tool. It helps you organize your symptoms before meeting with a clinician so you can have a more concrete, productive discussion about what you are experiencing and what questions to bring to your provider.

This appendix does **not** predict what your brain map will show. Mapping symptoms to candidate EEG patterns before the recording is done puts the cart before the horse: the same symptom profile can arise from different brain configurations, and the same brain pattern can appear under very different clinical labels. Predicting the map from a questionnaire reverses the logic this book is built on. The map is the measurement. These symptom lists help you describe your experience clearly so your clinician can integrate it with what the recording actually shows.

Think of this appendix as preparation for a conversation, not a decoder ring. You describe your experience. Your provider measures your brain. Together you compare the two and decide what, if anything, to do about it.

The screening instruments below (PHQ-9, GAD-7, ASRS, PCL-5, ISI) are validated tools widely used in clinical settings. If you have not completed them formally, your provider may assign them at intake. Validated forms and scoring instructions are available from the original scale developers and reputable health organizations; use official versions rather than random social media quizzes.

PHQ-9 (Patient Health Questionnaire-9): Depression screening

The PHQ-9 is a nine-item depression severity screen used in primary care and mental health settings. Each item asks how often you have experienced a symptom over the last two weeks. You get a total score; higher means more severe depressive symptoms. It is a checklist, not a life sentence. Many people bounce between a few items without meeting full criteria for anything.

Symptom themes to notice and bring to your clinician:

Loss of interest, low pleasure, low motivation. If anhedonia leads your profile, note how pervasive it is: across all activities, or specific to certain domains? How long has it been this way? These details help your clinician interpret what the map shows.

Sad mood, hopelessness, feeling "down." Note whether this is constant or episodic, and whether anxiety runs alongside it. Mixed mood-and-anxiety presentations are common, and telling your clinician about both helps narrow the picture.

Sleep problems. Sleep is a fork in the road. Note which direction: difficulty falling or staying asleep, or sleeping too much and still feeling unrefreshed? The distinction matters clinically. Bring your sleep schedule, screen-time habits, and any sleep-medication use.

Fatigue, low energy. Note whether fatigue is constant or time-of-day dependent. Sedating medications, sleep loss, and medical conditions (thyroid, anemia, chronic illness) can all drive fatigue independently of mood. Mention these to your clinician.

Concentration and attention complaints. If cognitive fog shows up alongside depression, note whether it was present before the mood symptoms started or arrived with them. This helps your clinician distinguish mood-driven attention problems from an overlapping attention-deficit presentation.

Harsh self-criticism, guilt, rumination. If sticky, self-referential thinking dominates, describe what it feels like: repetitive loops? Difficulty letting go of mistakes? This is useful information for your clinician.

Appetite changes. Note direction (increased or decreased) and duration. Appetite changes often reflect medical, hormonal, or medication factors alongside mood.

Psychomotor slowing versus agitation. Note which direction: do you feel physically slowed down, or internally restless and agitated? The two can point in very different clinical directions.

Thoughts of self-harm. If you are in crisis, prioritize safety and professional help immediately. Call 988 (Suicide and Crisis Lifeline) or go to your nearest emergency room. A QEEG is not a suicide risk tool and should never replace direct clinical assessment.

Question to bring to your clinician: "These are the depression symptoms I score highest on. Can we look at whether the brain map shows patterns that might relate to these specific themes, and whether those patterns suggest a particular starting point for training or other intervention?"

Heterogeneity note. Depression is not one thing. People with similar PHQ-9 scores can have different brain configurations. If your score is high but your map looks unremarkable, that is data, not failure. It may steer the conversation toward regulation, behavioral supports, or further evaluation rather than toward a single training target.

GAD-7 (Generalized Anxiety Disorder-7): Anxiety screening

The GAD-7 has seven items about nervousness, worry, tension, and irritability over the last two weeks. It is brief and widely used.

Symptom themes to notice and bring to your clinician:

Nervousness, feeling on edge, fear that something awful might happen. Note whether these are constant or situational. Also note caffeine intake, stimulant use, acute stressors, and sleep quality, all of which can amplify anxiety symptoms independently.

Uncontrollable worry, worry spread across many topics. Describe the quality: is it a racing mind that jumps between topics, or a single worry that you cannot release?

Trouble relaxing. Note whether you can physically settle (body relaxation) even when the mind is busy, or whether both body and mind stay activated.

Restlessness, hard to sit still. Note whether this is physical (can't stop moving) or internal (feeling driven without external movement). The distinction is clinically useful.

Irritability, easy annoyance. A short fuse can reflect anxiety, sleep deprivation, sensory overload, or hormonal factors. Note the context.

Overlap with depression. GAD-7 and PHQ-9 scores often rise together. If both are elevated, bring both sets of observations to your clinician.

Medication and lifestyle. Benzodiazepines, SSRIs, stimulants, decongestants, and caffeine all affect the brain's electrical activity. A double espresso on the way to the lab can produce a temporary picture that does not reflect your baseline. Tell your provider what you took and when.

Question to bring to your clinician: "My anxiety symptoms are strongest in these areas. Does my brain map show anything that might relate to the anxiety picture, and are there patterns worth distinguishing from sleep deprivation or medication effects?"

ASRS (Adult ADHD Self-Report Scale): ADHD screening

The ASRS asks about inattention, disorganization, forgetfulness, restlessness, impulsivity, and interrupting. Adult ADHD is heterogeneous. A QEEG does not diagnose ADHD, and a normal-looking map does not rule it out. What the map can do is suggest which regulatory style your brain is using when you meet behavioral criteria.

Symptom themes to notice and bring to your clinician:

Inattention: drifting off, poor follow-through, careless mistakes, forgetfulness. Note whether inattention is global (everything) or context-dependent (boring tasks but not engaging ones). Note your sleep history, as drowsiness and attention deficits can look identical on both behavior checklists and brain recordings.

Hyperactivity / restlessness: fidgeting, difficulty staying seated, feeling driven. Note whether this is primarily physical or primarily a sense of internal pressure. Note stimulant medication timing relative to any brain recording.

Impulsivity: blurting, interrupting, difficulty waiting. Note whether impulsivity rides along with anxiety or frustration, or appears on its own.

Question to bring to your clinician: "I score highest on these ADHD symptoms. Can the brain map help distinguish which regulatory pattern might be involved, and can it help rule out sleep, anxiety, or other factors that produce similar symptoms?"

When the map looks "normal." A meaningful minority of people who meet ADHD criteria on careful history and rating scales do not show a dramatic resting QEEG deviation. That finding is still informative. It nudges the conversation toward executive strategy, sleep, mood, thyroid, vision, hearing, substance use, and other drivers of real-world performance.

PCL-5 (PTSD Checklist for DSM-5): Trauma screening

The PCL-5 tracks four symptom clusters tied to PTSD: re-experiencing, avoidance, negative thoughts and mood, and hyperarousal. Trauma-related brain activity is state sensitive. Someone hypervigilant during the recording may look different from someone numb or shut down on another day.

Symptom themes to notice and bring to your clinician:

Re-experiencing: intrusions, nightmares, flashbacks. Note the frequency, intensity, and whether they are more visual, somatic, or emotional. Note any head-injury history, sleep-loss patterns, and current medications, as these can independently affect the recording.

Avoidance of reminders, emotional numbing. Note whether you tend toward withdrawal and shutdown or active avoidance of specific triggers. Note any overlap with depressive symptoms.

Negative cognitions: guilt, blame, detachment, loss of interest. These overlap heavily with depression symptoms. If both PCL-5 and PHQ-9 are elevated, bring both.

Hyperarousal: startle, vigilance, sleep problems, concentration trouble. Note whether the hyperarousal is constant or triggered by specific contexts. Substance use, withdrawal, and panic can amplify this picture acutely.

Dissociation: depersonalization, derealization. If present, describe what it feels like. Report any neurological symptoms or medication changes to your clinician, as these can affect interpretation.

State versus trait. Trauma survivors can oscillate between wired and numb. A single recording captures one window. If your PCL-5 is high but the recording day was unusually calm or unusually flooded, say so. Your clinician may want to compare conditions or schedule a follow-up.

Question to bring to your clinician: "My trauma symptoms cluster in these areas. Can the brain map help distinguish what the nervous system is doing underneath, and does the recording reflect my typical state or a snapshot of a particularly good or bad day?"

ISI (Insomnia Severity Index): Sleep screening

The ISI asks about difficulty falling asleep, staying asleep, waking too early, satisfaction with sleep, daytime impairment, and how much sleep worries affect your life.

Symptom themes to notice and bring to your clinician:

Sleep onset insomnia (hard to fall asleep). Note your typical bedtime routine, screen use, caffeine timing, and whether the difficulty is a racing mind, physical tension, or both.

Sleep maintenance insomnia (waking through the night). Note how often and when you wake, and whether you can get back to sleep. If you snore or gasp at night, mention it, as sleep apnea is a medical issue, not something to "train through" on EEG alone.

Early morning awakening. Note whether this is new or longstanding, and whether mood symptoms are present. Circadian factors and mood disorders often contribute.

Daytime fatigue, sleepiness, impaired functioning. Note whether you are chronically sleep-restricted. If so, a recording after sleep stabilization may look different from a recording taken during a period of sleep debt.

When insomnia pairs with anxiety or depression. Expect overlap. Bring your ISI, PHQ-9, and GAD-7 observations together.

Question to bring to your clinician: "My sleep problems are mainly [onset / maintenance / early waking / daytime fatigue]. Does the brain map show anything that might relate to the sleep picture, and should we rule out medical sleep disorders before starting any training?"

Other sleep questionnaires. Clinicians sometimes use the Pittsburgh Sleep Quality Index (PSQI) instead of or alongside the ISI. Bring any prior sleep study results if you have them.

Complaint-Based Quick Reference

This section is for people who have not been through a formal screening process but know how they feel and want a starting point for the clinical conversation. The complaints below are common reasons people seek a brain map. For each one, we list a question worth bringing to your clinician.

Complaint	Question to Bring to Your Clinician
"I can't start things"	"Does my map show patterns related to initiation or frontal activation that might explain why getting started is so hard?"
"I can't fall asleep"	"Does my map suggest my brain is running too hot at rest, or is something else showing up that relates to sleep onset?"
"My mind won't stop"	"Is there a pattern on my map consistent with a mind that has trouble downshifting? What would training target?"

Complaint	Question to Bring to Your Clinician
"Everything overwhelms me"	"Does my map show anything related to sensory gating or arousal regulation that might explain the overwhelm?"
"I feel foggy"	"Does my map show slowing or underactivation that might relate to the fog, or could this be a sleep or medication effect?"
"I feel flat; nothing excites me"	"Does my map show a pattern consistent with low motivation or withdrawal? Is there overlap with the depression picture?"
"I can't stop checking"	"Is there a pattern on my map that relates to repetitive or sticky thinking?"
"I overreact to everything"	"Does my map suggest a regulatory or gating issue that might explain the intensity of my reactions?"
"Certain sounds make me rage"	"Does my map show anything in the temporal regions or in sensory processing that might relate to sound sensitivity?"
"I'm always on edge"	"Does my map show a hyperarousal pattern, and can we rule out caffeine, sleep, or medication as contributors?"
"I forget words / lose my train of thought"	"Does my map show patterns related to processing speed or temporal-region activity?"
"I miss social cues / sarcasm goes over my head"	"Does my map show connectivity or processing patterns that might relate to social-information processing?"
"I have to keep moving"	"Does my map show patterns related to motor inhibition or sensorimotor regulation?"
"Stimulants make me worse"	"Can we share my map results with my prescriber so they have another data point when reviewing my medication?"
"Everything takes forever"	"Does my map show anything related to processing speed or frontal efficiency?"

How to Use This Worksheet

1. Take the scale. Your provider may assign the PHQ-9, GAD-7, ASRS, PCL-5, or ISI as part of intake. If you complete a screen on your own, bring the full set of answers, not only the total score, so the themes stay visible.

2. For children and teens, use pediatric tools and pediatric-informed readers. This appendix centers on adult self-report scales. If you are arranging care for a minor, expect behavior checklists, parent and teacher reports, Vanderbilt-type forms, and other age-appropriate tools instead. Adult cutoffs and adult interpretations should not be pasted onto a child's map.

3. Notice your strongest themes. Circle the sentences that sound most like you: sleep versus energy, worry versus panic, inattention versus restlessness, trauma intrusions versus numbness. If the screener format does not feel like a natural fit, the **Complaint-Based Quick Reference** above offers a parallel starting point organized by how you would describe the problem in your own words.

4. Write down your themes and questions. Bring a short list to your provider: "These are my strongest symptoms. Here are the questions I want to ask about my brain map." The specificity of your observations makes the conversation more productive.

5. Let the map inform the plan, not replace the assessment. This worksheet tells you what to observe about yourself and what to ask about. Your brain map adds a layer of information that symptoms and questionnaires alone do not capture. Standard clinical assessment comes first; the map informs the training plan rather than the diagnosis or the prescription. When the two tell different stories, trust the integrated clinical picture: history, exam, other tests, and your lived experience. When they agree, you have a clearer starting point for understanding why certain symptoms cluster the way they do in your case.

6. Name comorbidity explicitly. If you flagged items on more than one scale, write that down as a short list: for example, "PHQ-9 sleep

+ fatigue, GAD-7 worry + tension, ASRS inattention." Comorbidity is the default in real clinics, not the exception.

7. Ask about norms and databases. Different software packages use different normative comparisons. A pattern that looks "red" in one engine may look borderline in another. What matters is both what pattern appears and how it was judged relative to age-matched peers under the same eyes-open and eyes-closed conditions.

We use tools like this every week to organize intake information. Used honestly, they reduce guesswork. Used carelessly, they become a new kind of label. Stay on the honest side: observations first, humility always, and a full QEEG before anyone sells you a protocol based on a questionnaire alone.

Appendix I: Consumer Quick Lookup

This appendix consolidates the practical action items from across the book into one reference. Tear it out, photograph it, or bookmark it. It covers the five questions we hear most often: How do I find a good provider? What should I watch out for? How much does it cost? How do I know if it's working? And what if my child is the one being assessed?

Finding a Provider

Start here:

- **Peak Brain Institute** (www.PeakBrainInstitute.com): the authors' practice, with locations in Los Angeles and remote services available.
- **Neurofeedback.space** (neurofeedback.space), a searchable global directory of verified neurofeedback providers, hardware vendors, and educational resources. Filter by location, specialization, and remote availability.
- **BCIA directory** (bcia.org): Board Certification in Neurofeedback (BCN) is the field's best known credential, and it means the holder has met a defined training baseline. Treat it as one useful starting list, not as a quality filter. No research links it to better outcomes, and many excellent practitioners never pursued it. What matters more is appropriate licensure, or documented supervision, for the kind of work you need. Chapter 17 covers that distinction.
- **ISNR member directory** (isnr.org), the International Society for Neuroregulation & Research. Membership requires professional standing.
- **Your existing providers:** ask your therapist, psychiatrist, or primary care doctor. Neurofeedback works best when it coordinates with your other care, not when it replaces it.

Scripts for the first phone call:

1. "Do you do a quantitative EEG brain map before starting training, and which normative database do you use?"

    - You want "yes" and a specific answer (NeuroGuide, qEEG-Pro, or similar). If they say "we don't need a map," ask what baseline assessment they use instead. A thorough clinical intake with standardized testing can support a training plan, but starting without any assessment is a red flag.

2. "How do you choose protocols: based on my brain data, or based on my diagnosis?"

    - The answer should involve your individual QEEG patterns. "We do theta-beta training for ADHD" without looking at your brain first is the old model.

3. "How many sessions do you typically recommend before reassessing?"

    - Good range: 20–25 sessions before a re-map. Fewer than 15 is premature. More than 30 without reassessment is a yellow flag.

4. "What happens if I'm not responding?"

    - Listen for: re-map, protocol adjustment, referral. If the answer is "just keep going," that is a red flag.

5. "What are your credentials, and do you coordinate with other providers?"

    - BCN, QEEG-D, or licensed health professional (psychologist, LMFT, LCSW, MD) with neurofeedback training. Willingness to talk to your therapist or psychiatrist matters. For clinical work with diagnosed conditions, the provider should hold an independent clinical license or work under documented supervision by a licensed clinician (see Chapter 17 for the full scope distinction).

The Provider Scorecard in Chapter 17 gives you a printable checklist for comparing clinics side by side.

Red Flags

Walk away if you encounter any of the following:

- **Guaranteed outcomes.** "We guarantee improvement in 20 sessions." No honest clinician can guarantee neuroplastic change. Brains are individual.
- **No baseline assessment before training.** We use quantitative EEG because we believe it produces better-targeted training. Other clinicians build effective protocols from a thorough clinical intake with standardized testing. Either approach gives you a baseline. Starting without any assessment means no one can tell what to train or whether training is working.
- **One protocol for everyone.** If every client gets the same electrode sites and frequency targets regardless of their map, the clinic is running a commodity, not a clinical service.
- **Pressure tactics.** Urgency messaging ("your brain is deteriorating"), emotional manipulation of parents, or pre-paid session bundles with no exit clause.
- **No re-mapping.** A clinic that never repeats the brain map has no way to know whether your brain is actually changing. Expect a re-map around session 20–25.
- **Resistance to coordination.** If they won't talk to your therapist or psychiatrist, they are operating in a silo. Neurofeedback is strongest as part of integrated care.
- **Diagnosis from the brain map.** A QEEG shows patterns, not diagnoses. "Your brain map proves you have ADHD" is a reverse inference error (Chapter 1 of *The QEEG Field Guide* explains why). A responsible clinician describes patterns and discusses how they may relate to your symptoms.

Costs, Insurance, and Payment

Typical cost ranges (U.S., as of 2026):

Component	Typical Range	Notes
Initial QEEG assessment	\$500–\$1,500	Full QEEG with recording, processing, clinical interpretation, and feedback session. Range reflects variation in database, report depth, and included services. Some clinics bundle the first few training sessions.
Individual training session	\$100–\$250	45–60 minutes including setup. Frequency: typically 2–3× per week during active training.
Re-map (follow-up QEEG)	\$250–\$1,500	Usually at sessions 20–25, then as needed. Some clinics charge the same as the initial map, since it is the same work.
Typical initial course	\$4,000–\$10,000	20–40 sessions. Varies widely by region, provider, and complexity.

Insurance and reimbursement:

- Most private insurance plans do **not** cover neurofeedback as a standalone service. Some plans cover the QEEG assessment under EEG diagnostic codes (CPT 95957, 95816) when ordered by a physician.
- **CPT codes commonly used:** 90901 (biofeedback training, which includes EEG neurofeedback), 90875 / 90876 (individual psychophysiological therapy incorporating biofeedback, when provided with psychotherapy). Note: CPT 90912 / 90913 are sometimes listed in neurofeedback billing guides, but those codes are defined by the AMA for biofeedback training of the perineal muscles (anorectal or urethral sphincter) and do not apply to EEG neurofeedback.
- **Important:** This book does not provide billing or coding advice. CPT codes, coverage rules, and payer policies change frequently. Verify all billing codes with a certified medical coder and confirm coverage with your specific insurance plan before submit-

ting claims. The reimbursement information here is general background, not a billing guide.

- **HSA / FSA:** Neurofeedback is generally eligible for Health Savings Account and Flexible Spending Account reimbursement as a qualified medical expense, especially with a letter of medical necessity from your physician. Confirm with your plan administrator.
- **Superbill:** Even without direct insurance billing, most providers can give you a superbill (itemized receipt with diagnosis and CPT codes) for you to submit to your insurer for out-of-network reimbursement.
- **Ask upfront:** "Do you bill insurance directly? If not, do you provide a superbill? Which CPT codes do you use?" This conversation at intake prevents surprises.

Is It Working? A Self-Check Rubric

Progress in neurofeedback is rarely dramatic and sudden. It is usually gradual, sometimes invisible to the person experiencing it until others point it out. Use this rubric at three checkpoints: session 10, session 20–25 (re-map), and session 35–40.

Signs of progress (any 3 of these suggest real change):

- ☐ Sleep is measurably better, falling asleep faster, waking less, or feeling more rested
- ☐ Focus sustains longer in tasks you previously couldn't finish
- ☐ Emotional reactions are less intense or recover faster
- ☐ Other people notice changes before you do (spouse, therapist, teacher, coworkers)
- ☐ You're handling stress situations that used to derail you
- ☐ Energy is more consistent across the day (fewer crashes)
- ☐ Anxiety episodes are less frequent or shorter
- ☐ Your re-map shows spectral changes in the directions your clinician targeted

Yellow flags (discuss with your clinician):

- ☐ No subjective change by session 15, still early enough to adjust, and worth a protocol conversation
- ☐ New symptoms that weren't present at baseline (increased irritability, headaches, sleep disruption) lasting more than 2–3 sessions
- ☐ You feel better but your re-map shows no measurable change; this may mean the improvement has other sources, or that the QEEG metric being tracked isn't the right one
- ☐ Re-map shows brain changes but you feel no different; may need more time, or the symptom-brain gap may have other explanations (sleep, stress, medication)

Red flags (consider stopping or seeking a second opinion):

- ☐ No subjective or objective change by session 30, despite at least one protocol adjustment
- ☐ Worsening symptoms that your clinician cannot explain or adjust for
- ☐ Your clinician has not re-mapped and cannot articulate why
- ☐ You are being pressured to continue without a clear rationale tied to your data

Chapter 18 covers the full non-response picture. The short version: most apparent non-response is a protocol mismatch, not a property of your brain. If it is not working, the first question is whether you are training the right thing, not whether your brain is capable of learning.

The Parent Path

Everything above applies when your child is the client, with these additions:

Before the assessment:

- Keep your child's medication schedule stable for at least 2 weeks before the QEEG (don't start, stop, or change doses right before a brain map without medical guidance).

- Make sure your child sleeps well the night before; a tired child's brain map looks like an ADHD brain map (Chapter 14).
- Bring a medication list with doses and timing.
- Prepare your child: "They're going to put a cap on your head with sensors. It measures your brain waves, like a thermometer for your brain. It doesn't hurt."

During training:

- Sessions for kids are typically shorter (15–20 minutes of active training) with game-based feedback.
- Children don't need to understand what's happening. The conditioning works through the feedback loop, not through conscious effort.
- You may notice changes before your child reports them: better behavior at school, fewer meltdowns, easier bedtimes.
- Track changes with weekly notes; memory is unreliable across 20+ sessions.

Decision points:

- Request a re-map at session 20. Ask the clinician to show you the before-and-after comparison and explain what changed.
- If your child's teacher or therapist reports improvement but the re-map is flat, trust the functional data; not every clinical gain produces a dramatic Z-score swing.
- If nothing is changing by session 25–30, ask about protocol adjustment before buying more sessions.

Before Your First Brain Map

Treat the recording day like a mild experiment. These preparation steps help ensure the map reflects your actual brain, not yesterday's bad sleep or this morning's extra coffee.

- **Stimulant medications and modafinil** are ideally washed out before the recording, because they shift the EEG enough to obscure the brain's own patterns. In practice "two days without stimulants" means skipping only one day of medication: you take your normal dose the day before that, skip the day before the recording, and can resume right after the session. This is about data quality, not safety. Whether to hold any prescription is always a decision your prescribing physician agrees to, never one your neurofeedback provider makes. If your prescriber says not to interrupt, the clinician records on medication and interprets accordingly. For all other medications, do not stop or change them for the brain map without your prescriber's guidance.
- **Sleep normally the night before.** Sleep deprivation increases frontal theta and inflates the theta-beta ratio, two of the most commonly flagged metrics. A sleep-deprived map may look like an ADHD map even if you don't have ADHD.
- **Document your caffeine, cannabis, alcohol, and sleep-medication use.** These all affect the EEG. The clinician needs to know, because accurate interpretation requires it. The information is clinical.
- **Bring your medication list** with doses and timing (including supplements, OTC sleep aids, and anything you take regularly).
- **Eat something before the recording.** Low blood glucose increases frontal theta. Don't fast.
- **Ask how the clinician handles confounds.** A good response includes: asking about your sleep, substances, and medications; screening for drowsiness during recording; and noting these factors in the interpretation. If they don't ask, you should volunteer the information.
- **Expect the recording to take about 20–30 minutes** of actual cap-on time (roughly 10 minutes eyes-closed, 10 minutes eyes-open), plus setup and cleanup.

For Parents: The Stimulants-vs-Neurofeedback Decision

The question we get most from parents: "Should I try neurofeedback instead of, or in addition to, stimulants for my child's ADHD?"

This is not a binary choice, and it's not a decision this book can make for you. But here's a framework that gives you something concrete to bring to your prescriber:

Start here: What's the current situation?

Situation	Recommended sequence
Your child has no diagnosis yet and you want to understand the brain before choosing a path	Get a QEEG as a baseline before starting neurofeedback training. If medication is also being considered, share the results with your prescriber as one input alongside clinical assessment.
Your child is on stimulants, not responding well, or having significant side effects	A QEEG can inform the training plan and add context for your prescriber. Standard medical assessment guides medication decisions.
Your child is not on stimulants, school is struggling right now (failing grades, behavioral issues)	Discuss timing with prescriber. Stimulants act in hours; NF takes months. Immediate need may warrant immediate intervention.
Your child has done neurofeedback and needs a break or interim support	Stimulants can bridge while consolidation continues.

Key questions to ask your prescriber: 1. "What assessments has my child had so far, and are there gaps? Would a brain map add useful information for the training plan?" 2. "If we add neurofeedback, how should we monitor whether my child's response to the current dose changes over time? Who should I report changes to?" 3. "What outcome measures are we tracking so we know if things are improving?"

For Parents: School Coordination Scripts

A note on privacy and credentials before sharing brain map results with a school. What you share with teachers, counselors, or special education teams may become part of your child's educational record under FERPA, where it can follow them through their school career. Brain map results are also protected health information under HIPAA, and you control whether and how much to disclose. You can share general observations on your own, but clinical findings, anything involving diagnosis or treatment recommendations, should be presented by a licensed clinician. Ask your provider to prepare a summary letter or join the meeting directly.

Once your child has a brain map and is starting neurofeedback, these are the conversations worth having:

With the classroom teacher:

> "We recently had my child's brain mapped, and we're starting neurofeedback training to address [specific target: e.g., attention and impulse control / emotional regulation / sensory overwhelm]. This is different from medication; it works gradually over weeks and months, not immediately. We're tracking changes with a weekly behavior log. I'd like to share that with you monthly so we can compare your observations with the training progress. Could we set up a 10-minute check-in at the 4-week mark?"

With the school counselor or psychologist:

Lead with the performance testing, not the map. A continuous performance test measures what your child actually does on sustained attention and impulse control, which is the kind of evidence a school works from. The map is context for why, not proof of a diagnosis or a subtype.

"We have executive function testing from [provider name], including a continuous performance test. It shows [specific measured findings: e.g., sustained attention below age expectation, high response variability]. There is also a QEEG brain map, which our provider has explained to us as context for those results rather than as a diagnosis. My child is in neurofeedback training. I would like to know whether the accommodation plan matches what the testing shows. For example, if sustained attention is the measured weakness, should we revisit time-extension accommodations?"

With your pediatrician:

"My child is starting neurofeedback training in addition to [current interventions]. I want to make sure we're tracking all variables. Would you be willing to note any behavior changes I report at our 3-month check-in alongside the training timeline? And if the neurofeedback seems to be helping, I'd like to discuss whether any medication adjustments make sense at that point."

For Biohackers and Optimization-Oriented Readers (Devon's Toolkit)

If you're reading this book as a high-performer looking to optimize rather than treat a condition, here's a more direct practical guide.

Consumer EEG hardware worth knowing

None of these replace a clinical QEEG. What they can do: rough arousal monitoring during meditation, biofeedback training at home, HRV + EEG paired practice. Think of them as fitness trackers for the brain: useful data, not clinical precision.

Device	Ch.	Best use	Notes
Muse 2 / Muse S	4	Meditation feedback, sleep staging	Good entry-level; limited spatial resolution
Neurosity Crown	8	Cognitive state monitoring, developer APIs	Best for quantified-self tracking
OpenBCI (Cyton)	8–16	DIY neurofeedback, research-grade	Requires technical knowledge; research-grade signal
BrainBit	4	EEG + HRV in one device	More integrated autonomic picture

The honest caveat: Consumer devices can tell you whether your brain is calm or active. They cannot replace a clinical brain map for protocol selection. Use them for tracking; don't use them for diagnosis.

Meditation app + neurofeedback stack

One sequencing approach we use in practice (this is our preference, not an evidence-based prescription; no trial has compared this order against alternatives):

1. **First 20 sessions of neurofeedback:** no formal meditation requirement. Let the training do its work without adding another variable.
2. **Sessions 20-40:** begin a 5-10 minute breath-awareness practice on rest days. Basic: eyes closed, count breaths, restart when you lose count. You're rehearsing the attentional state the training is building.
3. **After 40 sessions:** if you're an experienced meditator returning to practice, you'll likely find the sits easier. If you're new, basic apps (Waking Up, Ten Percent Happier) work well as a parallel track.

If you already meditate or want to start meditating now, there is no reason to delay. The sequencing above reflects our clinical observation that some people find meditation more accessible after building a regulatory foundation, not a requirement.

The apps that pair best: Waking Up (Sam Harris) for analytical meditators; Headspace for consistency and habit formation; Ten Percent Happier for skeptics. The app matters less than the consistency.

Nootropics and neurofeedback: the honest opinion

The short version: the stack in Chapter 19 (sleep, exercise, assessment, training) has more evidence behind it than any supplement combination.

Some people use sleep and stress supplements alongside training. Forms and doses vary, and those specifics are conversations for your physician, not decisions to make from a book. If asked, Andrew's own preference for sleep support is magnesium glycinate. Caffeine before sessions is fine for most people; timing relative to sleep matters more than the amount.

A note on stimulant nootropics and neurofeedback: Modafinil behaves like a stimulant during training. Like other stimulants and like cannabis, it does not need to be stopped for neurofeedback, but it does need to be accounted for. As regulatory capacity improves, some people find that modafinil feels stronger, the same pattern clinicians see with prescription stimulants. If you notice the effect shifting, that is worth telling your prescriber. For other stimulant nootropics (racetams, high-dose noopept), evidence is limited; discuss timing with your clinician.

No-diagnosis optimization protocol (if you have no presenting condition)

Assessment first. Get a QEEG baseline. You're looking for subtle inefficiencies the brain is compensating for, not pathology. Chapter 15's discussion of coherence training and IAF applies here.

Recommended starting protocol:

- 20-25 sessions of QEEG-guided neurofeedback targeting whatever the map shows (typically: coherence optimization, alpha strengthening, sleep-architecture improvement if indicated)
- Re-map at session 20; compare to baseline
- If changes are visible and correlate with functional improvements: continue to session 40
- If no changes: discuss protocol adjustment before committing further

The periodization concept from Chapter 19 is the right frame: build phase, peak phase, consolidation phase. Don't train indefinitely without a plan.

References Cited

Arnold, L. E., Arns, M., Bergman, R., et al. (2021). Double-blind placebo-controlled randomized clinical trial of neurofeedback for attention-deficit/hyperactivity disorder with 13-month follow-up. *Journal of the American Academy of Child and Adolescent Psychiatry, 60*(7), 841–855. https://doi.org/10.1016/j.jaac.2020.07.906

Arns, M., Gunkelman, J., Breteler, M., & Spronk, D. (2008). EEG phenotypes predict treatment outcome to stimulants in children with ADHD. *Journal of Integrative Neuroscience, 7*(3), 421–438. https://doi.org/10.1142/S0219635208001897

Arns, M., de Ridder, S., Strehl, U., Breteler, R., & Coenen, A. (2009). Efficacy of neurofeedback treatment in ADHD: The effects on inattention, impulsivity and hyperactivity: A meta-analysis. *Clinical EEG and Neuroscience, 40*(3), 180–189. https://doi.org/10.1177/155005940904000311

Arns, M., Drinkenburg, W. H. I. M., & Kenemans, J. L. (2012). The effects of QEEG-informed neurofeedback in ADHD: An open-label pilot study. *Applied Psychophysiology and Biofeedback, 37*(3), 171–180. https://doi.org/10.1007/s10484-012-9191-4

Arns, M., Conners, C. K., & Kraemer, H. C. (2013). A decade of EEG theta/beta ratio research in ADHD: A meta-analysis. *Journal of Attention Disorders, 17*(5), 374–383. https://doi.org/10.1177/1087054712460087

Arns, M., Heinrich, H., & Strehl, U. (2014). Evaluation of neurofeedback in ADHD: The long and winding road. *Biological Psychology, 95*, 108–115. https://doi.org/10.1016/j.biopsycho.2013.11.013

Arns, M., & Kenemans, J. L. (2014). Neurofeedback in ADHD and insomnia: Vigilance stabilization through sleep spindle and circadian networks. *Neuroscience and Biobehavioral Reviews, 44*, 183–194. https://doi.org/10.1016/j.neubiorev.2012.10.006

Arns, M., Feddema, I., & Kenemans, J. L. (2014). Differential effects of theta/beta and SMR neurofeedback in ADHD on sleep onset latency. *Frontiers in Human Neuroscience, 8*, 1019. https://doi.org/10.3389/fnhum.2014.01019

Askovic, M., Soh, N., Elhindi, J., & Harris, A. W. F. (2023). Neurofeedback for post-traumatic stress disorder: Systematic review and meta-analysis of clinical and neurophysiological outcomes. *European Journal of Psychotraumatology, 14*(2), 2257435. https://doi.org/10.1080/20008066.2023.2257435

Barlas, D. (2021). A meta-analysis of the effect of neurofeedback on depression. *NeuroRegulation, 8*(2), 104. https://doi.org/10.15540/nr.8.2.104

Barth, B., Mayer-Carius, K., Strehl, U., Wyckoff, S. N., Haeussinger, F. B., Fallgatter, A. J., & Ehlis, A.-C. (2021). A randomized-controlled neurofeedback trial in adult attention-deficit/hyperactivity disorder. *Scientific Reports, 11*, 16873. https://doi.org/10.1038/s41598-021-95928-1

Berger, H. (1929). Über das Elektrenkephalogramm des Menschen. *Archiv für Psychiatrie und Nervenkrankheiten, 87*(1), 527–570. https://doi.org/10.1007/BF01797193

Boxum, M., Voetterl, H., van Dijk, H., Gordon, E., DeBeus, R., Arnold, L. E., & Arns, M. (2025). Challenging the diagnostic value of theta/beta ratio: Insights from an EEG subtyping meta-analytical approach in ADHD. *Applied Psychophysiology and Biofeedback, 50*(4), 655–666. https://doi.org/10.1007/s10484-024-09649-y

Braboszcz, C., Cahn, B. R., Levy, J., Fernandez, M., & Delorme, A. (2017). Increased gamma brainwave amplitude compared to control in three different meditation traditions. *PLOS ONE, 12*(1), e0170647. https://doi.org/10.1371/journal.pone.0170647

Breteler, M. H. M., Arns, M., Peters, S., Giepmans, I., & Verhoeven, L. (2010). Improvements in spelling after QEEG-based neurofeedback in dyslexia: A randomized controlled treatment study. *Applied Psychophysiology and Biofeedback, 35*(1), 5–11. https://doi.org/10.1007/s10484-009-9105-2

Callaway, T. G., & Bodenhamer-Davis, E. (2008). Long-term follow-up of a clinical replication of the Peniston protocol for chemical dependency. *Journal of Neurotherapy, 12*(4), 243–259. https://doi.org/10.1080/10874200802502060

Carmen, J. A. (2004). Passive infrared hemoencephalography: Four years and 100 migraines. *Journal of Neurotherapy, 8*(3), 23–51. https://doi.org/10.1300/J184v08n03_03

Carrick, F. R., Pagnacco, G., Hankir, A., Abdulrahman, M., Zaman, R., Kalambaheti, E. R., Barton, D. A., Link, P. E., & Oggero, E. (2018). The treatment of autism spectrum disorder with auditory neurofeedback: A randomized placebo controlled trial using the Mente Autism device. *Frontiers in Neurology, 9*, 537. https://doi.org/10.3389/fneur.2018.00537

Clarke, A. R., Barry, R. J., McCarthy, R., & Selikowitz, M. (2001). EEG-defined subtypes of children with attention-deficit/hyperactivity disorder. *Clinical Neurophysiology, 112*(11), 2098–2105. https://doi.org/10.1016/S1388-2457(01)00668-X

Clarke, A. R., Barry, R. J., Dupuy, F. E., Heckel, L. D., McCarthy, R., Selikowitz, M., & Johnstone, S. J. (2011). Behavioural differences between EEG-defined subgroups of children with attention-deficit/hyperactivity disorder. *Clinical Neurophysiology, 122*(7), 1333–1341. https://doi.org/10.1016/j.clinph.2010.12.038

Coben, R., & Padolsky, I. (2007). Assessment-guided neurofeedback for autistic spectrum disorder. *Journal of Neurotherapy, 11*(1–2), 5–23. https://doi.org/10.1300/J184v11n01_02

Coben, R., Linden, M., & Myers, T. E. (2010). Neurofeedback for autistic spectrum disorder: A review of the literature. *Applied Psychophysiology and Biofeedback, 35*(1), 83–105. https://doi.org/10.1007/s10484-009-9117-y

Collura, T. F. (2014). *Technical Foundations of Neurofeedback*. Routledge.

Colombo, M. A., Ramautar, J. R., Wei, Y., Gomez-Herrero, G., Stoffers, D., Wassing, R., Benjamins, J. S., Tagliazucchi, E., van der Werf, Y. D., Cajochen, C., & Van Someren, E. J. W. (2016). Wake high-density electroencephalographic spatiospectral signatures of insomnia. *Sleep, 39*(5), 1015–1027. https://doi.org/10.5665/sleep.5744

Cortese, S., Ferrin, M., Brandeis, D., Buitelaar, J., Daley, D., Dittmann, R. W., Holtmann, M., Santosh, P., Stevenson, J., Stringaris, A., Zuddas, A., Sonuga-Barke, E. J. S., & European ADHD Guidelines Group. (2016). Neurofeedback for attention-deficit/hyperactivity disorder: Meta-analysis of clinical and neuropsychological outcomes from randomized controlled trials. *Journal of the American Academy of Child and Adolescent Psychiatry, 55*(6), 444–455. https://doi.org/10.1016/j.jaac.2016.03.007

de Zambotti, M., Rosas, L., Colrain, I. M., & Baker, F. C. (2019). The sleep of the ring: Comparison of the ŌURA sleep tracker against polysomnography. *Behavioral Sleep Medicine, 17*(2), 124–136. https://doi.org/10.1080/15402002.2017.1300587

Egner, T., Strawson, E., & Gruzelier, J. H. (2002). EEG signature and phenomenology of alpha/theta neurofeedback training versus mock feedback. *Applied Psychophysiology and Biofeedback, 27*(4), 261–270. https://doi.org/10.1023/A:1021063416558

Erickson, K. I., Voss, M. W., Prakash, R. S., et al. (2011). Exercise training increases size of hippocampus and improves memory. *Proceedings of the National Academy of Sciences, 108*(7), 3017–3022. https://doi.org/10.1073/pnas.1015950108

Ferrarelli, F., Smith, R., Dentico, D., Riedner, B. A., Zennig, C., Benca, R. M., Lutz, A., Davidson, R. J., & Tononi, G. (2013). Experienced mindfulness meditators exhibit higher parietal-occipital EEG gamma activity during NREM sleep. *PLOS ONE, 8*(8), e73417. https://doi.org/10.1371/journal.pone.0073417

Ferreira, S., Pêgo, J. M., & Morgado, P. (2019). The efficacy of biofeedback approaches for obsessive-compulsive and related disorders: A systematic review and meta-analysis. *Psychiatry Research, 272*, 237–245. https://doi.org/10.1016/j.psychres.2018.12.096

Fisher, S. F. (2014). *Neurofeedback in the Treatment of Developmental Trauma: Calming the Fear-Driven Brain*. W. W. Norton & Company.

Friedrich, E. V. C., Sivanathan, A., Lim, T., Suttie, N., Louchart, S., Pillen, S., & Pineda, J. A. (2015). An effective neurofeedback intervention to improve social interactions in children with autism spectrum disorder. *Journal of Autism and Developmental Disorders, 45*(12), 4084–4100. https://doi.org/10.1007/s10803-015-2523-5

Fruchter, E., Goldenthal, N., Adler, L. A., et al. (2024). Amygdala-derived-EEG-fMRI-pattern neurofeedback for the treatment of chronic post-traumatic stress disorder: A prospective, multicenter, multinational study evaluating clinical efficacy. *Psychiatry Research, 333*, 115711. https://doi.org/10.1016/j.psychres.2023.115711

Gloss, D., Varma, J. K., Pringsheim, T., & Nuwer, M. R. (2016). Practice advisory: The utility of EEG theta/beta power ratio in ADHD diagnosis: Report of the Guideline Development, Dissemination, and Implementation Subcommittee of the American Academy of Neurology. *Neurology, 87*(22), 2375–2379. https://doi.org/10.1212/WNL.0000000000003265

Goessl, V. C., Curtiss, J. E., & Hofmann, S. G. (2017). The effect of heart rate variability biofeedback training on stress and anxiety: A meta-analysis. *Psychological Medicine, 47*(15), 2578–2586. https://doi.org/10.1017/S0033291717001003

Guler, S., Cohen, A. L., Afacan, O., & Warfield, S. K. (2021). Matched neurofeedback during fMRI differentially activates reward-related circuits in active and sham groups. *Journal of Neuroimaging, 31*(5), 947–955. https://doi.org/10.1111/jon.12899

Hamilton, J. P., Farmer, M., Fogelman, P., & Gotlib, I. H. (2015). Depressive rumination, the default-mode network, and the dark matter of clinical neuroscience. *Biological Psychiatry, 78*(4), 224–230. https://doi.org/10.1016/j.biopsych.2015.02.020

He, S., Everest-Phillips, C., Clouter, A., Brown, P., & Tan, H. (2020). Neurofeedback-linked suppression of cortical β bursts speeds up movement initiation in healthy motor control: A double-blind sham-controlled study. *Journal of Neuroscience, 40*(20), 4021–4032. https://doi.org/10.1523/JNEUROSCI.0208-20.2020

Hershaw, J. N., & Hill-Pearson, C. A. (2022). Changes in EEG activity following live Z-score training predict changes in persistent post-concussive symptoms: An exploratory analysis. *Frontiers in Neurology, 13*, 714913. https://doi.org/10.3389/fneur.2022.714913

Hill, A. R. (2012). *Measuring & Modulating Hemispheric Attention* [Doctoral dissertation, University of California, Los Angeles]. eScholarship. https://escholarship.org/uc/item/55c35139

Hill, A. R. (2026a). Five structural biases in neurofeedback-for-ADHD research: Why the evidence looks weaker than it should [Preprint]. *PsyArXiv*. https://doi.org/10.31234/osf.io/hb2eq_v1

Hill, A. R. (2026b). Frequency-specific operant learning in neurofeedback reveals distinct cortical mechanisms: Evidence from double-blind ERSP and ERP dissociations [Preprint]. *bioRxiv*. https://doi.org/10.64898/2026.04.13.718260

Hobson, H. M., & Bishop, D. V. M. (2017). The interpretation of mu suppression as an index of mirror neuron activity: Past, present and future. *Royal Society Open Science, 4*(3), 160662. https://doi.org/10.1098/rsos.160662

Hoedlmoser, K., Pecherstorfer, T., Gruber, G., Anderer, P., Doppelmayr, M., Klimesch, W., & Schabus, M. (2008). Instrumental conditioning of human sensorimotor rhythm (12–15 Hz) and its impact on sleep as well as declarative learning. *Sleep, 31*(10), 1401–1408. https://doi.org/10.5665/sleep/31.10.1401

Insel, T. R. (2013, April 29). *Transforming diagnosis* [Blog post]. NIMH Director's Blog, National Institute of Mental Health. The original post is no longer available from NIMH; archived at https://psychrights.org/2013/130429NIMHTransformingDiagnosis.htm

International Society for Neuroregulation & Research. (2025, June 20). ISNR CPT update. https://isnr.org/single-post/2025/06/20/isnr-cpt-update

Kamiya, J. (1968). Conscious control of brain waves. *Psychology Today, 1*(1), 56–60.

Kapur, V. K., Auckley, D. H., Chowdhuri, S., Kuhlmann, D. C., Mehra, R., Ramar, K., & Harrod, C. G. (2017). Clinical practice guideline for diagnostic testing for adult obstructive sleep apnea: An American Academy of Sleep Medicine clinical practice guideline. *Journal of Clinical Sleep Medicine, 13*(3), 479–504. https://doi.org/10.5664/jcsm.6506

Knyazev, G. G. (2013). EEG correlates of self-referential processing. *Frontiers in Human Neuroscience, 7*, 264. https://doi.org/10.3389/fnhum.2013.00264

Lansbergen, M. M., Arns, M., van Dongen-Boomsma, M., Spronk, D., & Buitelaar, J. K. (2011). The increase in theta/beta ratio on resting-state EEG in boys with attention-deficit/hyperactivity disorder is mediated by slow alpha peak frequency. *Progress in Neuro-Psychopharmacology and Biological Psychiatry, 35*(1), 47–52. https://doi.org/10.1016/j.pnpbp.2010.08.004

Lantz, D. L., & Sterman, M. B. (1988). Neuropsychological assessment of subjects with uncontrolled epilepsy: Effects of EEG feedback training. *Epilepsia, 29*(2), 163–171. https://doi.org/10.1111/j.1528-1157.1988.tb04414.x

Lehrer, P. M., & Gevirtz, R. (2014). Heart rate variability biofeedback: How and why does it work? *Frontiers in Psychology, 5*, 756. https://doi.org/10.3389/fpsyg.2014.00756

Lubar, J. F., & Shouse, M. N. (1976). EEG and behavioral changes in a hyperkinetic child concurrent with training of the sensorimotor rhythm (SMR): A preliminary report. *Biofeedback and Self-Regulation, 1*(3), 293–306. https://doi.org/10.1007/BF01001170

Lutz, A., Greischar, L. L., Rawlings, N. B., Ricard, M., & Davidson, R. J. (2004). Long-term meditators self-induce high-amplitude gamma synchrony during mental practice. *Proceedings of the National Academy of Sciences, 101*(46), 16369–16373. https://doi.org/10.1073/pnas.0407401101

Management of Posttraumatic Stress Disorder Work Group. (2023). *VA/DoD Clinical Practice Guideline for the Management of Posttraumatic Stress Disorder and Acute Stress Disorder* (Version 4.0). Department of Veterans Affairs & Department of Defense. https://www.healthquality.va.gov/guidelines/MH/ptsd/

MedlinePlus / National Library of Medicine. (n.d.). Delirium tremens. https://medlineplus.gov/ency/article/000764.htm

Misaki, M., Tsuchiyagaito, A., Guinjoan, S. M., Rohan, M. L., & Paulus, M. P. (2024). Whole-brain mechanism of neurofeedback therapy: Predictive modeling of neurofeedback outcomes on repetitive negative thinking in depression. *Translational Psychiatry, 14*(1), 354. https://doi.org/10.1038/s41398-024-03066-9

Monastra, V. J., Lubar, J. F., & Linden, M. (2001). The development of a quantitative electroencephalographic scanning process for attention deficit-hyperactivity disorder: Reliability and validity studies. *Neuropsychology, 15*(1), 136–144. https://doi.org/10.1037/0894-4105.15.1.136

Monastra, V. J., Monastra, D. M., & George, S. (2002). The effects of stimulant therapy, EEG biofeedback, and parenting style on the primary symptoms of attention-deficit/hyperactivity disorder. *Applied Psychophysiology and Biofeedback, 27*(4), 231–249. https://doi.org/10.1023/A:1021018700609

Moore, J. P., Trudeau, D., Thuras, P. D., Rubin, Y., Stockley, H., & Dimond, T. (2000). Comparison of alpha-theta, alpha and EMG neurofeedback in the production of alpha-theta crossover and the occurrence of visualizations. *Journal of Neurotherapy, 4*(1), 29–42. https://doi.org/10.1300/J184v04n01_04

Nicholson, A. A., Ros, T., Densmore, M., Frewen, P. A., Neufeld, R. W. J., Théberge, J., Jetly, R., & Lanius, R. A. (2020). A randomized, controlled trial of alpha-rhythm EEG neurofeedback in posttraumatic stress disorder: A preliminary investigation showing evidence of decreased PTSD symptoms and restored default mode and salience network connectivity using fMRI. *NeuroImage: Clinical, 28*, 102490. https://doi.org/10.1016/j.nicl.2020.102490

Ogrim, G., Kropotov, J., & Hestad, K. (2012). The quantitative EEG theta/beta ratio in attention deficit/hyperactivity disorder and normal controls: Sensitivity, specificity, and behavioral correlates. *Psychiatry Research, 198*(3), 482–488. https://doi.org/10.1016/j.psychres.2011.12.041

Ossadtchi, A., Shamaeva, T., Okorokova, E., Moiseeva, V., & Rozengurt, R. (2017). Neurofeedback learning modifies the incidence rate of alpha spindles, but not their duration and amplitude. *Scientific Reports, 7*, 5765. https://doi.org/10.1038/s41598-017-04012-0

Pan, N., Long, Y., Qin, K., Pope, I. Z., Chen, Q., Zhu, Z., Cao, Y., Li, L., Singh, M. K., McNamara, R. K., DelBello, M. P., Chen, Y., Fornito, A., & Gong, Q. (2026). Mapping ADHD heterogeneity and biotypes by topological deviations in morphometric similarity networks. *JAMA Psychiatry, 83*(5), 478–490. https://doi.org/10.1001/jamapsychiatry.2026.0001

Patel, K., Sutherland, H., Henshaw, J., Taylor, J. R., Brown, C. A., Casson, A. J., Trujillo-Barreto, N. J., Jones, A. K. P., & Sivan, M. (2020). Effects of neurofeedback in the management of chronic pain:

A systematic review and meta-analysis of clinical trials. *European Journal of Pain, 24*(8), 1440–1457. https://doi.org/10.1002/ejp.1612

Peniston, E. G., & Kulkosky, P. J. (1989). Alpha-theta brainwave training and beta-endorphin levels in alcoholics. *Alcoholism: Clinical and Experimental Research, 13*(2), 271–279. https://doi.org/10.1111/j.1530-0277.1989.tb00325.x

Peniston, E. G., & Kulkosky, P. J. (1991). Alpha-theta brainwave neurofeedback in the treatment of Vietnam veterans with combat-related post-traumatic stress disorder. *Medical Psychotherapy: An International Journal, 4*, 47–60.

Pineda, J. A. (2005). The functional significance of mu rhythms: Translating "seeing" and "hearing" into "doing." *Brain Research Reviews, 50*(1), 57–68. https://doi.org/10.1016/j.brainresrev.2005.04.005

Pineda, J. A., Brang, D., Hecht, E., Edwards, L., Carey, S., Bacon, M., Futrell, N., Suk, D., & Kraskov, A. (2008). Positive behavioral and electrophysiological changes following neurofeedback training in children with autism. *Research in Autism Spectrum Disorders, 2*(3), 557–581. https://doi.org/10.1016/j.rasd.2007.12.003

Rance, M., Zhao, Z., Zaboski, B., Kichuk, S. A., Romaker, E., Koller, W. N., Walsh, C., Harris-Starling, C., Wasylink, S., Adams, T., Gruner, P., Pittenger, C., & Hampson, M. (2023). Neurofeedback for obsessive compulsive disorder: A randomized, double-blind trial. *Psychiatry Research, 328*, 115458. https://doi.org/10.1016/j.psychres.2023.115458

Raymond, J., Varney, C., Parkinson, L. A., & Gruzelier, J. H. (2005). The effects of alpha/theta neurofeedback on personality and mood. *Cognitive Brain Research, 23*(2–3), 287–292. https://doi.org/10.1016/j.cogbrainres.2004.10.023

Recio-Rodriguez, J. I., Fernandez-Crespo, M., Sanchez-Aguadero, N., Gonzalez-Sanchez, J., Garcia-Yu, I. A., Alonso-Dominguez, R., Chiu, H.-Y., Tsai, P.-S., Lee, H.-C., & Rihuete-Galve, M. I. (2024). Neurofeedback to enhance sleep quality and insomnia: A systematic review and meta-analysis of randomized clinical trials. *Frontiers in Neuroscience, 18*, 1450163. https://doi.org/10.3389/fnins.2024.1450163

Rezaee, M., Effatpanah, M., Nasehi, M. M., Ghamkhar, L., & Barati, N. (2025). Assessing the impact of neurofeedback on cognitive function in individuals with autism spectrum disorder: A systematic review. *Iranian Journal of Child Neurology, 19*(2), 27–37. https://doi.org/10.22037/ijcn.v19i2.46578

Robbins, J. (2000). *A Symphony in the Brain: The Evolution of the New Brain Wave Biofeedback*. Atlantic Monthly Press.

Ros, T., Theberge, J., Frewen, P. A., et al. (2013). Mind over chatter: Plastic up-regulation of the fMRI salience network directly after EEG neurofeedback. *NeuroImage, 65*, 324–335. https://doi.org/10.1016/j.neuroimage.2012.09.046

Russo, G. M., Balkin, R. S., & Lenz, A. S. (2022). A meta-analysis of neurofeedback for treating anxiety-spectrum disorders. *Journal of Counseling & Development, 100*(3), 236–251. https://doi.org/10.1002/jcad.12424

Saxby, E., & Peniston, E. G. (1995). Alpha-theta brainwave neurofeedback training: An effective treatment for male and female alcoholics with depressive symptoms. *Journal of Clinical Psychology, 51*(5), 685–693.

Schabus, M., et al. (2017). Better than sham? A double-blind placebo-controlled neurofeedback study in primary insomnia. *Brain, 140*(4), 1041–1052. https://doi.org/10.1093/brain/awx011

Scott, W. C., Kaiser, D., Othmer, S., & Sideroff, S. I. (2005). Effects of an EEG biofeedback protocol on a mixed substance abusing population. *The American Journal of Drug and Alcohol Abuse, 31*(3), 455–469. https://doi.org/10.1081/ADA-200056807

Slater, J., Joober, R., Koborsy, B. L., Mitchell, S., Sahlas, E., & Palmer, C. (2022). Can electroencephalography (EEG) identify ADHD subtypes? A systematic review. *Neuroscience and Biobehavioral Reviews, 139*, 104752. https://doi.org/10.1016/j.neubiorev.2022.104752

Smit, D. J. A., Posthuma, D., Boomsma, D. I., & De Geus, E. J. C. (2005). Heritability of background EEG across the power spectrum. *Psychophysiology, 42*(6), 691–697. https://doi.org/10.1111/j.1469-8986.2005.00352.x

Smit, D. J. A., Wright, M. J., Hansell, N. K., Geffen, G. M., Martin, N. G., & Boomsma, D. I. (2006). Genetic variation of individual alpha frequency (IAF) and alpha power in a large adolescent twin sample. *International Journal of Psychophysiology, 61*(2), 235–243. https://doi.org/10.1016/j.ijpsycho.2005.10.004

Sorger, B., Scharnowski, F., Linden, D. E. J., Hampson, M., & Young, K. D. (2019). Control freaks: Towards optimal selection of control conditions for fMRI neurofeedback studies. *NeuroImage, 186*, 256–265. https://doi.org/10.1016/j.neuroimage.2018.11.004

Sterman, M. B., LoPresti, R. W., & Fairchild, M. D. (1969). Electroencephalographic and behavioral studies of monomethylhydrazine toxicity in the cat (Technical Report AMRL-TR-69-3). Wright-Patterson Air Force Base, OH: Aerospace Medical Research Laboratory.

Sterman, M. B., Wyrwicka, W., & Howe, R. (1969). Behavioral and neurophysiological studies of the sensorimotor rhythm in the cat. *Electroencephalography and Clinical Neurophysiology, 27*(7), 678–679.

Sterman, M. B., Howe, R. C., & Macdonald, L. R. (1970). Facilitation of spindle-burst sleep by conditioning of electroencephalographic activity while awake. *Science, 167*(3921), 1146–1148. https://doi.org/10.1126/science.167.3921.1146

Sterman, M. B., & Friar, L. (1972). Suppression of seizures in an epileptic following sensorimotor EEG feedback training. *Electroencephalography and Clinical Neurophysiology, 33*(1), 89–95. https://doi.org/10.1016/0013-4694(72)90028-4

Sterman, M. B. (1976). Effects of brain surgery and EEG operant conditioning on seizure latency following monomethylhydrazine intoxication in the cat. *Experimental Neurology, 50*(3), 757–765. https://doi.org/10.1016/0014-4886(76)90041-8

Sterman, M. B. (1977). Effects of sensorimotor EEG feedback training on sleep and clinical manifestations of epilepsy. In J. Beatty & H. Legewie (Eds.), *Biofeedback and behavior* (pp. 167–200). New York, NY: Plenum Press.

Sterman, M. B. (2000). Basic concepts and clinical findings in the treatment of seizure disorders with EEG operant conditioning. *Clinical Electroencephalography, 31*(1), 45–55. https://doi.org/10.1177/155005940003100111

Sterman, M. B. (2010). Biofeedback in the treatment of epilepsy. *Cleveland Clinic Journal of Medicine, 77*(Suppl. 3), S60–S67. https://doi.org/10.3949/ccjm.77.s3.11

Tan, G., Thornby, J., Hammond, D. C., Strehl, U., Canady, B., Arnemann, K., & Kaiser, D. A. (2009). Meta-analysis of EEG biofeedback in treating epilepsy. *Clinical EEG and Neuroscience, 40*(3), 173–179. https://doi.org/10.1177/155005940904000310

Tendler, A., Stern, Y., & Harmelech, T. (2025). Can amygdala-derived-EEG-fMRI-pattern (EFP) neurofeedback treat sleep disturbances in PTSD? *Brain Sciences, 15*(3), 297. https://doi.org/10.3390/brainsci15030297

Thatcher, R. W. (1998). Normative EEG databases and EEG biofeedback. *Journal of Neurotherapy, 2*(4), 8–39. https://doi.org/10.1300/J184v02n04_02

Toomim, H., Mize, W., Kwong, P. C., Toomim, M., Marsh, R., Kozlowski, G. P., Kimball, M., & Remond, A. (2005). Intentional increase of cerebral blood oxygenation using hemoencephalography (HEG): An efficient brain exercise therapy. *Journal of Neurotherapy, 8*(3), 5–24. https://doi.org/10.1300/J184v08n03_02

Treves, I. N., et al. (2025). Consumer-grade neurofeedback with mindfulness meditation: Meta-analysis. *Journal of Medical Internet Research, 27*, e68204. https://doi.org/10.2196/68204

Tsuchiyagaito, A., Misaki, M., Kirlic, N., Yu, X., Sanchez, S. M., Cochran, G., Stewart, J. L., Smith, R., Fitzgerald, K. D., Rohan, M. L., Paulus, M. P., & Guinjoan, S. M. (2023). Real-time fMRI functional connectivity neurofeedback reducing repetitive negative thinking in depression: A double-blind, randomized, sham-controlled proof-of-concept trial. *Psychotherapy and Psychosomatics, 92*(2), 87–100. https://doi.org/10.1159/000528377

U.S. Food and Drug Administration. (2019, April 9). FDA identifies harm reported from sudden discontinuation of opioid pain medicines and requires label changes to guide prescribers on gradual, individualized tapering [Drug Safety Communication]. https://www.fda.gov/drugs/drug-safety-

and-availability/fda-identifies-harm-reported-sudden-discontinuation-opioid-pain-medicines-and-requires-label-changes

U.S. Food and Drug Administration. (2020, September 23). FDA requiring boxed warning updated to improve safe use of benzodiazepine drug class [Drug Safety Communication]. https://www.fda.gov/safety/medical-product-safety-information/benzodiazepine-drug-class-drug-safety-communication-boxed-warning-updated-improve-safe-use

van Beijsterveldt, C. E. M., & van Baal, G. C. M. (2002). Twin and family studies of the human electroencephalogram: A review and a meta-analysis. *Biological Psychology, 61*(1–2), 111–138. https://doi.org/10.1016/S0301-0511(02)00055-8

Van Dongen, H. P. A., Maislin, G., Mullington, J. M., & Dinges, D. F. (2003). The cumulative cost of additional wakefulness: Dose-response effects on neurobehavioral functions and sleep physiology from chronic sleep restriction and total sleep deprivation. *Sleep, 26*(2), 117–126. https://doi.org/10.1093/sleep/26.2.117

Van Doren, J., Arns, M., Heinrich, H., Vollebregt, M. A., Strehl, U., & Loo, S. K. (2019). Sustained effects of neurofeedback in ADHD: A systematic review and meta-analysis. *European Child and Adolescent Psychiatry, 28*(3), 293–305. https://doi.org/10.1007/s00787-018-1121-4

van der Kolk, B. A. (2014). *The Body Keeps the Score: Brain, Mind, and Body in the Healing of Trauma.* Viking.

van der Kolk, B. A., Hodgdon, H., Gapen, M., Musicaro, R., Suvak, M. K., Hamlin, E., … Spinazzola, J. (2016). A randomized controlled study of neurofeedback for chronic PTSD. *PLOS ONE, 11*(12), e0166752. https://doi.org/10.1371/journal.pone.0166752

van der Vinne, N., Vollebregt, M. A., van Putten, M. J. A. M., & Arns, M. (2017). Frontal alpha asymmetry as a diagnostic marker in depression: Fact or fiction? A meta-analysis. *NeuroImage: Clinical, 16*, 79–87. https://doi.org/10.1016/j.nicl.2017.07.006

Voetterl, H. C., van Wingen, G., Michelini, G., Griffiths, K. R., Gordon, E., DeBeus, R., … Arns, M. (2023). Brainmarker-I differentially predicts remission to various attention-deficit/hyperactivity disorder treatments: A discovery, transfer, and blinded validation study. *Biological Psychiatry: Cognitive Neuroscience and Neuroimaging, 8*(1), 52–60. https://doi.org/10.1016/j.bpsc.2022.02.007

Voigt, J. D., Mosier, M., & Tendler, A. (2024). Systematic review and meta-analysis of neurofeedback and its effect on posttraumatic stress disorder. *Frontiers in Psychiatry, 15*, 1323485. https://doi.org/10.3389/fpsyt.2024.1323485

Wan, F., Nan, W., Vai, M. I., & Rosa, A. (2014). Resting alpha activity predicts learning ability in alpha neurofeedback. *Frontiers in Human Neuroscience, 8*, 500. https://doi.org/10.3389/fnhum.2014.00500

Wan, H., Chen, B., Li, X., & Bu, J. (2026). Effect of EEG neurofeedback therapy on addiction disorders: A systematic review and meta-analysis. *Addiction, 121*(2), 225–238. https://doi.org/10.1111/add.70164 (PMID: 40798852.)

Westwood, S. J., Aggensteiner, P.-M., Kaiser, A., Nagy, P., Donno, F., Merkl, D., et al.; European ADHD Guidelines Group. (2025). Neurofeedback for attention-deficit/hyperactivity disorder: A systematic review and meta-analysis. *JAMA Psychiatry, 82*(2), 118–129. https://doi.org/10.1001/jamapsychiatry.2024.3702

Wyrwicka, W., & Sterman, M. B. (1968). Instrumental conditioning of sensorimotor cortex EEG spindles in the waking cat. *Physiology & Behavior, 3*(5), 703–707. https://doi.org/10.1016/0031-9384(68)90139-x

Zafarmand, M. H., Farahmand, Z., & Otared, N. (2022). A systematic literature review and meta-analysis on effectiveness of neurofeedback for obsessive-compulsive disorder. *Neurocase, 28*(1), 29–36. https://doi.org/10.1080/13554794.2021.2019790

Zhao, Z., Yao, S., Zweerings, J., Zhou, X., Zhou, F., Kendrick, K. M., Chen, H., Mathiak, K., & Becker, B. (2021). Putamen volume predicts real-time fMRI neurofeedback learning success across paradigms and neurofeedback target regions. *Human Brain Mapping, 42*(6), 1879–1887. https://doi.org/10.1002/hbm.25336

About the Authors

Andrew Hill, PhD, a UCLA-trained cognitive neuroscientist, founded Peak Brain Institute. His 25 years in the field include 25,000 QEEG brain maps, roughly 10,000 clients, and doctoral work on a double-blind, sham-controlled neurofeedback protocol. He teaches, consults, and hosts the *Head First* podcast.

Madeleine McCann is a Senior Neurofeedback Coach and Southeast Program Manager at Peak Brain Institute, pursuing a Master of Education in Mental Health Counseling at the University of Miami.

Peak Brain Institute operates in Los Angeles and offers remote services. The authors' commercial interests are set out in the front matter, under What We Have a Stake In.

One Last Thing

If any of this helped, take the free **Reader Kit** with you: the full-color brain-map plates, the questions to ask any clinic, the Provider Scorecard, and a bibliography we keep current. The kit asks for a first name and email to deliver the materials; your email is used only for kit delivery and occasional book-related updates, and you can unsubscribe at any time. If you prefer not to provide an email, the Provider Scorecard and conversation scripts are in Chapters 5 and 17 of this book.

Scan with your phone's camera
or visit **peakbrainpress.com/nfb-bonus**

Your brain has a pattern. Now you know how to read it, and what to train.

www.ingramcontent.com/pod-product-compliance
Lightning Source LLC
LaVergne TN
LVHW010711061126
851857LV00014B/1137
* 9 7 8 1 9 7 1 4 0 2 0 8 6 *